The Glass Monolith

JON KEITH EVANS

Table of Contents

Acknowledgement

Without the help of The Glass Monolith Fellowship individuals named, as well as countless others, here and in other dimensions—I acknowledge that this work, dedicated to them, would not have been produced. The Fellowship works for the people to assist them in elevating their consciousness during this apparent time of transition on planet Earth. Let man seek knowledge and guidance from the Infinite God—his own inner nature—not from the debilitating, mental chaos and darkness of his mind or anyone else's.

This text is not fictional; it is a *vorla* (from the higher consciousness) and is therefore a higher truth that cannot be dismissed as such. Still, it will be misunderstood by some in the three-dimensional world. One has to understand what is being said.

Gratitude

Cheryl K. Wash and Lynda

Bruce, of Highest Good

Publications, Imprint

Publishing and

cover designer,

Barron Steward- all for their creative and publishing support.

The Glass Monolith

Introduction

People frequently talk about hitting a "Glass Ceiling"!

I, on the other hand, would hit a Glass Monolith. Most insidiously, it wasn't until the age of 47 that my Glass Monolith could be identified.

This Author detested the movie 2001: A Space Odyssey because of its preoccupation with symbolism versus telling the actual story. There is, however, one part of the movie that is appropriate for our discussion, even though I hated it when it was presented in the movie. In several scenes, from the monkeys to the astronauts, a monolith was depicted as a barrier, a brick wall, or a partition.

At least you could see the monolith depicted in 2001: A Space Odyssey. In the period that followed, the Author finally completed my nightmarish Undergraduate curriculum; however, my problems were not yet completely resolved. That Glass Monolith was Asperger's Syndrome—a kissing cousin to Autism! I also suspected Hyperlexia ONLY because ABC/WLS-TV presented a news segment about it. At the time of my diagnosis, I asked my doctors about it, and yes, that suspicion was also confirmed! It was as if I would run into a Glass Monolith—not just a glass ceiling!

Another reason for subtitling this book "The Glass Monolith" was that there was a perpetual barrier between This Author and not only normal social functioning, but also a viable career. I could understand it if I were younger. In my adulthood, I could suck it up and buckle down. My persuasive ability was always a joke.

Advisory: The names of some of the characters described have been either altered or changed to prevent embarrassment to them and/or their families.

The timeline for this book is between May 9, 1982, when I got my Bachelor's Degree—plodding along and not knowing that I even had Asperger's—through May 25, 2001, when my Asperger's was discovered. The Epilogue phase occurred between that period and a conference called Telecom 2003, which took place on or about March 2003.

May 9, 1982, Los Angeles Olympics, May 25, 2001

How My Asperger's Was Discovered

Re: Job Readiness Training and Placement Program

Dear Mr. Evans:

This letter is to inform you that you have been referred for the Job Readiness Training/Placement Program of Christ Hospital and Medical Center's Vocational Services Department. I would like to invite you to a four-day program that will help you complete applications, develop a resume, learn effective interviewing techniques, and explore job strategies. You are currently scheduled for the next training session, which will begin on January 10, 2000, and continue through January 13.

 We will meet at Christ Hospital and Medical Center in Room 022W on the ground floor:

The schedule is as follows:

Jan.10, 9:00 a.m. to 1:00 p.m.

1

Jan. 11, 9:00 a.m. to 1:00 p.m.

Jan. 12, 9:00 a.m. to 1:00 p.m.

Jan. 13, 9:00 a.m. to 1:00 p.m.

Kindly confirm your participation in the program by contacting me at (708) 346-5400. If you have any questions regarding the Job Readiness Training/Placement Program, please do not hesitate to call me. I look forward to meeting with you.

JS/mck cc: DHS/ORS

Related to the Evangelical Lutheran Church in America and the United Church of Christ.

The first day started off innocently enough. It was a group setting. There were several persons in the group—the names of which I do not remember. One person was a hockey fan, however. Come to find out, so was Jeremy.

I don't recall any of my fellow members appearing to be outwardly disabled. However, I didn't appear to be outwardly disabled either; yet here I was at a facility for the disabled.

Jeremy's assistant was White, very young, and very innocent-looking. Her hair was very long and brown. Her face was smooth and almost angelic-looking. She was of moderate build and was neither waifishly thin nor, as the lechers would say, "stacked". Her name was Melissa Bos. Melissa dressed in a non-provocative, conservative manner, irrespective of the type of outfit she wore.

During the first session, Jeremy did all the talking, while Melissa assisted by passing out flyers and speaking only when directed by Jeremy. That first session had a wrinkle I didn't expect. However, I could see some semblance of the method to the madness once the exercise began.

The case was Desert Survival. The object of the exercise was to prioritize items from a given set that was listed. These items were all that would be provided to the group members on a hypothetical basis. Our job was to rank the items from most important to least important during a hypothetical case of desert survival from 1 to 10. After we finished the exercise, we were to compare our results with what a panel of experts would say.

The answers were surprising. For instance, I based my answers on the premise that it was best to get out of the desert as soon as possible. Come to find out, the last thing I should have done was to run or move in any way. Instead, the experts advised that the best tactic would be to signal for help and ensure the signal was always visible. Running to a place of safety would've expended such large amounts of energy in so hostile an environment that I theoretically would not have survived.

There was another exercise in which we were to invite a set number of notable people, living or dead, to dinner. We had a choice as to whom we would choose. This was more of a flight of fancy than something related to job readiness.

There were also some administrative matters that had to be taken care of, such as notifying workshop participants about fire escapes and emergency procedures, providing emergency telephone numbers, and scheduling. We were also advised about when lunch would be served. Each session lasted a whole day. Daily attendance was mandatory to complete the program and to advance to the Job Club. Also, it was expected that each member would participate in the Workshop.

On the participation part, Jeremy had NO problem with me. The trouble was that there were many times when I thought Jeremy was full of it! For instance, Jeremy contended that in times of protracted unemployment, it would be better to take any job at all—even if that meant being a cashier in a supermarket or some other menial position. Jeremy also contended that the advertised job market was not, nor should be, the only game in town. He also contended that it was necessary to cold canvass for jobs.

What Jeremy failed to realize was that one of the people in that workshop could say, "Been There! Done That! Seen It! Tried It, and, unfortunately, Failed It!" That person was This Author! For instance, I explicitly told him, "I applied for a job as an Audio Consultant at a high-end stereo outlet because I liked stereo and home theater. I took the test and got all but one question right. I was still rejected because they said I didn't have any retail experience. Ironically, some of these employers think that I'm going to "fly the coop" as soon as I do find the decent job that I can't find anyway." Jeremy noted that I frequently used the phrase "Devil's Advocate" to describe my job search experiences or when I disagreed with him.

Jeremy held his ground, contending: "Well, in a case like that, you should go to places like Circuit City, Best Buy, and even Target. Then, if you want to go to places like that, you can."

The next day, Jeremy again mentioned some other features of a job hunt, such as the way you might be dressed, experience, and other straightforward issues. Mostly, however, Jeremy mentioned the importance of the "fit." He seemed to emphasize the importance of that "fit" as an issue. It was then that I mentioned my research project.

One of the issues I raised with Jeremy was the subject of rejections without interviews. For instance, there were times when I would submit a resume or job application and receive a rejection letter within twenty-four hours. I would not get the interview. His response was that cases like that were a simple numbers game—nothing more. Again, I thought that he was full of it!

He contended that a rejection letter from an employer was a "positive learning experience!" The reason why I thought Jeremy was full of it was that learning requires a measure of objectivity. No one can maintain a level of objectivity when that person is experiencing unemployment. Factor in the type of protracted unemployment that I was experiencing, and that objectivity will further erode. Factor a wife and/or children into the equation, and you have an even further erosion of objectivity. In my case, I was totally dependent on an aging, ill mother. Anymore "positive learning experiences" could prove to my detriment.

When I said that further "positive learning experiences" could prove to my detriment, I meant that I could easily see myself in a scenario where I could wind up on the street with NO job, no income, no outlooks at getting a job, and penniless—effectively, destitute or possibly suicidal. With my luck, I saw my mother dying while all of this was happening— unless I pushed hard to circumvent it.

The third day put me in a dilemma. I had an interview as a Technical Writer at the now-defunct Arthur Andersen. This branch of the firm was near the Edens–Interstate 94 junction in far northern Cook County. Fortunately, all I had to do was jump on the Tri-State Tollway. It was less than half an hour north of Christ Hospital, despite Christ Hospital being located in the southwest suburbs.

I arrived so early that I spotted an automotive division of Motorola on the way. Therefore, I was able to drop off a copy of my resume at Motorola. Then, I was off to my original interview.

I was still well within ample time when I reported for my original interview at Arthur Andersen. I met with the receptionist, then

5

straightened up in the restroom. I picked up the latest issue of Time Magazine while I waited.

The interviewer's assistant called me in. To my delight, I was offered tea, and it came with lemon on top. I finished it, then went in for my interview. It was at that point that I did something stupid.

Marciea advised me NOT to use the samples of my work that I had. These samples were mostly from my post-baccalaureate work, with the grades already included. My strategy was to demonstrate that I consistently achieved good grades on my work. Marciea contended that they were no good because of the editor's marks and grading. Since they were the only samples of my work, I took no Technical Writing samples at all. I also asked questions about software quality control, as I had experience in that area. However, I was told that Arthur Andersen already had someone in place to handle software quality control. Although I thanked Arthur Andersen for the interview, I should not have been, nor was I surprised, when I received a rejection letter from them just two days later.

It would've been far better for me always to have some sample of my work with me. That way, if samples of my work were called for, I could readily present them and show the employer my thought processes. Samples of one's work make for a process that would be efficient for both the employer and the job seeker.

Little did I know that my life would undergo a major change starting the next day!

An Executive Decision–Part Two: "You Have an Illness!"

Speak of the devil! The next and final day of the Job Readiness Workshop at Christ Hospital Vocational Services Unit would touch on the very subject of interview preparedness.

Christ Hospital's Vocational Services Unit had a novel plan for showing the importance of interview preparedness. While each person waited for their mock interview, we all watched a video about interview preparedness. In one case, the video showed a so-called "Valley Girl" of the 1970s and early 1980s. They had a talk and style that was caricaturized. The video used that style to show how NOT to approach a job interview.

Then, the video shifted to a woman who was more appropriately attired and behaved suitably. The video showed her as having her work samples available when the interviewer requested them. With those thoughts, the video implied that the interviewer would choose the second candidate.

Melissa was more than familiar with this video and even asked: "Did it show the 'Valley Girl' yet?" The plan was that we would all dress in interview-appropriate attire. We would then be videotaped and critiqued as we conducted our "mock interviews."

I let the others go first. After all, I just had an interview the day before, and even Jeremy thought that it would be more appropriate to let the others go through the process first. Then, it was my turn. A full-sized VHS camcorder was set up on a tripod, ready to go. I presumed that Jeremy turned the camera on before calling me in for the interview. I gave him my resume. "When he asked me why I wanted to be a Technical Writer, I gave him my standard answer— that on one hand, I had an intense interest in Science and Technology. On the other hand, I had proven writing skills. I told him that my reason for wanting to be a Technical Writer was to combine these two areas. After I gave my standard answer, Jeremy asked me:

"Approximately how many interviews have you been on?"

"I would say I've been on about fifty interviews," I said:

7

"About fifty?" asked Jeremy.

"About that," I said

Jeremy didn't seem surprised. However, what he said to me was a surprise. He said, "Here's the thing. You have an illness. You're trying too hard. You go off on a tangent. What happens during an interview is that an employer gets freaked out."

"I think you confuse 'Personality Disorder' with 'Character Flaw'. I urge you to once again apply for disability–OK? Everybody gets rejected. Christopher Reeve would even get rejected! You might need to be on medication. That's not going to make you a zombie."

Jeremy continued: "I've scheduled you for an appointment with Ms. Roland at your DORS office next Wednesday. I'll be there with you." I had once again hit a Glass Monolith. Make that slammed!

Author's Side Notes:

What made this experience so painful to me was that it reminded me of my kindergarten year. I was forcibly pulled out of line rather than leave on that final day with the rest of my class. Later, I learned that I was suspended for one year, with the prevailing excuse being that I was not ready for first grade.

At the Owasippe Scout Reservation, during my early teens, I took and completed what was called "The Swimmer's Test." It was a grueling 100-yard trial that included 25 yards of backstroke. However, I was given a non-Swimmer's classification, rather than a "Swimmer's" classification, because I completed the bulk of the course underwater. No one told me that doing the course underwater was illegal!

Now, it was déjà vu all over again! I felt that I was being singled out once again.

The worst was yet to come. First, Mom bantered that I should apply for Disability and/or Public Aid. It didn't make any difference to her that I would have to put up with surly Negroes with broad behinds and bad attitudes. It didn't matter to her that I would have to wait for maybe hours on end to get seen. She thought I should take a book to read. In her mind, she had to go through it— what made me so different? Mom also felt that the money was mine, so why not collect it?

My position was that if I earned my own money, I didn't have to make any excuses or apologies. I saw Public Aid as not only a sellout, but also self-prostitution. As for disability, I was the type of person who could only take so much rejection before deciding that something was not worth it.

Besides a heated debate with Mom, I also had to make that dreaded meeting the Wednesday after Christ Hospital Vocational rejected me. I arrived at the DORS office first. Secondly, Jeremy came in. We both sat in the waiting area, waiting for Ginnie Roland to receive us. While we waited, I gave him the rejection letter I got from Arthur Andersen and sarcastically told him, "Here's another positive learning experience!"

When Ginnie came out to receive us, we all retreated to a conference room in the back. It was then that she repeated the same sentiment to me that Jeremy had expressed on the previous Thursday. She then decided that I would NOT be allowed to receive any more services from the Department of Human Services until, and unless, I sought counseling. The irony of the matter was that I just ended a relationship with a psychologist who was Black, male, and an absolute ding-a-ling! This was the same counselor that Bess Robertson, a counselor I knew earlier, recommended. For instance, when I told him that my major problem was my inability to establish a career, he scoffed at me, insulted me and went off on irrelevant tangents. For instance, he contended that I needed to stare into a mirror, declare that I loved myself, and kiss myself. Needless to say, not only was such an exercise silly, but it was also downright irrelevant.

I only had four meetings with this ding-a-ling. However, when he failed to show up for a meeting that I arrived on time for, I had had enough of him. I went to the DORS office and was granted a petition to fire him.

Now, I was being told to risk dealing with another possible ding-a-ling psychologist or risk losing services. I couldn't take it. To make matters even worse, the subject of psychoactive medication came up. When I brought up the point of what I had been doing, as far as testing and whatever medications I was on, Ginnie thought I was missing the point. In the end, Jeremy's judgment stood. Unless I replaced my psychologist, I'd get no services.

So, there I stood. I was pulled out of I AM CARES and was rejected from Christ Hospital's Vocational Services Unit. Now, any services rendered by the Illinois Department of Rehabilitation Services was held hostage.

My first task was to contact the Client Services Administrator to appeal my case. This time, I received prompt action, even though I had to wait a couple of weeks to schedule a meeting. Once I did, I met with Ginnie, her supervisor, and the Client Services Administrator. However, I'd get nowhere. Ironically, the Client Services Administrator thought that there was more that I should've been doing in terms of training and classwork.

So, I had to bite the bullet and get myself another psychologist. I shuddered at the possibility because the only affordable Mental Health facilities were the same community health facilities that I found abhorrent. Even more insidiously, I couldn't just get an appointment. First, I had to have a long-winded orientation session before being assigned a psychologist. That orientation session was held en-masse with a lot of other people with varying degrees of problems. Worse yet, there was the same Ms. Samuelson from Halsted Street that I had to fire back in 1986 for the same reason why I had to dump the last nitwit I had.

The en-masse orientation session was held at the Roseland facility. It was moderated by a Black counselor who drove a red BMW 6-Series Coupe. You wouldn't know he had social work or psychology credentials by the polluted English that he used. He also had a tendency to insult the group whenever one of us made a mistake or omission. For instance, he'd say, "Yawl the worst group I ever saw!"

Once I got past that session, fortune would smile on me at last. For starters, I did NOT get Ms. Samuelson as I feared. Secondly, and most importantly, I got a Black woman who had some semblance of sense about her. She wasn't into the type of irrelevant nonsense that caused me to dump Ms. Samuelson and that nitwit. In fact, I could work on some issues with her very well, thank you!

Once I had stabilized that situation, I then telephoned Christ Hospital's Vocational Services Unit. This time, I wanted to speak with Gloria Moreno, Jeremy's supervisor. However, Ms. Moreno had already gone on maternity leave. Fortunately, I would meet with a substitute for Gloria. Her name was Diane Bazan.

At the risk of perhaps getting shot, I'd describe Ms. Bazan as looking quite like actress-talk show moderator Sally Jessy Raphael. Even her voice was similar. Ms. Bazan was quite civil to boot. Once I explained my situation to Ms. Bazan, she called Jeremy in to explain why I was barred from Placement Services.

Jeremy finally came up with the reason why he had doubts about my ability to perform on the job. It was the research project I told him I was working on. Once he came clean, I said to him, "Alright. Maybe that might not have been appropriate for me to mention that, but still, to shut me out like that?"

Jeremy continued, "I became concerned that Jon might have an illness and that he needed to get treatment before he could continue to receive services."

Ms. Bazan then interceded, "Jon, we have to make sure that if we send somebody out with a disability, that whatever disability they might have doesn't interfere with their ability to do the work. Now, in your case, you have an illness. That doesn't make you a bad person. It's not your fault, unless you don't get help for it." She concluded, "If your counselor tells us that it's alright for you to receive services, we would be more than happy to let you back into the Job Club." (That was the name of their Placement Services.)

Although I was unable to break the Glass Monolith that separated me from getting Vocational Services, I got more consideration from Ms. Bazan than from any of the other principals to date. I also gained a better understanding of why I was initially barred from receiving Vocational Services. With that, our meeting adjourned. However, we kept in touch.

As for Jeremy Sadlier, I was initially furious and hurt with him. In the long run, however, He would ultimately bring me closer to the answer to what my Glass Monolith was. Ironically, I'd still have to wait fifteen more months before finding out. However, he was part of the process that led me to find out.

Speaking of Christ Hospital, Mom had started going to Christ Hospital's clinics. There were a couple of times that I drove her out there. The only problem I had with it was that it was the same hospital that pronounced Norman dead on arrival. That left me wondering how

Mom would react. Fortunately, it was no different from the other facilities she had been to.

Roseland Mental Health Center had an on-staff Psychiatrist. He wanted to know if I would need any medication. I turned it down. As I have stated many times before, I did not want to end up the way former First Lady Betty Ford did. Secondly, NO medication could help me with my career issues. Those career issues were at the core of my problems.

If there were problems with my brain function, and if psychotropic medications could help such brain function, I was amenable to using medications ONLY if I had a baseline medical examination that included an EKG (Electrocardiograph) and an EEG (Electroencephalograph). Otherwise, there was NO WAY I was putting dope into my body-period!

Author's Side Note:

Technically, Alcohol, Tobacco, and even Caffeine are psychotropic drugs or medications. They are all mood-altering.

Technically, ALCOHOL, TOBACCO, AND CAFFEINE ARE DOPE!

This Author's concern was that once I were to start using any form of psychotropic medication, legal or not, without the tightest safeguards, that I would wind up on the road to substance abuse! (Domino Theory)

I made my feelings about psychotropic medications known to Ginnie Roland. She argued that I had effectively undergone these evaluations during my first sleep study. She thought that I was merely putting up roadblocks. I must counter-argue that the brain is the Central Processing Unit (CPU) of the human body. Once the CPU is damaged, the entire computer becomes unusable. Any type of mood-altering or psychotropic drug, legal or black-market, has the potential of ruining the CPU bar none!

13

When I started at Underwriters Laboratories in 2000, I developed a different set of problems. For the first week or so, I was highly proactive—until I committed the logic error that led me to mistake Lory Littlefield for a woman. Then, I acted as a mindless "yes man" who didn't bother checking for errors. For instance, I even missed Rich Winton's editor's marks and other salient instructions. This series of operating errors was so severe that it caused Winton to "write me up" and give me a negative performance review.

I was now terrified. I was fired from a company for much less than what Rich charged, and didn't even have the benefit of a warning about my work performance to boot!

I was even more frightened when Rich told me that he had notified Atul. I said, "Oh no! When I learned that Rich conferred with John Hawley, the Section Manager.

The next morning, I got an email from Richard O'Sullivan, the Chief Personnel Administrator for all of Underwriters Laboratories. Rich asked that I meet with him the following week. Prior to this period, I had never met Mr. O'Sullivan.

It was that email that sent me into a complete state of panic. I figured that if the problem was so serious that it would warrant my meeting the Chief Personnel Administrator of the Company, I was on the way out. I took Christ Hospital's Vocational Services Unit up on its offer to send help if it would prove the difference between me keeping the job and me getting terminated. When I told Ms. Bazan about my predicament, she agreed that if they were going to have me meet with the Chief Personnel Administrator of the Company, the company was, indeed, about to "term" me. It was at that point that I told Christ Hospital's Vocational Services Unit to intervene on my behalf.

The worst was yet to come. While Rich and I were working on something, John Hawley came to my cubicle. Hawley asked to see both of us. Once Rich and I got to Haley's office, Mr. O'Sullivan was already there. "Could this be the end?" I thought to myself.

It was shortly before this meeting that I had telephoned the Vascular Research Unit at NU Hospital. I was checking to see that some funds I had allocated from my paycheck were going towards Stroke research for Minorities. While I was on the call, however, I was put on hold and then disconnected. When I called back, I complained about being disconnected. Now, O'Sullivan has a complaint from NU Medical that I came off in a demanding way. His view was that I embarrassed the Company. At that point, I groaned. "What else could go wrong?" I thought to myself.

John Hawley was concerned that the time I spent making follow-up calls to NU was time taken away from my work, until I told him that I made the follow-up calls strictly during my lunch period.

Then O'Sullivan told me of another complaint against me. This time, it was coming from the adjacent cubicles to me. My neighbors had been complaining that I was so loud that they couldn't conduct their business.

At first, I wanted to scoff at that complaint. However, in light of the severe charges that had already been lodged against me, I considered myself in no position to respond to those complaints. I had to listen to what O'Sullivan had to say. Meanwhile, John Hawley merely told me to "zip it!"

O'Sullivan got back on the subject of my phone call to Ms. Bazan at Christ Hospital and added: "Just because I'm going to meet with you next week, doesn't necessarily mean the ax is going to fall. It might,

15

but not right away. In the meantime, we'd like to take care of it ourselves, without the need for any outside intervention."

I left John Hawley's office, grateful that I still had my job, for the moment. I spent the weekend in my room thinking to myself about what was going wrong. I didn't tell Mom because she would've ridden me like a bucking bronco. She kept me on a short leash, and any mistake I made was magnified.

However, I had some fences to mend. For instance, the first thing I did was to write a letter of apology to NU Hospital and to the internal department that referred me to the NU Medical section. I also submitted a copy of that letter of apology to Mr. O' Sullivan. I then submitted that letter to those various departments. As I was about to start work, Mr. O'Sullivan appeared once again. He thought that it was unnecessary to send the various copies I sent.

About three hours later, I kept my appointment with O'Sullivan. I was under the impression that Rich would be joining us. I was wrong. It would be strictly O'Sullivan and this Author. It was at that point that I told him that I would go and seek medical and/or psychiatric attention for the issues that emerged while I was at work. I would then keep O'Sullivan apprised of all findings and developments. O'Sullivan agreed with this approach.

My first step was to telephone NU Medical's Neurology Department. It was there that I was able to set up an appointment for a complete neurological evaluation. Come to find out, it was in a department called Neuro-Behavior. However, I had to wait. I also telephoned Christ Hospital and Ms. Bazan. Although there was a bit of a wait at Christ for such an evaluation, she thought that I was taking an excellent tack in addressing the problem.

I visited at least two websites about the side effects of Claritin. BOTH of those sites described MEMORY LOSS as a possible side effect. "Could this be the reason why I would have a problem with my work performance?" I thought. I paid a visit to the Industrial Nurse to find out further.

According to the Industrial Nurse, it was not common for Claritin to cause the memory drop-offs that I was experiencing. However, it was more than possible for the drop-offs to occur.

After I conferred with the Industrial Nurse, I paid a visit to Rich's office, along with the necessary proof. Rich was skeptical at first; however, given the magnitude of the problem, he begrudgingly gave me the benefit of the doubt.

I stopped taking the Claritin in the following days after my conference with the Industrial Nurse. The operational errors, while not coming to a screeching halt, also diminished in number. In fact, I would be working on a couple more projects that Rich had in mind. Rich ultimately liked my work.

Richard C. Winton To: Stephen P.

Woyner/NBKIULI@ULI, Gary J.

11/08/00 05:26 PM Manzella/NBKIULI@ULI, Steven G.

Modlin/NBKIULI@ULI cc: Atul J. Shah/NBKIULI@ULI, Jon

K. Evans/NBKIULI@ULI

Subject: (Waterlab) Spreadsheets

Gentlemen:

As discussed today, I have developed the Waterlab Sample Selection spreadsheet format. I created two spreadsheets: one for Group A and another for Group B. They are in the S:\fus directory.

The internal screens contain all the information we need to fill in the left part of the spreadsheet—that is, everything except the samples to be selected. Fields on the internal screen can be copied into the spreadsheets. I believe this is the preferred way to do this because it reduces the likelihood of typo errors. Jon Evans has begun transferring info from the internal screens to the (Group-A) spreadsheet; the process seems to be working well. I have asked him to continue and finish populating that spreadsheet with (internal) info for all the (Group-A) clients. He should be able to finish this by the end of the day on Thursday or possibly Friday morning, and then start working on the internal clients for the (Group-B) spreadsheet.

Please review the Waterlab Sample Select.xls spreadsheet and provide feedback on it ASAP. I don't want Jon to continue until we all agree this format is what we want.

I will be in the office Thursday morning and then out for the rest of the week, returning Monday.

Richard Winton

Engineering Group Leader - 3OI6CNBK Underwriters Laboratories Inc. (Wording is altered to avoid embarrassment to Underwriters Labs and to comply with Secrecy Statutes.)

I also took Underwriters Laboratories up on its network of professionals that help employees deal with personal problems. It was here that I discovered a psychologist and counselor with an office just a scant few blocks from NU Medical. I was sold on him for simplicity's sake.

It was here that I got an unexpected revelation.

According to him, the experiences and events I was experiencing at UL that caused Rich to write me up were actually the delayed effects of Norman's death. It was a sudden death that occurred on 9 November 1999.

After the write-up, I would wind up serving two masters. I did some finishing work for Rich in Water lab. But Rich also had me work for Calibrations. In the morning, I had my Water lab work. In the afternoon, it was Calibrations.

While my situation at Underwriters stabilized, I would lose my sister on Thanksgiving, Saturday, 25 November 2000. Two days later, I would lose my paternal Uncle, Emmanuel Evans I. I had the three days of Bereavement Leave, plus the weekend. That left me with a total of five days off work. On the Monday after we laid Emmanuel Sr. to rest, and held Marciea's Memorial Service, I had an appointment with NU Medical's Neurobehavior Unit. There, I submitted to a complete Neuro-Psychiatric Evaluation, save for the Minnesota Multiple Personality Profile, or any other tests involving my personality issues.

I reported on time, and was met by a young, svelte, White woman who was fully covered. She didn't have the perkiness of actress Melissa Joan Hart in her series, Sabrina. Instead, this lady had a calmer form of pleasantness. She was a post-doctoral resident Neurologist by the name of Amber Christie.

I went there somewhat prepared. For instance, I took out two small pieces of a plastic-encased clothesline that I just happened to have on hand. I thought that if I could visually show Dr. Christie an example of some of the issues I had with social functioning, it would prove very beneficial in giving her an immediate understanding of my problem.

Author's Side Note:

As a young teenager, I was in the Boy Scouts. I took a test in which I had to demonstrate how to tie a Square Knot. My scoutmaster had a friend who asked me to do the demonstration. He pulled out a handkerchief. I said that scoutmaster's friend: "Alright! Where's the other rope?"

My scoutmaster's friend IMMEDIATELY, and UNEXPECTEDLY, was able to tie the Square Knot, using his single handkerchief alone!

Meanwhile, I expected that the only way to tie a Square Knot was by connecting two ropes! The picture of a Square Knot in my Boy Scout Manual led me to believe that you needed two ropes to tie a Square Knot, since the book said that Square Knots were used to tie small boats to moorings.

Little did I know that Square Knots were also used to tie Tourniquets in the event of bleeding injuries—until my scoutmaster and his friend told me.

I began my meeting with Dr. Christie by advising her that one of the issues I faced in my job at Underwriters was the problem of "logic errors". I then showed Dr. Christie how I tied a Square Knot using the two lengths of rope I had. I then showed Dr. Christie how my scoutmaster's friend showed me how he was able to tie a Square Knot using a SINGLE length of rope! In so doing, I duplicated the demonstration that my scoutmaster's friend gave. Dr. Christie, at that point, was hooked on my demonstration. Suffice it to say, the ploy worked.

Dr. Christie's interest piqued when I told her about my previous testing and history. She had me do a few tests on current events and history. I had no problems with these tests, and Dr. Christie noted that.

The next test that Dr. Christie had me do was a sequencing of letters and numbers. I was to recite that sequence forward first; afterward, I was to recite it going backward. It was here that both of us noticed that I wasn't as sharp going backwards as I was going forward. She also had me take a test called the Trail Making Test. Here, I was to draw a line to a designated point using either the shortest path or a certain sequence of dots. I didn't do too badly in this test.

There was one test that I found odd. However, I could see the method to the madness in retrospect. For instance, Dr. Christie had me name types of animals as quickly as I could over one minute.

Dr. Christie gave me one test where I met my Waterloo. It was Arithmetic. In this test, I was to give the answers to common and uncommon arithmetic problems verbally. If it were simple addition or subtraction, I was fine. As I progressed to higher-level arithmetic, I informed Dr. Christie that using a paper and pencil was necessary for me to solve the problems. Dr. Christie also gave me a second chance to think more carefully about it.

I was also tested on copying simple to complex shapes. Dr. Christie noted that it took me some time to study the shapes and figures. However, I had a minor issue duplicating the figures.

Perhaps the most telling tale about my problem occurred when Dr. Christie recited two stories to me. She then asked me to tell her what I remembered about the stories.

On the very first story she read me, I was able to recall quite a bit of the information from the story. Then, I ran out of information that I could readily recall. Dr. Christie then asked: "Is there anything else?"

At that point, I strained my memory. However, I was able to glean a few more details about the story.

Strangely, on the second story, I had considerable difficulty retaining information in the first place and was able to glean even less when Dr. Christie asked me what else I could remember.

At that point, Dr. Christie said: "I think that this is more developmental than volitional."

One of the things that worried me was that the memory drop-offs I was experiencing what might have been the onset of what I called "Brain Rot"! That would either be senility or even Alzheimer's Disease.

Dr. Christie, however, said: "If it were Alzheimer's Disease, I could've read those stories to you 200 times, and you still would not have remembered it. Instead, what you have is an Information Processing Disorder. What it is, is that sometimes some of the information you do retain, while other parts of the information can go right over your head; it's as if it was never there!"

Dr. Christie added: "I don't think you are Autistic, because you do connect with people, whereas people who are autistic simply do not. What you do need, however, is an environment where there might be a little more structure."

I asked Dr. Christie, "Is there any possibility that I might be Hyperlexic?"

"THAT'S VERY POSSIBLE," said Dr. Christie.

I came away from that evaluation feeling that I got two for the price of one. First, I got a very nice lady to work with. Most importantly, I got a clearer idea about what my Glass Monolith truly was. As I thought about the evaluation Dr. Christie gave me, I would more and more compare myself to my Laser V/Tech 486 Computer with about twenty gigabytes of hard drive memory! This computer was blazing fast while

I had the obsolete Windows 3.1 on it. When I installed Windows 95, it was slow, until I installed its maximum RAM of 32 Megabytes.

Author's Side Note:

The Intel 486 Microprocessor was a very reliable microprocessor. However, it was very slow! The fastest it could perform was 100 Megahertz! Even then, that was only if the end user retrofitted an Overdrive Processor to the computer! There was also a 133-Megahertz Overdrive Processor. However, Intel did NOT manufacture this processor, and there was one knowledgeable computer technician who warned that a 133 Overdrive Processor was prone to system lockup! At the time I had this evaluation done on me, second and third generation Pentium-class computers had already become the de facto standard among microcomputers, and even my DX-4 100 would become hopelessly obsolete!

That explanation seemed good enough for me. For instance, my seventh-grade principal bitterly complained: "Your rate of reasoning is very low." However, this nun hated my guts, period! Given the context of my evaluation with Dr. Christie, it could be that this nun was right.

Mom also liked the explanation that Dr. Christie gave when I told her about this evaluation. She also thought that I was, at times, slow. However, there were times when she felt that I was so highly knowledgeable that I should consider teaching as a vocational objective. Mom also lamented about the "flak" that she took in trying to get answers for some of the developmental problems I faced. That flak came from family members, doctors, teachers, and others.

Mom could also identify with an ABC/WLS-TV News Report that came on. It was about Information Processing Disorder. Like an idiot, however, I failed to tape it. If I was not mistaken, my S-Monitor had just blown a video output diode. As a result, I couldn't use the monitor to arm my VCR to record the News Final.

I was so comfortable with Dr. Christie's explanation about my problem that I barely remembered that I had to keep my promise to Mr. O'Sullivan. I also consulted the Industrial Nurse about the problem.

During this time, I also kept in touch with Ms. Bazan at Christ Hospital's Vocational Rehabilitation Unit. She was delighted to learn that the heat was off when I told Ms. Bazan about Ms. Roland's plans to close my case, she explained that it was standard procedure to close out a client's case once that client finds work and holds the job down for three months.

Ginnie Roland and I had a light-hearted meeting when I saw her shortly after that phone call. I told her about Marce's death and some of the other issues I was facing, and that was that. Then, we parted company.

My birthday was coming on 3 January 2001. It would be my 47th birthday. The last thing I wanted to do was to make a 50-mile trek on the morning of my birthday. Hence, I chose to burn one of the three vacation days I had. I also believed that people should have their birthday off from work.

Instead, I chose the time off to pay a visit to my old therapist, Patricia Sawyer. It was Ms. Sawyer whom I spent many a session with; first was during the aftermath of the Phone-Co Robbery, when I was accused of being the bandit. Next came the time I was fired from Ameritech.

This time, however, I was merely keeping Ms. Sawyer apprised of my situation, at her request, from time to time. I had to remind Ms. Sawyer that she had asked me to keep in touch with her because she asked me why I was seeing her.

I filled Patricia Sawyer in on what life was like since the last time I saw her. I mentioned my near scare at Underwriters and the deaths in my family that occurred. I also mentioned that I saw Dr. Amber Christie at NU Medical's Neurology Unit. There, after submitting to an evaluation, I received a diagnosis of Information Processing Disorder, and she also confirmed the possibility of Hyperlexia as well.

I described the Information Processing Disorder to Ms. Sawyer in terms of the Laser/V-Tech 486 Computer I still had. I described myself as having lots of memory, but very poor processing speed in terms of my thought processes. I also told her that I was like a 486 with about 20 gig of hard drive!

Author's Side Note:

The maximum hard drive that a 486-based computer with an Overdrive Processor could handle was a paltry 2 Gigabytes!

My explanation of my condition bothered Ms. Sawyer. She asked me to wait in her office, and I did, for about thirty minutes! When Ms. Sawyer came back, she told me that she had every reason to believe that the reason for the difficulties I was having at work was due to the deaths!

Ms. Sawyer was also perturbed that there was no follow-up appointment made after my diagnosis. To that end, Ms. Sawyer asked me to set up an appointment with Dr. Diana Harrison, an MD/ Ph.D. Neurologist. Dr. Harrison was in the same department where I got my initial evaluation from Dr. Christie. Ms. Sawyer thought that I would like Dr. Harrison once we met. With that, Patricia Sawyer commended me for keeping her apprised of my situation, and my visit with her was over. However, per Ms. Sawyer's instructions, I set up an appointment with Dr. Harrison. I would be in for a three-month wait. However, I took the appointment.

I found Dr. Christie's assessment of my neuro-psychiatric function credible enough to break the news to Dr. Bennett Leventhal at the University of Chicago. Unfortunately, he was unable to track down Dana Rivers, whom I met from Project Strive's Chicago Division. Dana told me that she would be moving on to the University of Chicago.

The University of Chicago

5841 S. Maryland Avenue, Chicago, Illinois 60637

Child & The Harris Center for

Adolescent Psychiatry Developmental Studies 5 January 2001

John K. Evans (Southfork Ranch).

Chicago, Illinois

Dear Mr. Evans:

Thank you very much for your letter of 9 December 2000. I appreciate you sharing your information with me. I am pleased that you have been able to find some answers to these important questions about your life and your functioning. I am only too sorry that you were not able to share this with your sister before she died. I only hope that you can use this information to make your life more productive and satisfying.

I would very much like to do the favor for you that you have asked. However, I am finding it a bit difficult. In your letter, you asked me to find Dana Rivers for you. At this point, I have not been able to locate Ms. Rivers at the University of Chicago. If you have any idea where I might find her, let me know, and I will do my best to try to locate her. In the meantime, I wish you the very best for a happy and prosperous New Year.

There was a Christmas party in late 2000. The Water lab insisted I join the lunchtime party. It was within about an hour or two after that lunchtime party that a Blizzard hit! Underwriters Laboratories would close before mid-afternoon!

Unfortunately, I'd stay stuck in Northbrook between about 2:00 PM until 6 PM! The blizzard affected and canceled trains inbound into Chicago.

Once I finally got home, Ms. Case, a friend from my former Ameritech/Illinois Bell Telephone days, was angry with me for not responding. Even after I told her that I was caught up in that Blizzard, her response was: "Do you see my point? I have been more of a friend to a Black person than anybody, and for you not to answer my call?"

Why such a venomous response? Remember! Ms. Case didn't know I was caught up in the Blizzard! Nevertheless, I'd commit a logic error that ultimately ruined our friendship!

HERE IS THE LOGIC ERROR!

During a break at work, I telephoned the authorities in the area of Lockport and asked them if they do what is commonly known as a "Wellness Check", a "Well-Being Check", or a "Welfare Check". The authorities assured me that they did. I then told the authorities why I suspected that something was amiss with Ms. Case. I inadvertently embarrassed and then alienated Ms. Case!

If anyone might have needed a "Welfare or Well-Being Check", I should have. For starters, my Cough-Variant Asthma was going wild, and on one occasion, I went to the Medical Department immediately upon my arrival at work, coughing all the way! The Industrial Nurse understood what I needed before I even said a word. There was also a morning in which I came in to work with a temperature of 101 Degrees

Fahrenheit! The Nurse Practitioner cautioned me to return later that day do determine whether the fever would break, which it did.

Another health practitioner who was worried about my welfare was Diana Harrison, MD/Ph. Ph.D., at Northwestern Medical Center's Neuro-Behavior Division. I kept my appointment with her on 21 April 2001.

I showed up on time, and in a short time, out popped a middle-aged White woman who was slightly taller than This Author. Her hair was short. She was covered from head to toe and wore a pair of brown slacks. Those slacks matched the rounded toe jazz oxfords that she wore. That lady was Diana Harrison, MD/Ph.D.

Like an idiot, I made the mistake of not taking my Square Knot sample to that meeting with me, as I had when I met with Dr. Christie. Instead, I assumed that Dr. Christie made Dr. Harrison aware of the Square Knot model I presented to Dr. Christie.

Instead, I was still dumbfounded and upset by the fiasco with Ms. Case, so I mentioned the chain of events that led to everything going wrong. Most importantly, I told Dr. Harrison that the fiasco with Ms. Case was a "Logic Error" on my part, and that I had a propensity towards such "logic errors"

Dr. Harrison responded: "Have you considered the possibility that you might be Autistic?"

"AUTISTIC?" I inflected interrogatively.

"Yes, Autistic-things like Non-Verbal Language Disorder; Asperger's Syndrome," said Dr. Harrison.

At that point, I was stunned. I posed that very question to the Center for Personal Development. At that time, AUTISM WAS

CATEGORICALLY RULED OUT by the Center for Personal Development-NOW IT WAS BACK AGAIN!

I managed to collect myself a few minutes after Dr. Harrison posed the autism question to me. I then asked her: "Is there any possibility that I might also be Hyperlexic?"

"ABSOLUTELY," said Dr. Harrison.

Dr. Harrison continued: "It isn't just Hyperlexia by itself. Instead, all of that is part of the Autistic continuum."

Dr. Harrison had me set up a follow-up meeting with her. In the meantime, I immediately wrote Diane Bazan back at Christ Hospital Vocational and gave her the lowdown.

I was able to get that follow-up meeting on 25 May 2001. During that meeting, Dr. Harrison told me:

"Jon, I contacted another colleague of mine, sort of a third party, and this doctor told me: "This person is DEAD BANG POSITIVE FOR AUTISM!" "Meanwhile, I had taken several written questions to Dr. Harrison. One of the questions I posed to her was this: "When I was in school, I was very good at science. Ironically, I was bad at Math. Could Information Processing Disorder have anything to do with this?"

"ABSOLUTELY," said Dr. Harrison.

"Could it account for why I had such a rough time in college?" I asked

"ABSOLUTELY," said Dr. Harrison.

Meanwhile, Dr. Harrison had already put together a tentative treatment plan for me. She suggested a couple of counselors who were specialists in Adult Autism. Dr. Harrison also wanted me to see a developmental specialist up in Skokie.

Both Dr. Harrison and I agreed that my original plan for getting a baseline neurological evaluation that included a physical examination should continue as planned.

It was evident, even during my sorry Undergraduate career, that I would frequently hit a Glass Monolith. NOW, MY GLASS MONOLITH HAD A NAME TO IT. THAT NAME WAS AUTISM SPECTRUM DISORDER!

Meanwhile, I'd run a gamut of feelings. First off, I started off humbled. On the outside, many of my friends, friends of the family, and family members depicted me as someone who was either intelligent or articulate, or both.

In reality, that was simply a facet of the Autism Spectrum Disorder kicking in. On the other hand, there were many of my enemies, detractors, classmates, and even my father, who declared that I lacked common sense! It was evident that both sides were credible!

One of the reasons why I thought that both sides of people's perception of me seemed credible was that I was now spending scads of time between Calibration Records projects on the net. Here, I would be researching Autism Spectrum Disorder and its related problems. As for the Hyperlexia, I would also be spending scads of time researching it, and it all would fit in.

Meanwhile, back at home, I told Mikey about what happened. Mikey told me that I was "in the mix for 45 years." In his mind, it seemed that there should be a way around these issues so that I could function like everyone else. Shortly after that call, Mom told me that Milton said that a lot of these things we know about Autism only came out very recently!

Perhaps, the most important thing that Mom said in all of this was: "You can't blame anybody or yourself!"

Even a classmate by the name of "Goldilocks" contended that I was "socially ignorant" during a bout of verbal sparring and trash talk.

The paradox was that just as I was being humbled, if not humiliated by the findings on the Internet about characteristics of Autistics, I was also grateful that I had found the answer to what my Glass Monolith really was.

I rented a car and dropped in on Ms. Bazan at Christ Hospital's Vocational Services Unit. Although it was a bit of a stretch for Ms. Bazan to say, "Isn't that wonderful?" I knew what she was talking about. I had an inkling that I might have had a problem after my disastrous undergraduate career. However, I figured that all I had to do was to put that nightmare behind me and secure a stable, decent-paying job. However, once I had a job, those problems would not go away.

What Ms. Bazan was talking about when she said, "Isn't that wonderful," about my diagnosis, was quite simple. In both of our minds, most people think that the answer to major life issues is to "drown the fourth in a fifth", as the late WVON Radio Commentator Roy Wood might say, or use dope. The finding of my Autism Spectrum Disorder, under the circumstances that it was diagnosed, actually reinforced my belief that the use of psychoactive medications, in today's society, is way too excessive. More often than not, those psychoactive medications, dope, alcohol, anabolic steroids, sexuality, and religious fanaticism (both Western and Eastern) are mere smokescreens for more deep-seated issues, such as my Glass Monolith!

Self-talk and PMA (Positive Mental Action) Advocacy are fine. However, my concern is that simply thinking positively and talking positively is like putting a paint job, costing hundreds of dollars, on a clunker! Couple self-talk and/or PMA with an assault on core issues, and more desirable outcomes may result.

I wasn't even aware that I might have had a problem until that ABC/WLS-TV News Report came out on Hyperlexia in 1990. Even then, I had to do some legwork to determine if my suspicions at least had merit. Marciea, meanwhile, was delighted with me for seeking the counsel of Dr. Leventhal and for looking back into my background for the answer to my developmental history. It was also Marciea that was exhorting me to have myself tested for Autism! Although I scoffed at her contention for reasons of maintaining objectivity, Marciea would ultimately prove correct! Even now, I could hear her smiling from her urn and saying: "See Jon! What'd I tell you?" Now it was May of 2001, and only then was it confirmed that I did indeed, have a problem.

What I was grateful for was "The Answer"! Therefore, I knew what Ms. Bazan was talking about when she said: "Isn't that wonderful?" My ten plus year search to find what my Glass Monolith was, was over.

To underscore how important, it was for me to have found what my Glass Monolith was, I even sent a "Thank You" present to Ms. Case-despite her anger with me for that botched well-being check that I made.

That leads to one final point in this chapter.

I learned that in Greek Mythology, there was a Greek soldier/hero by the name of Pyrrhus. Pyrrhus's army won his battle. However, Pyrrhus was mortally wounded during that battle. Pyrrhus eventually died-as did my friendship with Ms. Case. As a result, victories that are won at great costs are now referred to as "Pyrrhic Victories!"

But what do you expect from someone who did complete his Undergraduate-at the expense of my credibility, my self-respect, and my career direction?

After the Knowledge, More Change Would Loom.

Once I hit the motherlode, however, I found myself playing inside of the motherlode for a little while. For instance, I posed an assortment of questions, alternative issues, and observations to Dr. Harrison, snowing her in the process.

Dr. Harrison was busy on my case as well. She already had me contact a consultant in Skokie. This consultant was a developmental specialist. Her specialty was in dealing with cases such as mine. In fact, I started that process by telephoning her and sending her a fax from my office. In turn, the consultant was more than happy to respond to me. However, I had to wait. I'd not get the appointment until later in September.

Now that I was settled into my Van Pool, I had only to deal with my newly found findings of Autism. I got a call from one of the consultants that Dr. Harrison recommended. That consultant posed a question to me that I thought was noteworthy. She asked if I had a "life partner" I presumed that to mean something like a spouse or a girlfriend. I told the consultant that if I had a "life partner" without having made anything of myself, that the end result would be some form of catastrophic spiral that would or could include domestic violence. The consultant scoffed at my theory and wondered if distorted thought patterns could be a part of the problem with me.

The consultant and I engaged in a lot of other small talk. However, it was generally pleasant. I sent a follow-up letter to the consultant. During that follow-up letter, I correctly described myself as a cross between Einstein and Cartoon Network's Johnny Bravo! I elaborated on particulars that have made me part of both extremes.

I was a man of ironies. I battled feelings of immaturity. I seemed to be bombarded by those feelings. They seemed to come from anywhere and anyone. To make matters more insidious, I should've been the one that would either hold down the job that Conrad had or held down a position as a Lab Technician for a considerable time. My having to clear up a personal bankruptcy didn't help matters either.

I also had to think, however, that if I were truly immature, I would NEVER have earned my post-baccalaureate in the first place! During most of that coursework, I was carried by my work ethic! If I were also immature, I would never have earned the confidence of John Hawley or "The Singing Boss," Both of whom were a delight to work with.

Per my promise to Mr. O'Sullivan, I called a joint meeting between him, the Nurse Practitioner, and me! For the meeting, I also included the same video on Hyperlexia that I taped ten years earlier. The plan worked to an exacting T. I was able to explain to Mr. O'Sullivan what my problem was and convey possible medical ramifications to the Nurse Practitioner.

After I lost my job at Underwriters due to restructuring, part of my strategy was to reach out to Christ Hospital's Vocational Services Unit. Diane Bazan was very happy to meet with me, as was Melissa Bos, a former assistant to Jeremy Sadlier. Now, she was a major player at the Vocational Services Unit in her own right. Ms. Bos and Ms. Bazan were now conducting the Job Club referral sessions that were held weekly. Although I was still not in the Club, Ms. Bazan had no problem with letting me use the service's job leads, computers, and database.

Ms. Bazan also assisted me and insisted that I reconnect with the Illinois Department of Rehabilitation Services immediately. She drafted a letter stating that I had been under the Department's care before and needed the assistance again.

I also touched base with Dr. Harrison again. For one thing, I still had that appointment with that developmental consultant in Skokie that I had to visit. What I failed to get, however, was a three-way meeting with the consultant and Dr. Harrison at Dr. Harrison's office.

What I did get was a visit with Dr. Harrison and an additional doctor named Paul Darren. He, too, was a Neurologist Diagnostician. I posed many of the questions I left for Dr. Harrison and got a surprising answer to one of them. For instance, I asked about getting a baseline test for neurological function. I insisted on such a test to determine if I had any form of neurological disorder. I also insisted on a baseline test before I was prescribed or administered ANY form of psychoactive medication.

Dr. Darren told me that the problem with a baseline test of neurological function was that something as simple as a meal or a cup of coffee could throw off such a test! What Dr. Darren, Dr. Harrison, and I all agreed on was that I have that general medical examination with a battery of neuro-psychiatric testing. I had this set of tests scheduled for 1 October 2001.

Meanwhile, Ms. Bazan was getting very upset-NOT with me, but with the Illinois Department of Rehabilitative Services. They had yet to reinstate my file and update my case to status. She demanded that I "crab at them" to get the business done. In the meantime, Ms. Bazan would introduce me to a new player in the Christ Hospital Vocational Services scheme of business. She was a student from the Illinois Institute of Technology. She had long hair and was very attractive, though very covered. She always wore black and white. Her name was Rawda.

It was during that period that I finally touched base with the consultant that Dr. Harrison wanted me to see. But there was a problem. This consultant used what was called an "Interactive Metronome." The idea behind the interactive metronome was that timing was highly important in helping people with learning disabilities. Autism was one such learning disability that the Interactive Metronome was touted to help.

In the Interactive Metronome, the idea was to clap at the precise moment that a computer directs the patient to clap. The computer could then record how the patient would respond to the directive to clap. If it were on time, there would be no problem. If the patient clapped out of time with the computer's directive beat tone; there was a problem.

The Interactive Metronome had its critics. One such critic was the same Bennett Leventhal, MD/Ph.D., that I chatted with back in the Summer of 1991! This was also the same Bennett Leventhal who opened up the possibility that I might have the same Autism that ultimately turned out to be true! This time, Leventhal expressed reservations about the Interactive Metronome just a scant few weeks after Dr. Harrison suggested that I test out on the machine.

According to Leventhal, the Interactive Metronome was nothing more than a glorified music lesson! However, the consultant explained that Dr. Leventhal's objection to the Interactive Metronome is that it might be seen as a universal panacea, rather than the diagnostic tool that it was intended to be.

In very late September 2001, I went out to the Osten Developmental Institute in Skokie. There, I was met by a very kind lady who was the consultant. Not surprisingly, there were many children at this institute.

In a twinkling, I was taken to a back room where the computer was located. My hands were connected to a network of wires. Those wires, in turn, were connected to an ordinary PC.

Then, I had some headphones placed on me. This headset carried a pilot tone that I was supposed to respond to. That response was made possible by clapping my hands, and thus, completing a circuit that the computer picked up.

Once I was hooked up, the consultant turned on the computer and the pilot tone. It was a single tone, at first. It was a dull-sounding tone in the key of C. All I had to do was listen to it and respond to it. Once I could get a read on a rhythm, I could even anticipate when to move my hands to clap.

Then, the consultant got sneakier. She would introduce not one, but two tones! The object of this phase of the exercise was to respond to one test tone and disregard the other! That second tone was a cowbell.

I had to focus and concentrate harder. However, I was able to work the two test tones without a tremendous amount of difficulty.

The acid test came when I had to respond to an electronic floor mat while responding also to the original test tone. This I did by stamping my feet when directed by tone, as well as to continue to respond to the original thud in the key of C! It was here that things got a little crazy- and, come to find out, a little informative. Once the computer spit out its results, it showed that I was coming in slightly ahead of the test tone! In deference to Dean Skuza from Popular Hot Rodding Magazine Television Magazine, I was probably "red-lighting"-without the quarter mile drag strip to race a car on!

The ladies at the Osten Developmental Institute had one final test for me. For this test, I had to stand on a wooden board. That board, in turn, would be placed on top of a cylindrical tube that was strong enough to hold my weight.

I got up on the board and cylinder teeter-totter with nary a problem. I was able to balance myself with very little difficulty. However, the consultants had another wrinkle to throw in! They had me place a beanbag in my right hand. They then asked me to toss the beanbag over my head and to try to catch the bag with my left hand. This was tricky enough on solid ground. However, they had me do this exercise while I was still on the teeter-totter!

I was able to pull it off, although the shifts in weight because of the throws had me a touch concerned. The real acid test came when the consultants asked me to do the throws on the teetertotter without looking at the path of the beanbag! I was to look straight ahead! It was here that I began to get unstable while I was doing the exercise.

I got through the exercises without additional drama. After the exercises ended, the consultants explained some options that could apply to my treatment. To that end, I attempted to set up a conference call while I was supposed to be at Dr. Harrison's office for an appointment. In the meantime, the consultants had some reservations about an adult being evaluated and tested at an office that was designed for children! Ultimately, I would learn that services for adult Autistics were lacking, compared to services for children who were Autistic!

On 1 October 2001, I first got the stitches taken out of my head after hitting it against a low billboard! That doctor was also kind enough to look over the results of my Dopplers from the Legs for Life Nationwide Screening program. She then performed a more comprehensive inspection of my circulatory system than I expected, and had blood chemistry done on top of that. Once that was taken care of, it was off to the Neurological Clinic where I was to meet with Dr. Paul Darren for my comprehensive Neurological Evaluation and physical.

Dr. Darren had an assistant from Nigeria join him. She, like Dr. Christie, was a postdoctoral fellow named Nancy Folisade. Dr. Darren and Dr. Folisade would form a tag team that could conduct the evaluation.

Phase One of the evaluation was an interview and family medical history. It was here that I was pretty thorough in my description. I let Doctors Darren and Folisade know about Marciea's Shy-Drager Syndrome, and let them know that she was atypical compared to the demographics of the usual sufferer. Dr. Darren understood but emphasized the atypical part. Also discussed was any substance abuse history within the family. I had none, but my family did!

Phase Two of the evaluation concerned a series of memory retention tests, recall tests, assembling face models, and visual puzzles. When it came down to the memory retention and recall tests, I stumbled a bit, and Dr. Folisade had to intervene before she allowed me to continue.

I described my long-term memory and told the team that I was better at it than my short-term memory. When I gave the example of Enzo Ferrari's poor customer service to Ferrucio Lamborghini, Dr. Folisade seemed riveted.

Next was the physical examination phase. It was here that Dr. Folisade took over. It was a once-over-lightly examination, just enough to check the neurology and motor functions, and to listen to my heart; that was it. Finally, Dr. Darren recommended that I have another Sleep Evaluation done on me to complete the process.

I had that Sleep Evaluation done on me during the week of 12 October 2001. I decided that I would make an adventure of it. First, there would be dinner at a downtown restaurant. Then, I would move on to NU Medical for the evaluation.

What I found a touch daunting was my choice of restaurants. I chose Catch Thirty-Five, at 35 West Wacker Drive. The trouble was, the minimum price for a typical meal at Catch Thirty-Five was thirty-five Dollars-plus! That thirty-five dollars plus was probably going towards paying for the ambience of the restaurant. For instance, there was a piano at the front of the place. There was also exotic seafood such as sea bass and tilapia; you name it.

Fortunately for me, there was also a seafood salad mini-entrée/appetizer. It was huge. I made do with that, lemonade, and an apple pie, and called it a meal. The damage was a scant $20.00. I made sure that my drink would be caffeine-free. Otherwise, it would've disrupted the results of my Sleep Evaluation.

After a couple of hours of window shopping, I reported to NU Medical for the Sleep Study. It was around 8:30 PM. I followed the directions on where to report and which elevator to take. That was important because although the medical center was the same, the building was all new.

Once I reported to the Sleep Clinic, I was met by a night nurse, who put me into my room. Once she familiarized me with what I would need, I was allowed to shower in the nearby bathroom. I knew not to wet my hair. I was then turned over to a male Technician of East Indian descent who just happened to be adopted by Westerners. He hooked me up to the assortment of monitors I would need. I then watched the 9 and 10 PM News, and the Sleep Evaluation started after that. My evaluation would conclude at 6 AM, and I hopped the Metra Electric home afterward.

This Sleep Evaluation, like my other two evaluations, proved abnormal. It also showed the presence of Sleep Apnea. I was not surprised by this finding. What I did find surprising was that a link was, at least, implied between sleep difficulties and Autism Spectrum Disorder! Could it be that the reason for my Autism was my inability to sustain sleep?

One of Dad's favorite stories was how he admonished Lottie, his sister, not to wake me as an infant. However, she impulsively wanted to play with me. However, Lottie was the one who had become sleepy while I was still going strong, even though it was the middle of the night! Most insidiously, Mom would send me over to a neighbor's house so that she could get some sleep!

The findings of the Neurological Evaluation concluded that I had Pervasive Developmental Disorder, but remember! Pervasive Developmental Disorder is part of the Autistic continuum! One of the characteristics of PDD includes motor difficulties, such as tying a necktie or catching a batted ball, as I reported to Dr. Darren. Another characteristic of PDD includes issues such as difficulties in interpersonal relationships!

These findings were reported to Dr. Harrison. In the meantime, Dr. Darren and Dr. Folisade seemed delighted to have had me as a patient. They thanked Dr. Harrison for the referral and pledged any further assistance to me if the need arose.

After Thanksgiving 2001, I was finally able to have my case reinstated at the Illinois Department of Rehabilitation Services. This time, however, I had to attend an Intake Meeting as if I were a new member who had to be initiated in the first place. As luck would have it, the same Ginnie Roland who had been with me through my trials with Christ Hospital's Vocational Services Unit and their initial rejection of me would conduct this intake.

Ginnie was delighted that I had found out what my Glass Monolith was since I left her cadre. There was some doubt as to what my problem was while I was with her. Her thoughts were that now that it was known that I had Autism Spectrum Disorder, the picture was clearer in terms of how to best work with me. I agreed with her.

What Ginnie did have reservations about was my continuing with Christ Hospital's Vocational Services Unit. It was expensive. Ginnie worried about cost considerations. However, Ginnie also knew that I had a relationship with Christ Hospital's Vocational Services Unit, and that any change from that relationship would prove disruptive. I agreed with her on that front as well.

Dr. Harrison had me meet with a vocational specialist by the name of Julius March. A couple of weeks after my meeting with Dr. March, the Occupational Consultant in Evanston, I got a call from Dr. Harrison that came on the answering machine. By this time, the year 2001 had crossed into the year 2002. That call said: "Hi Jon. This is Dr. Harrison calling from NU Medical. I got a call from the Occupational Consultant last week. And he went over the evaluation. He recommended that you NOT return to work at this time, and that you apply for Disability and get cognitive rehabilitation services, and he also concurred with my diagnosis. So, he recommended rehab services, which you have had some involvement in, and applying for Disability through your local Social Security office, and that's what you should do. You might also contact your local community mental health service office as well. It's Roseland Mental Health Center."

I picked up the phone while Dr. Harrison was still talking and introduced myself. Then, Dr. Harrison elaborated further on the consultant's contention that I shouldn't even be looking for work at all!

Dr. Harrison told me that she had asked the consultant about my near success at Underwriters. However, Harrison told me that the consultant thought that the case of Underwriters was a matter of simple luck on my part!

Meanwhile, I couldn't believe what I was hearing. Since the message was still on the answering machine, I transferred it to a tape recorder. I then played it for Mom.

Mom's position always was also that I should apply for Disability! She felt that since I had "emotional problems", I wasn't lying.

I scoffed at Mom's contention because any emotional problems I was having would resolve themselves with a stable job and a stable career. I was effectively on my way to that goal when I got cut. Let us not forget. The bizarre, unusual, and profound difficulties I had during my Undergraduate would give anyone "emotional problems". I believed that I had to suck it up and get myself together!

On the more practical side, I was already rejected twice for Disability. The reasons for my rejection were that my problems were NOT significant enough to warrant getting Disability!

Most importantly, I was always the type of person who could only take so much rejection before I decided that what I was

doing was NOT worth the effort. In this case, the multiple rejections for Disability were leading me to believe that unless I were like the late actor Christopher Reeve, in his final eight years of his life, I would have NO chance at getting it, not that I could necessarily blame the decision-makers. There was already an overabundance of people who were experts at subverting a public program for personal gain. This Author could cite so many examples that are relevant to this story, but would be compromised.

Mom, however, thought that I should go back and reapply. She also asserted that I was "no more than anybody else." She believed that I had no right to decide to give up the way I was doing it. Mom also contended that "People that just got off the boat can get it. Why can't you (meaning This Author) get it?"

Mom concurred with Jeremy Sadlier from the Christ Hospital Vocational Services Unit. Now, she was concurring with the dub I took from the answering machine. She held that I had no business spending so much time on the computer looking for job leads. Since Mom wanted as much time as I could give her on demand, i.e., for errands, running with her, housework, or yard work, I was getting into conflicts with her while I was looking for work. Now, Mom had the ammunition.

What was more insidious than Mom's contention that I should NOT continue looking for work was that I was now getting a new counselor from DORS. Ginnie Roland would now transfer to a remote regional office. Although Ms. Roland assured me that the person I would have replaced her on my case would be brought up to speed, and that there wouldn't be any discontinuity in my care. I wasn't so sure. My new counselor, Laquinda Phelps, was young, Black, and appeared to be fresh out of college! That, to me, spelled trouble! My suspicions were confirmed when this new counselor effectively froze any further employment assistance without a clarification from Dr. Harrison!

I fared worse when I visited the Illinois Education and Training Center less than a week later. I consulted with Toni Randall. I showed her the chart of occupations that autistic individuals should enter and avoid, and told her about my meeting with Dr. Harrison's consultant. When I told her that I was counting on coming to a final, firm solution for balancing all of the parameters that I mentioned, Toni contended: "I don't want to get you into a situation that could 'set you up' if you know what I mean." Toni contended that any training program I would get into would "set me up" for failure! It didn't matter that I had shown her the Temple Grandin Internet article that showed her where Autistic and Asperger's patients could do well. I was too much of a hot potato for an employment-training program.

When I brought the problem back to Ms. Bazan, I was beginning to think to myself: "Thou Too Brutus?"

44

Bazan had thought about referring me for a lead as a Technical Writer in Cicero. In light of the reservations that the consultant had about me looking for work, she felt compelled to abort that referral.

So, it came down to this. Either I get a clarification about what Dr. Harrison's consultant said, or I will have my case held hostage again, as it was when Jeremy had concerns after the initial Job.

Readiness Workshop and training. However, once I notified Dr. Harrison, she got right to work on it, and here is that Letter of Clarification:

Northwestern Medical Faculty Foundation

675 North St. Clair Street

Chicago, Illinois 60611

2/20/02

Laquinda Phelps

Ill.. Dept. of Human Services DORS 8840 S. Stony Island Ave.

Chicago, IL. 60617

Dear Ms. Phelps:

I am writing this letter on behalf of Jon Evans, whom I have consulted over the past several months. I am aware that you do have copies of my evaluation and office notes.

Jon requested a "letter of clarification" regarding my recommendations. Please note that the patient was also in consultation with Julius March, Ph.D., regarding his symptoms, which are consistent with Asperger's Syndrome. Jon is unable to afford private treatment with Dr. March and was referred to you.

Dr. March indicated to me that he felt Jon needed extensive job support to function in any capacity in competitive employment. "Jon has difficulty interpreting social cues, gleaning the most salient features from information presented to him, and tends to be overly inclusive of details. These challenges have interfered with his ability to remain gainfully employed in the past, and he needs help from your department as he seeks employment about these issues. I do feel that it would be appropriate for your agency to support Jon in psychotherapy in addition to supported employment services."

Dr. March further recommended that I apply for Disability benefits in the meantime, as he works on the above issues.

Sincerely yours

Diana Harrison, MD/Ph. Ph.D.

Consulting Psychologist

Cc: Jon Evans

Check the irony of what the Letter of Clarification said. "…and tends to be overly inclusive of details." If I were tending to be overly inclusive of details, what was I doing forgetting things, and/or failing to detect things? I believe that a better description of my problem would be either that I was detecting things that I could leave out or failing to pick up things that I needed to. In a meeting with Dr. Harrison, she even modified one of my goals as being paying "appropriate" attention to detail.

To simplify matters, I will define my problem as zigging when I should zag, and zagging when I should zig.

The first thing I did was to take my copy of my Letter of Clarification back to Christ Hospital Vocational Services Unit, and Ms. Bazan's office. I was now back in business. Ms. Leander had no problem with my continuing with the Job Club either.

Despite my getting a Letter of Clarification from Dr. Harrison, I would hit another Glass Monolith. I repeatedly attempted to contact Toni Randall at the Illinois Education and Training Center. However, she never returned my telephone calls, faxes, or my E-Mails.

My Career Monolith

I made good on my promise not to march down the aisle on Graduation Day. I was too disgraced to take the walk in a cap and gown. My academic career spanned a whopping 8 h years, and four universities. There were also three stopping off points-Wright College, Northwestern University, and Governor's State University to pick up some necessary coursework. My first intent was to attend Loyola University. However, I fit in socially, but NOT academically at Loyola. The yardage at Chicago De Paul University was tough. However, at least I could get it. I had to move on to the University of Detroit in an attempt to complete an Engineering curriculum. I ran into an academic lynching instead. Finally, I had to settle for a Bachelor of General Studies Degree Roosevelt University in Chicago to save face! If my undergraduate career were a car, it would 've been the TC sports car that was jointly built by Chrysler and Maserati! Note: The Chrysler/Maserati TC bombed!

My mission was to use a university education to prepare myself for the working world. I was kicked out of both a Physics and an Engineering department -dismissed as a common wannabe. Although I tried to shore myself up by taking technical courses, the fact of the matter is that Liberal Arts students are the last to be hired by industry. Therefore, my mission failed-miserably.

Now that I put my Undergraduate years behind me, the sailboat that was my life needed a daggerboard-fast!

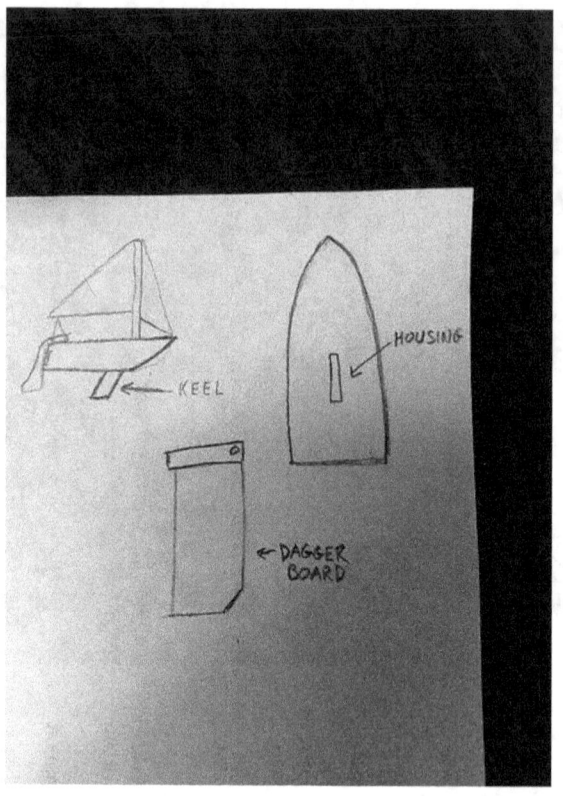

I thought that the Cable Television industry would be my deliverance.

Of all the major metropolitan areas that had been wired for Cable Television, Chicago would be, or be near, dead last! Not only were there technical issues, but there were some political issues as well. I even tried to get into the act with my proposal to implement Cable Stereo.

During this time (1982), the closest you could ever come to Cable Television was what was called Subscription Television. This type of television was broadcast over ordinary analog airwaves. However, you needed a special decoder and a monthly subscription to keep that decoder active. There were two competitors. ON-TV was one, and Spectrum was the other.

ON-TV and Spectrum used ordinary broadcast channels that were either NOT being used by the networks or were in use once the local channels went off the air for the night. For a while, even ABC/WLS-TV (Channel 7) had an arrangement with a Subscription Television provider. However, the name escapes me currently.

I smelled a ground-floor opportunity in Cable Television; so, did many other people. To that end, an outfit called Minorities in Cable and New Technologies was formed. I found out about Minorities in Cable and New Technologies through the Chicago Sunday Tribune.

Their first meeting was at Columbia College, which was just a hair's breadth south of my alma mater, Roosevelt University! I posed a written question to the panel: "What kind of background is necessary to get into the Cable industry?" The answer I got was- "Any"!

I was momentarily immensely encouraged by that response. I graduated with six hours of Electronics, with three more hours of Physics/Electricity and Magnetism. Intuitively, I would not have had any problems with Cable TV construction or installation? I was even naïve enough to think that I could parley my experience as an Operator for the old Illinois Bell Telephone Company into a Customer Service job in the Cable industry.

Regarding my Glass Monolith in the Cable industry, I was slowed down and held back by where I lived and by politics. It took a lot of political wrangling before there could be any discussion about Cable Television in Chicago. Ironically, Chicago's suburbs already had some form of Cable Television. Meanwhile, Chicago had not even decided how the Cable Television booty would even be divided.

Chicago did not want just one company to control all the Cable TV for the city. Instead, it tried to break the city up into several regions. Each separate region would control all Cable TV for that region. Here, too, there would be a considerable degree of wrangling and politicking. Meanwhile, all I could do was sit on the sidelines and wait.

In addition to my track stories, I also told Byron about my misadventures during college, and what to expect when he got there. While my stories certainly peaked Byron's interest, he then posed a simple question for me. He asked: "What are you?"

I could not answer Byron. It was clear to me that I was in serious trouble! Oh, I was able to weasel out of that situation by explaining that I had to settle for a Bachelor of General Studies degree, but the fact of the matter was that Byron touched on the very crux of my situation.

I was like a sailboat with its daggerboard missing, since I graduated with a degree, but without the skills the industry accepts. This type of situation predisposed me to hit Glass Monoliths.

If the Cable Television industry was one way to find my daggerboard, another one appeared to be in a new program at Roosevelt University, which was developed at or about the time I graduated. Roosevelt University had developed a curriculum in Electronics Engineering Technology. In it, the student would complete the compulsory General Education courses at Roosevelt, plus a few Physics and Electronics courses. That student would then move on to the Illinois Technical College across the street (NOT to be confused with the Illinois Institute of Technology). There, the student would complete the hardcore electronics training.

When I discussed the idea of my being in a curriculum like that with Prof. Walton, the chairman of the Physics Department at Roosevelt

University, he stated that I might as well go through the full four years of college all over again! Still, it was an option I kept in my hip pocket.

I did discuss various career options with officials of not only the Illinois Department of Rehabilitation Services, but a few agencies they worked with as well. Unfortunately, these officials focused more on my personality issues than my need to acquire specific skills that are industry acceptable.

After learning of a program by the Chicago Opportunities and Industrialization Center on 73rd and State Street, I went there. Their program was in Auto Mechanics. Since I was an Auto buff, I thought I'd find some solace here.

I presented my resume to the receptionist, then was told that I was too advanced for the program, even though I only had a Liberal Arts/General Studies degree. Instead, I was referred to their professional division, where I was more UNLIKELY to qualify for their openings.

While I was scoring very well on the U.S. Government's Clerical Examinations, I failed the Air Traffic Controller's Examination. I had to wait and wait, and wait to find out that I failed, and even then, only after a telephone call to one of the FAA's personnel, Alvin. There was one section on the test in which guessing was strongly desired. I was very conservative in my guessing.

My failure in the Air Traffic Controller's Examination raised this point. Whenever I encountered a job I found worth having or wanted to go the extra mile to get, I would either struggle with it or fail at it miserably. Anytime anything came up worth having, I would fail miserably or run into something that would block me from it; again, The Glass Monolith and I would always meet.

Author's Side Note:

For instance, on 2 April 1979, I got a terrific job as a Metallurgical Lab Technician for Pheoll Manufacturing Company, on Chicago's West Side. On 25 April 1979, the Chief Metallurgist would call me out and fire me because I was, in his words, "too slow" or "can't work with my hands". Although the charge was bogus, I was still out of work. Even more insidiously, I would never again get another job in the ferrous metals industry.

I eventually got a temporary full-time job as a Control Clerk for the U.S. Internal Revenue Service on 13 June 1983. Since my job at the Internal Revenue Service was only temporary and terminable at any time, I kept looking for work. During my lunch hour, I applied to Showtime-Teleprompter, a division of Group W Cable. Here, I thought I would be a shoo-in for finding a job. It was not.

Meanwhile, I was still touching base with the outfit Minorities in Cable and New Technologies, even to the point of joining the organization. I walked over to their office on my lunch break from the IRS. Oddly, the moderator of Minorities in Cable and New Technologies walked in, saw me, and admonished the receptionist about leaving the door unlocked.

The meetings came next. Often, we would meet after work in places like Columbia University and the Americana Congress.

I felt super strange at this meeting, especially since one of the gentlemen welcoming me told me to go sit down and have a drink. Remember. I was, and still am, a total abstainer. I felt even stranger after many Black women of various backgrounds came in and immediately broke off into their cliques. I sat alone.

This meeting had one saving grace, however. The name of that saving grace was Charles Hoard. Hoard was working for Continental Cablevision, one of the groups vying for a Cable TV license. Continental Cablevision was the sole bidder for Region Five of the five regions of Cable television that Chicago was divided into. Region Five included the West Pullman/Stewart Ridge area, where I lived.

Charles Hoard was sitting alone as I was. However, when he and I met, he was more than happy to chew the fat with me about some of the issues I had relative to getting into the Cable Television industry. We traded names and business cards, and I was well on my way. The mission was accomplished.

Continental Cablevision would team up with a minority-based outlet called Stellar Communications Incorporated. My understanding of this partnership was that Stellar Communications was Black owned and operated.

As for the other players, Group W would take the Northwest Side, while a group that is now, at the time of this writing, RCN Communications would take the Lakefront, and soon, Region Four, where my old home in West Englewood was. Alliances changed. Oftentimes, Cable groups would pull out of their respective areas that they would vie for. That would make a slot available for another Cable outfit to take over.

In terms of the Minorities in Cable and New Technologies, every member would hit that Glass Monolith I frequently spoke of. You see, approval of these deals required the approval of the Chicago City Council-the same Chicago City Council that was embroiled in Council Wars. Council Wars was compared to the movie Star Wars and was a battle between the first Black Mayor of Chicago, and the Chicago City Council.

It was around that time of this meeting, or shortly afterward, that the City Council approved the bid by the Stellar-Continental Cablevision group for Region Five, the far South Side of Chicago. This area included where I lived. However, there was no joy among the Blacks at that meeting. The moderator of Minorities in Cable and New Technologies expressed no joy. He was unhappy for some reason. Word had it that there wasn't much minority participation from the Stellar portion of the alliance. I couldn't be sure.

Marciea thought that my problem could easily be solved by simply taking a course in AUTOCAD, a series of programs in Computer Aided Drafting. She cited cases of friends who, according to her, were supposedly making huge incomes by taking this short course. I was skeptical, citing potential Glass Monoliths due to a lack of experience. I also stated that nowadays, industry wants people with a definite skills base, not patchwork courses. Since I only graduated with a degree in General Studies, I was at the most significant risk for rejection.

My career problems would compound in October 1984. At this time, I was working at Alpha Metals Corporation, a non-ferrous manufacturer of low-temperature alloys. However, my inability to multitask so overpowered me that I was committing a series of operating errors-unlike Pheoll, where I committed few, if any. I got a written warning that threatened termination. After it was determined that I was not suitable for the job, I resigned from Alpha, then went back to The Center for the Training of the Disabled.

I still lacked functional skills, predisposing me to have to take jobs of this nature. But Bess Robertson of the CTD contended that the "ability to verbalize" is a skill. She arranged a group meeting in which a panel of peers grilled me. These peers contended that I lacked self-confidence, rather than hard skills.

I must respond by saying that people who can verbalize are pennies a dozen, NOT a dime a dozen. The "ability to verbalize" is an INTANGIBLE!

INDUSTRY IS INTERESTED IN "HARD SKILLS" AND EXPERIENCE-NOT INTANGIBLES!

Cade McNown DID NOT LACK CONFIDENCE IN HIMSELF- Cade who? Yet, as a quarterback for the Chicago Bears, he was a laughingstock! Industry wants the Staubach! Certification in a "hard skill" would make me a Staubach.

In late 1984 or early 1985, I discovered a program at Sangamon State University in Springfield, Illinois, through a job fair I attended. This program was more like Telecommunications Management. Most importantly, this was a Graduate, not an Undergraduate program. My second choice would be to go to Illinois Technical College, which, at that time, was across the street from Roosevelt University! The Illinois Technical College offered various programs in Electronics. With those Electronics programs, I was sure that I could either find a job or open up my own independent business.

Part One of my plan was to check out the Illinois Technical College first. Here, I met a charming, relatively young White lady by the name of Wendy. She wore clogs and slacks and was moderately dressed. Her hair was short and blonde.

Our conversation was quite pleasant and even light-hearted. Wendy asked if I would've considered teaching Electronics. I told Wendy that I had no problem teaching Electronics whatsoever. However, without the skills and training in Electronics, that would be a moot point. However, I mentioned that I did have a degree from Roosevelt, but no skills. It was then that Wendy decided to have me consult Aminul Karim, the Dean at the School. Karim believed that, because I had my

General Studies Degree from Roosevelt already, the best course to take would have been the Dual Degree Program that Roosevelt University's Professor Walton discouraged me from Walton thought that I might as well have taken a full four-year course.

Part Two would be a little more involved and would require the help of Mom's credit card. Here, I would take a Greyhound bus to Springfield's Sangamon State University (now changed to the University of Illinois at Springfield). I would come back that same evening by Amtrak. First, I had to telephone Sangamon State to make the appointment for a visit. Then, I had to be sure that I was on the Greyhound bus. Fortunately, Greyhound Bus Lines had a satellite terminal at the 95th Street CTA Rapid Transit Terminus.

As I got off the bus and was about to pull into the station, a young, very attractive White woman stood in my path. She came up to me and asked: "Are you Jon Evans?" When I replied: "Yes, I am...", she said: "We're here to take you to Sangamon State."

In a twinkling, she, her colleague, and I were in a car and off to the campus of Sangamon State University. Once there, I would meet with the Chairman of the Communications Department. Meanwhile, the lady who was so nice as to pick me up would disappear to her work.

This program was in Communications. However, the eye was mainly focused on Communications Media Systems, such as Satellite media, Broadcasting, and newer but related technologies. There was a Co-Operative type of fellowship arrangement. There was NO guarantee of a job after graduation. However, there would be enough networking as part of the package that the odds would, according to the officials, favor me.

After lunch at Sangamon/UIS, I conferred with the Chairman again, then headed on my way to Springfield-Amtrak. The Chairman revealed that while the problem of crime didn't come close to that of Chicago, Springfield, too, had its moments.

However, most of these moments were the result of rowdy elements from the campuses.

I now had to decide between the former Sangamon State University (now the University of Illinois at Springfield), and the joint program between Roosevelt University and a proprietary school called the Illinois Technical College.

Had I chosen Sangamon UIS, I would've wound up with a Master's degree if I were successful. However, there was only a guarantee of being introduced to the network. There was NO guarantee of a job; there was also no guarantee of employability.

Roosevelt/ITC only promised another Bachelor's degree in addition to the one I had. However, certification in Electronics Engineering Technology and its accompanying Bachelor's degree would've left me eligible for licensing as an Electronics Technician. The FCC also had licensing for such technicians. Most importantly of all, I theoretically had the opportunity to put myself to work as an Electronics Technician, if only a TV or radio repairman a/la Dad. With that, I could at least support myself.

My goal was quite simple. The economy was a patent joke. I needed to position myself so that if I were to lose my job at any time, I could still support myself. To do that, I had to be skilled. Certifications by license would either help or be tantamount to a union card.

My decision would NOT be an easy one. Had I chosen Sangamon UIS at that time, I would've beaten Milton to a Master's! As a result, I would've been the first person in my family to have earned an advanced degree!

But what good would it have been to beat Milton to a Master's if I couldn't land a job? Remember! A whopping 90 percent of the job market was CLOSED to me because I lacked practical skills. This ineligibility for such a large percentage of the job market was, in my mind, my Glass Monolith!

The Roosevelt/ITC Program seemed to offer me a better chance of breaking my Glass Monolith than the Sangamon/UIS Program. Therefore, I chose Roosevelt/ITC.

I started the Roosevelt/ITC program in the Summer of 1985. As I started the course, I looked up the backgrounds of the professors I'd have, one of them being Professor Norman Cannon. I also noticed that Professor Cannon did not have any form of collegiate training, either at the Junior College level or the University level. Yet, Professor Cannon was teaching a course that could be used for credit towards a University Degree at Roosevelt University.

This was a dual-certificate program. Successful completion would result in both a Certificate in Electronics from the Illinois Technical College and an actual Bachelor of Science in Electronics Engineering Technology from Roosevelt University.

I thought to myself: "Shades of De Paul University"! Remember. DePaul had several cooperative or dual degree programs with several other universities around the country, not just in the state.

I got a 96 in the Electronics Midterm and did almost as well with Printed Circuit Fabrication. Ultimately, I got a B in both courses. But because I used up my eligibility for Undergraduate Student Loans, I could go no further. Now, once again, I was jobless, school less, and rudderless.

The trouble with chronic, protracted unemployment is that one day looks like all the other days in one's life. One month looks like all the other months in one's life. Monotony comes as standard equipment.

There were two exceptions.

One exception was that I once again got an employment solicitation from the United States Internal Revenue Service. But there was a catch. It was for what was called intermittent work as a Taxpayer Service Representative. Intermittent work meant, in their eyes, that I had to be available at a moment's notice. Even more insidiously, I could work one day, then be off the next, or several more days in succession. The job would NOT be the friendly confines of the 20th Floor!

But even more insidiously, the job was so precise, and the standards so strict, that I could be charged with deficiencies even though it did not appear that I was doing anything other than by procedure. That's because one of the standards used to judge an Intermittent Taxpayer Service Representative was the time it took to complete a call.

I was already fired once on allegations of being slow. I did NOT want another entity, private or public, to allege slowness on my part; So, I declined the job.

As I was exiting the floor where the Pre-Orientation Session was taking place, I was shown another Intermittent job. This one was in Collections. However, the standards were the same. Furthermore, there was NO reinstatement eligibility for either of the Intermittent jobs. As a result, I declined that job too.

I felt that if I were to take another Government job, I should have at least had what I had as a Temporary Control Clerk back at the friendly confines, no less.

Mom thought that maybe I could've taken one of the two Intermittent jobs, then worked my way through it, or up. Little did she know that such thoughts were, at best, wishful thinking!

Matters would become worse before they would become better. For instance, the former Conrad Hilton Hotel was being remodeled, refurbished, and renamed the Chicago Hilton and Towers. Meanwhile, I am not sure whether I submitted my resume or filled out an application for a Telephone Operator's position at the new hotel. Anyhow, I got a call from Rick Roles of the newly refurbished hotel, asking to see me.

There was still a lot of dust and debris to navigate to meet Rick at his location. Nevertheless, I managed, and he gave me an interview and a sample test on how to direct someone to the Chicago Hilton and Towers. Rick assured me that I did an excellent job on the sample test and asked me:

"When can you start?"

I responded: "When can you start me?"

"We'll call you." Said Rick.

Time grew closer and closer to the opening of the new Chicago Hilton and Towers. Yet, I heard nothing. Meanwhile, Mom told me, "Don't call them. They told you they'll call you."

A few weeks later, I received a call from the Minorities in Cable and New Technologies. Through them, I got a referral for an interview at Cablevision in Oak Park. I was to see Rose Smith.

I can't see what I did wrong during the interview. I was dressed to the nines, I listened more than I talked, although I did ask Ms. Smith why Cablevision wasn't in on the upcoming Cable TV development in

Chicago proper. Rose responded that such a foray would've been too massive an undertaking for such a small company. I never realized that it was that small.

Several days passed without an answer. When I couldn't take it anymore, I telephoned Rose and asked about the status of my application. She informed me that a letter was in the mail.

That letter arrived on the afternoon that I called. Unfortunately, it was a Rejection Letter!

I never renewed my membership in Minorities and Cable and New Technologies again. First, I was pre-screened out of any interviews at their job fair. Then, I was rejected after receiving a referral from the organization. I paid my membership dues, yet I was treated as if I were a non-member, or even a pariah, by the organization!

Speaking of the Cable TV industry, a new development has emerged. The Stellar/Continental Cable Television alliance was bought out by an outfit called Tele-Communications Incorporated (TCI) lock, stock, and barrel. TCI was based in Denver, Colorado, and was a huge conglomerate. If I wanted a job in the Cable Industry in Chicago, I would have to sever my ties to a very willing Charles Hoard and talk to officials of TCI in some way.

TCI had set up a Physical Plant at an abandoned car dealership on 57th and Western Avenue. I saw someone and was advised to return the next day at 7 AM because the supervisor covering the construction end of that was to leave for Detroit shortly after.

I admit to dragging my feet. I arrived later than 7 AM, and the supervisor was already gone. I blew it! It was just that simple. I also blew a large salary. The salaries for construction were running as high as $31K annually!

Marciea, my sister, had doubts about whether I should've even vied for jobs like Cable Television construction anyway because of my health.

Mike, my brother, had me stay with him in Hawaii for a few months. It was at this time that he wanted me to explore some employment possibilities there-as well as to consider helping him with his music career. I didn't realistically think that I could relocate to Hawaii, plant roots, and establish a career. It just wasn't going to happen! In fact, I always held that relocation was tantamount to running away from a person's problems, unless those problems were addressed beforehand.

But now what? Yes, I did resume my job search as I did before I left. However, I was just as much without direction career wise as when I first left for Hawaii. I had considerable time to mull over what I wanted, and needed to do next. Unfortunately, with the Thanksgiving and Christmas holidays of 1986, the only thing I could do was to mull over my future.

1986 would end and 1987 would begin without any change.

I went back to the former Illinois Bell Telephone Company on a cold canvass. Bess Robertson suggested that maybe I reconsider a return to the old Ma Bell, back when I was working with her. I had taken a test for their Operator's job before leaving for Hawaii. Mom had made that suggestion before I left for Hawaii.

During the first week of February 1987, I got a call from someone named Ms. Godmond at Illinois Bell. She suggested I come in and fill out an application. I included my resume. I thought that maybe this time, I would climb out of my rut. Little did I know that another Glass Monolith awaited me. It was a form-written postcard that said that I was rejected.

It seemed illogical for Illinois Bell to ask me to fill out an application, only to reject me shortly after I completed the application. When I went to their Personnel Office, they explained that anytime a resume was included with an application, that application was immediately referred to Management Personnel, where there were NO openings whatsoever.

I gave up in disgust as I stormed out the door. However, once I got home, I received another call from Ms. Godmond. Mom took the message and passed it along to me.

When Mom told me that Ms. Godmond called, I told Mom that was "bull (plop)"! I told Mom what happened when I went down to Illinois Bell and how they told me that they never had anything.

Therefore, she effectively told me to climb back on the horse that I had been thrown from. Mom insisted that I return Ms. Godmond's phone call despite what I was told and what I was going through.

This time, I was able to get in touch with Ms. Godmond, and with that, I learned I was to come in for processing, including a Medical on 10 February.

I got the job as an Operator again. Unfortunately, I had to work in the South Suburban area. That presented itself with a host of transportation issues that almost cost me my job. I was put on Extended Probation. When I finally cleared Probation, I looked to get out of Number Services entirely, or at the very least, get out of South Suburban Remote #1.

To that end, I applied for a couple of transfers-one upgrade, one lateral.

The upgrade transfer involved a test for the Central Office Technician. Instead of working with people, as I was doing, I would be working with telephone circuits. I had enough Electronics courses, so I qualified to take the test. However, I would hit one of those insidious Glass Monoliths once the time came for me to take the test.

The test was based on speed. You only had half an hour to complete the many entries in the test. I had an inkling that my lack of speed would prove to be my ultimate undoing. However, Ms. Magurney told me not to sweat it. Ultimately, I would fail the test by one lousy point!

This was NOT the first time that this would happen. I would take a test at AT&T for an Account Executive. The result was the same. For one reason or another, I would fail that test, too. If it were a job worth having, I would fail the test for that job. There were no ifs, ands, or buts about it.

I ultimately got a Lateral Transfer from South Suburban Remote #1 to East Midway Drive in Chicago, and held it from late 1988 to late 1993, when it would eventually close. I transferred to the Illinois Center Office. On the morning of 23 August 1994, I sat at a remote workstation, right next to a pillar, no less, and I got into an incident with a Junior Service Assistant that alleged that I was talking too loudly. I had had enough. I hit a Glass Monolith. It was that incident that prompted me to explore going back to school for career enhancement.

As I stated, during my ill-fated attempt at Engineering, I developed an ability to write. Couple that with courses I already had in Science and Technical Communications, and it looked very attractive to me. At that time, there was a demand for Technical Writers.

The Technical Communications Department was relatively new at the Illinois Institute of Technology. It was only in existence since about the mid to late 1980s. I would visit their annual Open House each year during the early 90s but vacillated about pulling the trigger-until the episode with Kay made my mind up for me. I was leaning towards some form of continuing education. The question was-what type?

Ms. Hampton, the Group Secretary, told me not to worry about my poor academic record. Although the Dean of the Graduate School brought the subject up, I was ultimately accepted. Just about two weeks after I had conflicted with Kay, I was in class.

There was only one class I could take, for the time being. It was the basic Technical Writing course. The class was so large, and so many other majors needed the class, that it ultimately closed to everyone except Technical Writing majors, which I had declared as my major.

That was different during my second semester at IIT. Speaking of dealing with people, one of the most prominent areas that Feinberg stressed was the concept of Corporate Culture. This wasn't a completely foreign concept to me. However, as a Technical Writer, Feinberg seemed to imply that the idea of Corporate Culture would be one of the most critical concepts to pick up.

My work in Technical Writing was particularly important after I was fired from Ameritech. I'd battle for months to find another job, and often, employers would use my firing from Ameritech against me. The Technical Communications curriculum was the only thing that enabled me to keep my sanity during the period of my firing.

Speaking of which, the next and final step in my Technical Communications curriculum was to figure out a way to perform the mandatory internship. This internship carried only one credit hour. I had to register for it. However, I now had the money for it. Thanks to Dr. Feinberg, I had only hit a Paper Monolith, rather than a Glass Monolith.

There were summer programs held at the Illinois Institute of Technology. These summer programs were geared towards getting more high school students interested in the field of Manufacturing Technology and/or Manufacturing Engineering. In fact, the Illinois

Institute of Technology was working in consort with Daley College of the City Colleges of Chicago chain. The plan was for those to first take care of core courses and curricula, then move on to the Illinois Institute of Technology to finish a four-year degree program.

There had to be some form of accountability for the progress of the summer programs at the Illinois Institute of Technology. There also had to be some way to show that accountability. That's where Professor Feinberg and, ultimately, Yours Truly, would come in.

Accountability requires documentation. That would be my job.

I got a call in early June of 1996. Dr. Feinberg telephoned and told me that the Manufacturing Engineering Department needed people to take notes on the summer programs. In a twinkling, she had me come down to campus to meet two other people that I would be working with.

One such person was Dr. Peter Johnson from the Chemistry Department. He was White, very astute, and had a Dick Tracyish look about him. Dr. Johnson and I hit it off immediately. I talked to him about my early background and was quite candid in telling him that I made the mistake of seeing science and the math as separate areas, rather than seeing them as allied fields. Dr. Johnson assured me that the programs that they were conducting would get that type of mindset out of youngsters' minds quickly.

The second person I would meet was Dr. Jerry Field. Dr. Field was a shorter, very conservative, White gentleman with a background that varied from Manufacturing Engineering to Marketing/Sales. He and I also engaged in some small talk as we went from the Humanities/Technical Writing Department to the Manufacturing building to pick up some materials I would need.

Dr. Feinberg also had me registered to sit in on some staff sessions to stay current with the latest technologies. One such session dealt with Hypertext Markup Language, the language that sets up routines such as buttons, clicking on icons, etc, and what would turn out to be my favorite, MPEG!

The upshot of Feinberg's delightfully fiendish plan was that I would now be working that one-hour internship I would need to graduate. To sweeten the deal, I would get paid for it! Just two-and-a-half months after I was officially fired from Ameritech as an Operator, I would be working again, albeit briefly, and at a substantial loss of pay, no matter. I figured that once I completed my internship, I could vie for bigger, better, and more lucrative things.

I was more or less on call. If there were any sessions of the summer programs, that would be when I would come down to school. I would sit in on the sessions, take notes, and otherwise make myself available to help out in any way I can for the staff.

Speaking of the staff, I would have two or three other members. They were graduate assistants who were there to help the students and introduce them to Manufacturing Engineering.

During that first session, I hung out with Dr. Feinberg. During this session, I worked with her to set up a framework for the upcoming report. I had set up a preliminary framework. Feinberg also had set up a framework. Between the two of us, we ultimately put together a baseline abstract of what the summer programs at the Illinois Institute of Technology would accomplish.

Once the actual program was underway, things got busy fairly quickly. For instance, the Chicago Urban League sponsored tours of the summer programs offered by the Illinois Institute of Technology. As for the students, they were from the inner city! We also met at the

Manufacturing Technology Department. There, someone on staff of Oriental descent showed the students around and explained the required courses.

Since I was still looking for a job, I took advantage of any possible opportunity to put my name out there and network. To that end, I met with a dapper, stocky Black man by the name of Jules Packnett, one of the representatives from the Chicago Urban League.

Meanwhile, back at the sessions, I would get a more intensive education about Internet use above what I was already doing.

Dr. Johnson was very detailed and very dynamic in his description of the history of the Internet and even taught me a few things about its use. Remember. I was sitting in on the sessions. For instance, I knew very little or nothing about search engines before this session. Thanks to Dr. Johnson, I found the Alta Vista search engine very effective in my searches for the things I was interested in. Once Dr. Johnson turned the computers over to the students, they were finding such web sites as "prurient interest "sites to web sites on the rap/hip-hop group, Bone Thugs N'Harmony! There was another morning session. At this session, Professor Keith McKee from the Manufacturing Engineering Department sat in. At this point, the Manufacturing Engineering program was starting to look very inviting, even to me.

I was already starting to consider what to do with my life after I completed my internship and was looking at a host of options. Should I go into Manufacturing? Should I go for a full-blown Master's? Should I get out into the industry? Whatever my options were, I saw my impending Certificate in Technical Communications as a "strike point." Once I established that "strike point", I could then address my options.

Professor McKee agreed and was more than happy to meet with me. Ultimately, he would prove very beneficial.

Meanwhile, the summer sessions would take a change. Instead of the early morning, there would be a few afternoon and evening sessions. I got a call from Feinberg for a late afternoon session to take place. Feinberg also wanted me to meet regarding my future.

Before that late afternoon session started, Feinberg and Dr. Field met with me, and her concerns were aired.

Dr. Feinberg was concerned about my level of experience. She thought that a better tack to take would be to combine my Technical Writing training with Sales/Marketing. Her rationale was that I spoke well and got along well with people. That's when Dr. Field met with me. According to him, Sales/Marketing was the last thing that companies would be likely to cut back.

I got leery at that point. Whenever I thought of Sales, I thought of hucksters such as Minister Louis (Fraud-A-Con)!

Philosophically, if something must be sold, maybe that product is not worth buying. I felt differently about a type of environment when describing a product or technology. For instance, I would not mind giving a seminar at a high-end Audio/Video outlet to describe High-Definition Television, advances in speaker technology, or Bluetooth.

I was also leery because industries that reject people for lack of experience really use that as a subterfuge for committing employment discrimination. For instance, everyone lacks experience until they get that experience in one way or another.

Ascension Thursday

In the Roman Catholic Church, the Feast of the Ascension was marked forty days after the Resurrection of Jesus Christ. This ceremony was always celebrated on a Thursday. Ascension Thursday is usually celebrated in the middle to late Spring.

71

The only difference between Ascension Thursday in the Roman Catholic Church and my feast of the Ascension was that my version of it was a touch belated. It was, however, just as sweet.

Also, consider that when the Allies won World War II, they referred to the surrender of Japan as VJ Day, while they referred to the surrender of the European Axis nations as VE Day. Since I was in an absolute war, why not refer to my version as V-IIT Day?

My version of Ascension Thursday started with a bright and sunny Thursday morning in late August 1996. I turned in my materials for the last time and met with Dr. Feinberg that afternoon. Feinberg already introduced me to a Black lady who would ultimately replace me. The program would continue well into Fall 1996.

As I met with Feinberg, she confirmed the credit hours I completed and that I was, indeed, eligible to receive the Certificate in Technical Communications. Feinberg then told me

that she would petition the Dean of the Graduate College to award me my Certificate. I did it!

There would be no formal commencement exercise or formal ceremony. No matter! I didn't need it. I celebrated this blessed day by jumping into my car and driving from Chicago's Illinois Institute of Technology to the Dominick's Food Store in Merrionette Park, Illinois. There, I purchased a raspberry flavored coffeecake and shared it with Mom and Ted.

I especially didn't need the music of "Pomp and Circumstance." I had a better song that I would choose as my graduation theme song. I chose Bob James/Fourplay's track Dream Come True! I played it on my car cassette player. This was much smoother.

At this juncture, at least I could tell Byron that I was now a Technical Writer. I trained for it. I am certified in it. I had finally found my daggerboard-or so I thought!

I would find out, the hard way was that just because I would find my daggerboard didn't mean that I would have an easier ride in trying to find work. Certainly, there were more companies willing to at least talk to me. There were also more companies that would send me letters of acknowledgement whenever I applied for their openings.

I mistakenly thought that I had a union card. Engineers, Computer Scientists, Chemists, Architects, Programmers, still had the pick of the litter. As for everyone else, it was "Catch as Catch Can!" Unfortunately, I was still in the "everyone else" category!

While everyone else could at least get something, I, on the other hand, would only get another collision with that now familiar Glass Monolith! For instance, just a few weeks after I scored my Certificate, I got a call from an employment agency on Chicago's Far Northwest Side. This was in an area between Cumberland Avenue and East River Road-the northwesternmost point in the corporate limits of Chicago.

However, once I got there, and interviewed with the people, there was a White lady who would introduce me to a new word- "skillsets".

She told me that they were looking for people who had things such as "PageMaker; FrameMaker," and "Microsoft Word." Although the agency had a training program for such matters, it was not currently in session. The upshot of that interview was that although I was certified as a Technical Writer, they still could not help me in any way.

Since I started getting the Society for Technical Communication's monthly publication, I pulled a lead for Technical Writers from a firm called Daasche and Thompson in Oak Park, Illinois. However, when I got a call from them, I was told to come back to them after gaining two years of experience. That was the minimum experience that they would consider or accept.

I got very little solace at a job fair at the Marriott in or around September or October of 1996. At one booth, the representative laughed at me when I told him that I knew Microsoft Works, rather than Microsoft Word. I did not have Microsoft Word on my computer.

At that same fair, I saw a potential opportunity. During my training at Technical Communications, my class visited a very prestigious firm downtown called Whittman-Hart. This company hired Technical Writers in many capacities. However, there was a group of Black Generation X males who were at that booth. They took a look at my resume, then threw it back to me, claiming: "You haven't got enough experience!"

I was faced with a dilemma. I was able to find a part-time job at the campus television station. The pay was low. However, I at least had some pin money. I even picked up another night on which to work. Instead of three hours per week, I would wind up working six. That proved problematic. I still needed to give myself some time to find work in my field.

One of the biggest ironies occurred while I was doing my job search. I registered with a temporary agency. There was one possible Technical Writing assignment that did turn up. The client company was Ameritech! I said that agency that there was bad blood between Ameritech and me, and I regrettably had to turn that assignment down!

It was with that thought in mind that I attempted to get a Metallurgical Lab Technician's job at an industry called Taussig in Skokie. However, the interviewer asked me: "Why should I hire someone for a lab technician's job at just $19,000 a year, when you just might find a

Technical Writer's job a few months down the road paying twenty-five dollars an hour?"

I said to that interviewer that I am just too tired of looking for work. It had been four months since I had graduated, and still, nothing was happening.

But the interviewer responded, "Everybody feels that way."

I still did not get the job.

I was also lashing out.

1996 would roll into 1997 with the same results. It was also at that time that I had attended my first Society for Technical Communication meeting. This one was an Independent Consultant's meeting. Unfortunately, I didn't know that these were Independent Consultants and not sources of employment.

In the Pre-Spring of 1997, there was a General Membership meeting of the Society for Technical Communication at the William Tell Inn in a suburb called Countryside. I arrived early and met an early twenties graduate from the University of Illinois at Chicago (formerly Circle Campus). He was white and thin.

As we chatted, I mentioned buzzwords such as the types of software I was unfamiliar with. After this graduate stepped away to the cash bar, from the buffet line, a relatively tall White woman slipped up behind me and spoke in a low, haunting voice: "You should try to pick up Microsoft Word. I think that's the most important."

I began to think about what she said as I sat with several other women at my table and had dinner with them. They seemed happy to take my resume. The dinner wasn't bad either.

As dinner concluded and the announcements were made, I found out a little more about that mystery woman. Her name was Anna Miller. She was on the Education Committee of the Chicago Chapter of the Society for Technical Communication.

All the Committee Chairmen/Chairwomen sat at a long table at the entrance to the dining room. As I concluded the meeting, I stopped at that table and presented Anna with my resume. Her interest peaked. She insisted that I exchange contact information with her.

That weekend, Anna telephoned me. When she told me that she thought that I had excellent credentials, I promptly told her "Ha!" She then faxed some changes that she thought that I should make to my resume. It took two tries. Come to find out, I had to set up my computer NOT only to receive the faxes, but to also set the computer up to print out the faxes on my computer! There were some Glass Monoliths that I could break just not enough.

My training for what Anna suggested would come in the oddest way. For instance, as I visited my E-Mail, I hit some spam! However, that spam would deliver some important, timely, and relevant information. The spam was from the Illinois Education and Training Center at the campus of the old Wilbur Wright College on the Northwest Side of Chicago.

This training center was funded by the State and dealt with those who were involuntarily displaced from their jobs. That, of course, would include me! Therefore, I made further inquiry.

My first step in the process was to take the L-Subway and bus to Wright College and the IETC. Come to find out, I had to take a qualifying test first. Even college graduates had to take this test. Formerly, they were granted an automatic exemption.

On Shrove Tuesday, 1997, I met with Marge Pietraszek, an intake counselor who would work with me. I marveled at her ability to speak fluent Polish. She and I also developed a rapport.

Since I was still struggling to find a job in my field, I was considering retraining in other areas of industry that were in demand, such as a Machinist or other skilled trades. Marge, however, thought that I had enough as it was. In her words, "Why mess around?"

It was with these thoughts in mind that she recommended that I train in the use of computer applications software. That software included the same Microsoft Word that the STC's Anna recommended earlier. The package also included Typing skills, PageMaker, and Windows 95. I already had Harvard Graphics and CADKEY.

I drove away from the Illinois Education and Training Center with some semblance of direction.

I would go to great pains on my resume to ensure that any claims I make are supported by some record or documentation. For instance, it wasn't enough for me to say that I had Microsoft Word. I made sure I mentioned what kind of Microsoft Word I really had. In my case, I would have Microsoft Word 97 on my resume.

Meanwhile, back at the Illinois Education and Training Center, I was introduced to a new player in my efforts to find work. Her name was Marquita Hynes. Marquita was young, gracious, White, and shorter than me.

At the Illinois Education and Training Center, some facilities enabled job seekers to look for a job. That included Internet access, telephones, fax machines, and scanners.

It was at the scanner that I would hit a Glass Monolith. I could scan my resume. However, I could not make any changes to my resume.

Although I could scan it, the Optical Character Reader that Wright College had was in WordPerfect! I, on the other hand, only knew Microsoft Word. I knew nothing about Word Perfect! I couldn't even use the floppy disk I had with me. The proctor inside was insistent that she could not help me. Marquita tried to assure me that the difference between Microsoft Word and WordPerfect was simply a matter of different icons. However, I was still too intimidated. I remembered the steep learning curve I went through to pick up Microsoft Word.

The entire Summer of 1997 was fraught with this same type of futility. However, when I declared my program a failure to Marge, she was quick to disagree. She had a variety of reasons that I don't remember. However, how do you resolve a burgeoning economy with the Glass Monolith that I was hitting? I had a problem, and there was no looking at it through rose colored glasses!

I had that same excuse thrown at me when I applied at AT&T's Cable Television division, which was conducting a mass hiring event in 1999. That involved me having to drive out to a location in Niles. Once I arrived there, there were throngs of people. Some of those people were being interviewed on the spot! Probably, some people were being hired on the spot. Unfortunately, I fell into neither category.

I named several categories of work that the company had that interested me. I put those categories on my application. That included a training position since I was a Technical Writer.

However, when I inquired about the training job that was posted, I was told that a hold was put on that job! Here is another example of the Glass Monolith I would run into.

The nonsense about being overly qualified is just that-nonsense. What should a company care if I can do the work, will do the work, and give an honest day's work for an honest day's pay? What should a company care if I can report to work without unexcused absences or tardies? However, AT&T's Cable division decreed that because of my background, I would not be suitable for a Customer Service job with them.

Author's Side Note:

There is some semblance of justice. Not long after this incident, AT&T sold its Cable division to Comcast.

Weeks would turn into months in 2000. Finally, I scored a potential breakthrough in late April. I tested well with a temporary agency. They sent me out to Xerox just northeast of O'Hare Field. There, I would work as a Data Entry person in the Sales Department.

These jobs were Temp-to-Perm. However, the job did require training.

The hiring was quite massive. This facility had a cafeteria and a training room. It also had an instructor from Seattle that would conduct the training classes. Those classes would be paid.

The system that we would be using was strictly based on the old DOS (Disk Operating System) rather than on the Windows I was more familiar with. Therefore, I found training on it, and using it to be an absolute trial. My other classmates had a better time of it. Sometimes, they would help me on the nuances of the system.

The good news was that I was able to detect some of the errors I was making. The bad news was that the instructor noticed that I was having difficulty using the system. She told me, "I'll give you a couple of days." With that, I immediately telephoned the temporary agency. The coordinator who was handling the Xerox account told me that he would be out to Xerox right away to see to the problem.

After I came in from lunch, I learned that I was removed from the assignment. However, I was admonished that I was eligible for further assignments because I didn't let the situation deteriorate to the point that I was fired. Sadly, however, I would get no further assignments from this agency.

I attended numerous job fairs since leaving Ameritech, and especially after I earned my post-baccalaureate degree. However, responses were very sporadic. I would submit resumes via the information I gleaned from the fairs. Sometimes, I would get acknowledgement letters and cards. Sometimes, I would get rejection letters within a matter of hours or days after I submitted my resume. Sometimes, the representatives would reject me on the spot! Rarely would I get an actual interview because of a Job Fair.

However, as an adult, I still needed to eat, clothe, and shelter myself. That meant that I was dependent on the same society that was rejecting me. Besides that, my biggest motivation of all was that I did NOT want to spend the rest of my life as a Ghetto Geek! That was the conundrum I faced.

I got a call from Manpower Temporaries that would've helped me get out of that "Ghetto Geek" trap. It was a temporary position for a Technical Editor. There was even the option for the client company to retain me as a permanent employee. Ironically, that client company was Ameritech!

While I nailed down that interview, I made a follow-up call to Underwriters Laboratories and got another interview. It was for a test for a position called Technical Correspondent. That required a typing test.

So, there I was, in a two-cushion shot. My day consisted of driving out to Ameritech's facility out by the same Interstate 90 that took me to the Molson Indy Vancouver! After that, I'd drive to Underwriters Labs.

When I got to Ameritech, I was met by a svelte, petite, perky White lady by the name of Kristi. She had her assistant show me the facility. This facility was light years from the "boiler room" and "jungle music" type of atmosphere that was my job at Ameritech's South Suburban Remote, Midway Drive, and River West offices. There was even a fountain in the central atrium because it was found that the "white noise" that was generated was more beneficial than other types of noise.

There was another irony. As I was shown a typical workstation, one of the ladies at that workstation recognized me. She was from the Society for Technical Communication. Therefore, she knew me from a few meetings I attended.

After the tour of the facility, Kristi's assistant gave me a test sample for me to edit. I was to phone the assistant when I was ready. If I had any questions, that same number also applied.

It was a highly peaceful environment where I worked. I did the best I could with it as far as making the edits were concerned. I concentrated on every element I could think of. Then, I handed over my test and hit another one of my now-famous Glass Monoliths.

In Kristi's mind, I was more of a "Creative Writer" than a hard-core Technical Editor. It was for that reason that I was turned down.

I had more luck when I arrived at Underwriters Laboratories later that morning, to early afternoon. I took my time and was as thorough about filling out my application and paperwork. Then, I took the typing test.

The copy and my actual work were directly above each other. That led to some issues in deciding where to focus my attention. Nevertheless, although I was slower than I would've been if the copy were in a more typical position, I still eclipsed the minimum typing speed requirement for the job.

I met with the same lady that I met at Oakton College's Job Fair and was told that I would be eligible for an interview.

The next day, I telephoned Manpower Temporaries about the Glass Monolith I hit during Ameritech's Technical Editing test. I told Manpower about the bitter breakup that I had with Ameritech when I was at River West in 1996. Given that, I surmised that they found out about me and rejected me.

Manpower scoffed at that theory. In their mind, Ameritech was looking to take on the Temp permanently. However, there were issues concerning the payment of a fee for services. In Manpower's mind, Ameritech was very picky about who they wanted. According to Manpower, it was for that reason, and not any bad blood from previous work at Ameritech, that I was rejected.

While I was working my two-car hiking stints, I was called on to another interview with Underwriters Laboratories. After this interview, I felt as if I was a whipped puppy! I left Underwriters, and instead of taking the Tri-State Tollway home perhaps, to save money, I took Sheridan Road, and Lake Shore Drive from Northbrook instead. When I got home, Mom asked how the interview went, and I told her the truth. What else could I tell her? I certainly wasn't going to kid myself.

That night, I decided to write a Thank you letter to the lady that set up my interview at Underwriters in the first place. I included a letter of clarification with that Thank you letter. A few days later, this lady called, and told me that the letter of clarification was not needed. Instead, she asked me to fax in copies of my credentials such as my

Post-Baccalaureate Certificate, and my Certificate from Advanced Careers Training Centers. This, I did.

In the meantime, I got yet, another phone call from Underwriters Laboratories. This time, it was to set an appointment for a physical! I wanted to schedule the appointment for later that Wednesday afternoon, August 23, 2000. However, the same lady I met at Oakton College, scoffed. I had to make it earlier. That meant that there would be NO hiking cars that afternoon in Crestwood. During the physical, a question came up because the EKG seemed to indicate an abnormality that I had to spend the next day investigating.

The next day, a Friday, I dared to call Sally. Had I cleared my drug test? Had I received the medical clearance I needed to start work that Monday?

The answers to both questions were YES!

It took an unheard of four years from the time I got my Post Baccalaureate Certificate in Technical Communications to the time I got my start on a job in Technical Communications! There were some intermittent jobs in the time between that. Nevertheless, there was a long drought that was finally over.

I'd hold that job down for precisely 49 Weeks. Then I'd lose the job in a restructuring. Fortunately, Underwriters Laboratories offered a series of Outplacement sessions. Ironically, these sessions were sponsored by the same outplacement firm of Challenger Gray and Christmas that I corresponded with. Also ironically, these sessions were at a Holiday Inn just to the northwest of Underwriters Laboratories. As my bus passed Pfingsten Road, I made it a point not to look at the building where I once worked. At those sessions, some of my thoughts about my employment and professional background came to surface.

For instance, I was also perturbed that I either had to accept being the "nigger of the company" or not work! This perception is a very caustic and insensitive thing to think, much less to write. However, it seemed that unless I could get a "nigger of the company" job, I could get no job at all! For instance, I applied for jobs such as Central Office Technician, Network Administrative Clerk, and Installer positions at Ameritech. I was blocked because I failed to pass the test by one point. Alternatively, I was told that the jobs were not available or that I could not move due to a "freeze on movement". Yet, I could hold down the Directory Assistance Operator's job that I was increasingly growing to hate and would be hated in return!

The paradox was that it was now becoming tremendously difficult for me to get a "nigger of the company" job as a stopgap measure. Employers felt that I would "fly the coop" as soon as something better came along, which NEVER took place.

Bob Ewing, the coordinator of the Outplacement Sessions, however, advocated for "nigger of the company" jobs because of the networking aspects. According to him, a "nigger of the company" job, as This Author calls it, could lead to a better job down the road.

This Author never met, nor spoke by telephone, to James Challenger of the outplacement firm Challenger, Gray, and Christmas. However, I read many of his articles. According to the articles, James Challenger advocated going against the grain.

For instance, James Challenger had disdain for the advertised job market, or for responding to leads solely by computer or by the newspaper. According to him, the best way to look for a job was to press the flesh. By that, James Challenger meant you went to the department head and met with him about jobs. You attend meetings, socials, and events. You got into circulation. You did not go by way of the direct route.

I had a problem with what James Challenger advocated in his articles. For instance, without a job description, I had NO way of knowing if I had the right to even apply for a particular job of my interest. For that, I needed a job description. If there is anything in the job description that would eliminate me from the job, I did not want to go through the embarrassment of vying for it and receiving an inevitable rejection!

Think about it. Roger (The Artful Dodger) Staubach would NOT have made the Hall of Fame by throwing into multiple coverages on receivers and consequently running up a bunch of interceptions. Any quarterback worth his salt would spot the field for an open receiver before throwing the ball. In the case of The Artful Dodger, he could also spot an alley that an offensive lineman would cut open, then run through it. Even then, if he were to try to run the ball without that alley cut open, The Artful Dodger would've wound up getting a "close inspection of the turf"!

Similarly, This Author was tired of failure. I had too much of it already, I wanted no more! That's why I thought Bob Ewing was full of bull (plop) by advocating cold canvassing, interviews where the likelihood of success was low, or otherwise running the gauntlet.

Bob Ewing said that a job seeker should practice interviewing techniques on a job that they would have no interest in. That way, he/she could get some feedback for when the job of a particular seeker's interest should come along.

That set my bull (plop) meter off! I recall visiting Operation Able, a firm that specialized in referring job seekers over the age of 55. According to Leo Kovitz, "You have to go through the 100 'no' to get the one 'yes'.

I strongly disagreed with Operation Able's Leo Kovitz, and I strongly disagreed with Challenger Gray and Christmas' Bob Ewing. I did NOT want to go through the 100 "nos." Instead, I wanted, if you pardon my football parlance, "one throw, one pass, and one touchdown".

The position of Challenger, Gray, and Christmas was that the advertised job market was highly competitive. Ironically, according to Challenger Gray and Christmas, the company in question is trying to fill the position as quickly as possible.

The next day, Ewing had us bring our resumes. Since I had several formats in printed form, and several more on disk, I was more than ready. Unfortunately, my computer was down, and I had NO access to computers that might have been available within the hotel.

I made the mistake of telling Ewing to direct me to whatever was next on the agenda because I was done. However, Ewing said:

"You're not done. What I want you to do is to change your resume. You're to put a description of yourself in it that'll get the employer's interest."

"That's Embellishment!" I said, with my bull (plop) meter now going wild!

"That's not embellishment," said Ewing. That's simply a way of getting your resume to stand out among all the rest."

Everything that Ewing advocated went against what I was reading in the newspapers and the Private Industry Council guidelines. For instance, Ewing advocated including outside interests and hobbies in resumes. My sources indicated that the inclusion of outside interests and hobbies was a no-no!

Ewing even advocated for my inclusion of my membership in the Society for Technical Communication, even though my membership had expired because I couldn't pay the annual fee! The only thing that Ewing and I agreed on was the inclusion of skill sets in the resume.

There were a series of four follow-up sessions after the outplacement session. For this, I would meet back at the hotel with a young, Black gentleman by the name of Sanders Dooley.

Dooley was a former Underwriters employee. Although Sanders held the Challenger, Gray, and Christmas company line, he was considerably more realistic about it. Therefore, we could see eye to eye, and we could come together on a strategy for getting back to work.

Meanwhile, back at Christ Hospital's Vocational Services Unit, I had a small crisis. I was looking in the databases when Melissa spotted a lead for a Technical Writer. It was at Griffith Laboratories in Southwest suburban Alsip. This lead was in the classifieds that week. However, I passed on it. The job requirements for the position explicitly stated that the applicant had to be **FLUENT** in French.

This Author took two years of French! I even won the French Award during my Sophomore Year of high school! I even used the French I learned at the 1976 Summer Olympic Games in Montreal, Quebec! However, fluency, in my mind, meant being able to speak at the mile-a-minute rate that native French, Haitian, and Quebecois can speak. I also thought that fluency meant being able to process the mile-a-minute language that French entails. I was not able to do this!

Melissa's position was that it was proper for me to vie for this job. Her position was that parallel jobs could develop under the radar.

I thought that Melissa's position was wishful thinking. However, I reluctantly composed a cover letter. I figured that I'd try to sell the fact that I learned my French, then put it to use at the Olympics. This I did in the cover letter. Here is part of what I wrote: *"I was fortunate enough to win the French award at Cathedral High School. However, the real French award came for me five years later, when I got a chance to use my French at the 1976 Summer Olympic Games in Montreal!"*

I presented my cover letter to Bos and Bazan, and Ms. Bazan jumped for joy! She was surprised and delighted that I spoke French and thought that I was a shoo-in for the job. However, I thought Ms. Bazan was smoking something.

I still had considerable doubts about my chances of getting the job. However, I had an idea: There was a lady in one of the offices who had an angelic look, favoring actress Jennifer Aniston. I had met her when I scored my job at Underwriters. She was low-key and not colorful. Consequently, I forgot her name at that time. My plan was to get an objective opinion about my cover letter before submitting it.

This Jennifer Aniston look-alike was more than happy to comply. With that, I left her office and continued to feel a little funny about submitting my cover letter to Griffith Laboratories. Since I was on the computer for some considerable time, I needed a break anyway.

After a few minutes, I returned to where I'd get my objective opinion. Here is what my Jennifer Aniston look-alike wrote: *"I was fortunate to learn French in high school. I also have some real-world experience in speaking French!"*

This woman of mystery added, "I would like to meet with you to discuss my skills further."

After I left that Jennifer Aniston look-alike's office, I felt less uneasy about submitting my cover letter, although I still did NOT like my chances at getting the job.

When Ms. Bazan discovered that I took this tack, she was also delighted. Come to find out, I had just met with the Coordinator for the Vocational Services Department, and her name was Lisa Leander! A few minutes later, Ms. Leander took a break and stepped out of her office. All three of us got acquainted again.

Getting an objective opinion about an issue as critical as a cover letter is a wonderful way to forge a relationship, whether business or personal. Here was one time I didn't have to experience a losing lesson to learn one.

It was also through the Bos that I got some insight into why Jeremy had some issues about me being in the Job Club initially. According to Melissa, Jeremy felt that the object of the game was to find a job, not to develop my research project. I also found out that Jeremy had reservations about me being in "competitive employment."

Dwight had his own ideas about what I had to do to get a job. One day, while Ted and I were talking about the job issue, his line was as follows. "You should just put a suit coat on, shoes shined, hair combed, nails cleaned. Go out every day to these places.

Dwight was a bit bossy. He was also naïve. For one thing, some gatekeepers will absolutely preclude personal visits to employers. Secondly, some employers will ONLY accept a fax, an email, or a mailed resume! Even back in the late seventies, employers were using blind advertising. That is, they gave any kind of information except where they were.

Dwight's position, as well as Ted's, was that 9/11, or "The Bombing" as I called it, made seeking a job an uphill climb, if not outright impossible. The tragedy of the matter was that they were right. Paradoxically, according to the terms of qualifying for Unemployment Insurance, I still had to actively look for work.

I had yet to get online. I still owed back bills on my telephone modem. In the meantime, I still had to equip my computer with a modem that would make it possible to connect to the outside world. I was still without it.

I had to buy myself a 56K modem first. Once I did that, I was now able to hook myself up. At first, I was using Mom's telephone line. However, I made it a point to use the line only at night. That way, I would be least likely to tie up her phone. However, when she found out that I had been using her phone lines, she was not happy.

So, I had to pay off my back modem bill and reactivate my own Internet service. Even that proved troublesome. For instance, I signed up for SBC's Dial-Up Internet Service. I didn't give a second thought to anything else as I was still on Windows 95. Unfortunately, I let SBC talk me into signing up for its DSL Service despite only having a Pentium 233!

Meanwhile, Ms. Bazan was getting very upset. It was NOT with me. It was, however, with the Illinois Department of Rehabilitative Services. They had yet to reinstate my file and update my case to status. She demanded that I "crab at them" to get the business done. In the meantime, Ms. Bazan would introduce me to a new player in the Christ Hospital Vocational Services scheme of business. She was a student from the Illinois Institute of Technology. She had long hair and was very attractive, though very covered. She always wore black and white. Her name was Rawda.

Over time, Rawda would take an interest in me and my case as time went on. She would even attempt to provide me with job leads. Unfortunately, the leads that she provided me with were way over my level of experience and/or skill set. Therefore, I could not respond to many of the leads.

Meanwhile, back at Christ, Ms. Bazan and Ms. Leander were also delighted that my case was finally reinstated at Illinois DORS. Ms. Bazan did, however, have another issue. She thought that I was "sitting on the pity pot!"

Shortly after my reinstatement at Illinois DORS, Dr. Harrison scheduled me to have an Occupational Evaluation done on me. For this, she had me visit a consultant who was in Evanston. He charged triple-digit fees for as little as forty-five minutes' worth of work!

There was a list of suggested occupations for people with Autism/Asperger's Syndrome. This list was found on the Internet. This list consisted of areas where such people could conceivably do well, and some areas those Autistics and Asperger's diagnosed patients MUST avoid like the plague! My plan was to take the findings of the specialists, the tests that I took at the Illinois Education and Training Center, this Internet list, and my academic background into account, and come up with a synthesis as to what career direction I should be heading.

I was also consulting Toni Randall at the IETC. She was a specialist who had been working on my case since I rejoined the IETC process. I went back to the Illinois Education and Training Center concurrent with my rejoining Christ Hospital Vocational, and after I left Underwriters. That process included a testing phase and an assignment of a counselor. Since I did very well on the test, I was assigned a counselor without needing any remedial work or care.

I started to cancel my appointment with this consultant in Evanston. After all, my finances were still strained, thanks to my inability to find work. Although I was drawing Unemployment Insurance at that time, I was still faced with some heavy demands. For instance, I needed the Internet for my job search. I really couldn't afford to pay for this appointment.

Ironically, I couldn't go another day without being, at least, pointed in some semblance of an appropriate career direction for me. I was sick and tired of having to look for work every few weeks or a few months. I had been running for over three months since I had left Underwriters—and counting! If other people can maintain a stable career, why can't I? I always felt, ever since my Undergraduate nightmare of a time, that I was never competitive with my peers. If I were going to break this pattern of existence, I felt that I had to buckle down NOW and address the issue.

It was with those thoughts in mind that I finished my visit to Roosevelt University's Placement Center and Job Service, and hopped the Elevated Subway to Evanston.

Once I got to downtown Evanston, I went to a small apartment building. This building was where the consultant lived. In a twinkling, I was met by a tall, White gentleman who I would estimate as being in his mid to upper 50s. His name was Julius March, Ph.D.

Finally, we could get to the career questions. It was here that this consultant had a wrinkle for me. I told him that I chose Technical Communications to be a liaison between the layman, or the common man, and the Engineers, Scientists, Technicians, or the so-called "geeks". March thought that instead of being a liaison between the geeks and the common man, I should, in his words, "be the geek."

I fared worse when I visited the Illinois Education and Training Center less than a week later. I consulted with Toni Randall. Toni contended that any training program I would get into would "set me up" for failure! It didn't matter that I had shown her the Temple Grandin Internet article that showed her where Autistic and Asperger's patients could do well. I was too much of a hot potato for an employment-training program.

When I brought the problem back to Ms. Bazan, I was beginning to think to myself: "Thou Too Brutus?"

Bazan had thought about referring me for a lead as a Technical Writer in Cicero. Considering the reservations that the consultant had about me looking for work, she felt compelled to abort that referral.

Meanwhile, Ms. Bos had some issues with my resume. I listed every skillset I had on the resume. I also listed my coursework, such as Physics, Math, Chemistry, Materials Science, Electronics, and software proficiencies. I also presented her with various types of resumes that I used at one time or another. I omitted such items as hobbies, outside interests, and avocations. In short, I only put the hard stuff on my resume.

Still, Ms. Bos the dlatmy resume was so loaded that she exclaimed: "lf l were an employer and I were reading resume I would immediately throw it out!"

Time and time again: I would be plagued by issues concealing my ability to take a test, Job Suitability, Speed Issues, Time Limits. Etc. If the job or career was worth having, I would hit a Glass Monolith in getting it. Do you remember die mythical Glass Ceding? Do you remember those spnbolic monkeys in 2001 A Space Odyssey? I was living It.

The Concept of The Logic Error

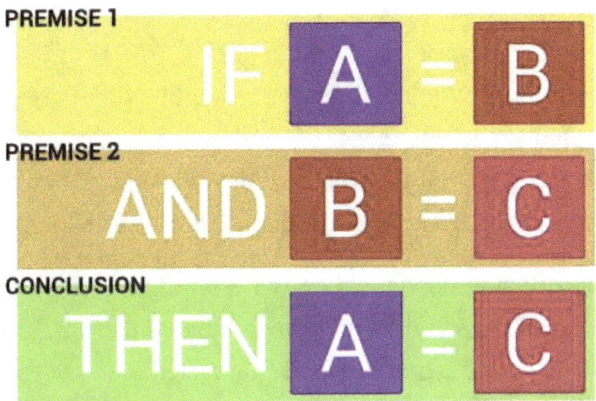

Through the auspices of the Illinois Department of Rehabilitation Services and the Center for the Training of the Disabled, I was referred to testing at an Urban Progress Center. They were actually called Urban Progress Centers during the late 1960s and early 1970s. However, they were in such blighted neighborhoods and usually served those who were "in the clique" the best. Anyhow, one of the counselors at the CTD insisted that I consider the COBOL programming course, which I eventually got steered into. This training program was conducted by a relatively large firm called Statistical Tabulating Corporation, or STAT-TAB, for short. This was back in 1983.

For this program, transportation via transit tokens was provided. The training would take about three months. After those three months, it would be possible to be placed at STAT-TAB itself.

The program was rigorous. If you failed the program, you were out. If you missed an excess of x days, you were out. Of course, if you were to go off on a fellow student or instructor, you were out. Homework was also part of the program.

The instructors for the program were a tag team affair. There were morning and afternoon sessions. There were also two instructors for the sessions. The head was someone by the name of Ray (Trick Question) Matlak. He would eventually be called "Trick Question" because of the types of questions he would ask on the tests. The other one was a short, White woman by the name of Patricia (Trish) Doherty. Trish was disabled, apparently due to Cerebral Palsy. However, her mind was as sharp as those who were able-bodied and able-minded.

There would also be guest speakers who would come in from time to time. These speakers would touch on issues concerning employment, COBOL, and their job experiences. It all varied.

There would also be visitors to the class. Although they would not lecture the class in any formal capacity, they would sit in with students to discuss various issues of the day.

Finally, we all had a den mother. Nitalia Rightout. She would take care of all of the administrative duties involving tokens, time put in, attendance, and would even offer to help students sometimes.

"Trick Question" gave the first assignment for homework. It was a flowcharting exercise. In this exercise, I spared not one detail; yet I still got in trouble for the assignment. I got a note saying: "Too Many Lines. Please Do Over."

When I made inquiry as to why I got the booby prize for this assignment. Come to find out, what "Trick Question" wanted was to for me to duplicate the flowchart on the previous page. The example on the preceding page had circles representing start and stop blocks. I had possibly no idea that they could be used as continuation blocks as well.

When I last did flowcharting for BASIC, we did all of the lines. Fortunately, this foul-up was very easy to fix.

Ms. Doherty, or TD, as I sometimes called her privately, alerted the class to the types of bugs common to computer programs. She would say: "There are two types of programming errors. There is the simple clerical error, in which you might forget to put in a symbol. Then there is the "Logic Error." "In a Logic Error, everything is just totally wrong, and you're way out in left field somewhere." Remember! Patricia (Trish) Doherty was disabled. Yet, she was more than capable of delivering a concept about programming that some able-bodied or able-minded persons could not.

The concept of a Logic Error stuck in my mind like Eastman 910 Adhesive, though in ways not immediately clear to me-AND WELL IT SHOULD!

Whenever you have a difference between what you might be thinking and what another person might be thinking, you have the presence of a Logic Error!

There had been too many instances of Logic Errors that I experienced. These Logic Errors affected not only my employment life, but also my academic and family life.

In the meantime, I had to introduce an incident that had me irate, and the customer, cool, calm, and collected, to the Open Forum Meeting that was being held at Midway Drive. This incident stuck in my mind like Eastman 910, a famous super adhesive! I needed to find an Area Code for a certain region of the country, but it wasn't there! Therefore, when an Open Forum meeting of Operators, Service Representatives, and other personnel was held, I easily had something to contribute to the meeting. In fact, I went first to make sure. The place I searched was so well-known that it should have been routine for me to find it in the database. However, it wasn't, and the Service Assistant concurred with me.

There was a panel of executives of Ameritech, who moderated the meeting. When I presented my case to the panel, the company President, Jim Eibel, asked what happened when I questioned the customer.

I told Eibel: "Had I questioned the customer, in this case, I'd have gotten killed!"

But Eibel countered: "That's exactly when you should've questioned the customer."

Meanwhile, John Corothers, Manager in Chief of Number Services, interceded and said: "I don't know what went on, or why you couldn't get that listing, but I will find out, and it will only take me about two minutes!"

I was finally going to get to the bottom of a potentially very serious incident and was happy about it. Therefore, I enjoyed the rest of the meeting, not needing to say anything further-and didn't!

Once the meeting concluded, all the Operators returned to their respective worksites. Before I started back, I consulted Ms. Cole about the potential sixth-day situation. Come to find out, the next day, a Friday, and a payday, was rescheduled off! Mark my word: One of the best possible situations to be in was to be scheduled off on payday.

As I met with Ms. Cole, Ms. Bennett informed me that John Corothers wanted to see me. I asked to meet with him away from the Operators, to prevent my speaking voice from disturbing others. Here, I'd hit a Glass Monolith. The Conference Room was busy, and, like an idiot, I didn't think to ask the Queen Bee to use her office for a few minutes.

However, there was a hallway behind the Queen Bee's office. Here, I'd get my answer.

It was a logic error on my part. Corothers told me that although I was thinking of a city, in truth, I was searching too wide an area! The computer was NOT programmed to search the type of area I was searching for!

Nevertheless, Corothers was true to his word. Therefore, I made it a point to send him a "Thank You" letter for the time he took out for me. Corothers countered that I should continue to make myself available to the Group Chief Operators in the event of any other problems, such as the ones that he uncovered. As I picked up, yet another commendation for attendance, both the Queen Bee and Ducky #2 noted how I conducted myself when Corothers and I met.

Speaking of my former role as a Directory Assistance Operator, I had an incident with a customer who ordered something. However, the address didn't immediately indicate that it was in Chicago. It was. Understandably, this customer was upset with me.

When I referred the matter to Al Bennett, one of the Group Chief Operators, she faulted me for not questioning the customer. However, I believed that to do that, I needed permission from the front office to use "What city please?" in my opening recording.

What did I go to Ms. Barker for?

Her response was: "These types of things have come up before, and frankly, I am getting tired of it! It's time for you to grow up!"

After a pause, Barker asked: "Have you ever thought about quitting?"

"I do want out of this department," I said.

"I'm not talking about a transfer; I'm talking about leaving the Company," said Barker.

After another pause, she said: "What you're going to have to do is to shape up. You're going to have to fall under constraints on doing the job, as we ask you to do. You're going to have to conduct yourself, like adults; that means, you're going to have to put controls on your voice, and your temper."

After another pause, Barker started in again, saying: "Frankly, if something like this were to continue, disciplinary action will be considered."

I was surprised at Barker's tirade. It was totally unexpected, and all because I requested permission to question a city in my opening recorded phrase. I listened, speaking only when Barker directed me to do so.

So why did I go to the front office about this issue? It was simple. If you took away something I needed to do a job, I could not have done the job! If I sound crazy, the late Cajun chef, Justin Wilson, openly stated that he positively could not cook without having Onions and Garlic!

I needed to have a locality identifier phrase. Without a locality identifier phrase, I would continuously run into problems with customers who want cities or suburbs not covered. Some customers even give a city or suburb at the last minute, without specifying the suburb. I could sometimes detect the problem because the street might not be contained in Chicago. However, that might not always be the case. Customers seeking listings in Berwyn, Illinois, a suburb of Chicago, were notorious for not specifying until the last minute.

Paradoxically, detecting when or whether a listing could be in a suburb or a different city involved some use of personal knowledge. Personal Knowledge was frowned upon by the front office! That, I could never understand.

For instance, in the case of Austin Boulevard, in Chicago, one side of the street could be the Chicago side, while the other side of the street could be the Oak Park side! Without personal knowledge, how could you tell? Also, Cumberland Avenue, Thatcher Avenue, and Pueblo Avenue are the same street! Without personal knowledge, how can you know which is what?

I also had introductory, or set-up, phrases that I regularly used. These set-up phrases ensured that I would fall under the guidelines of identifying the listing as directed by the front office. However, these phrases were frowned upon by Ducky and Ms. Barker. Ironically, Ms. Cole did not care about my use of set-up phrases.

Ducky even went so far as to say, "You don't need to set it up. Our customers set it up!" However, one of Ducky's criticisms of my technique was: "What you're worried about is insurance. What we're interested in is your efficiency."

Granted. There are practices and procedures that must be followed not only in Number Services, but in any organization. However, other Operators were engaging in extensive dialogue, even arguing with customers. I doubt that they were getting the heat I was getting just for using personal knowledge, or using atypical, but correct, phrases.

I am convinced that the front office wanted "cookie-cutter" Operators. That concept goes out the window for one reason: Perception! How does an Operator perceive the problem when he/she gets the problem? It may be a simple slam-dunk call, or it may be more involved. And yet, one of the principles of the "New Management" *was "Given the tools to do a job, our workers can do a first-class job!"* Right there, management contradicted itself!

One of the problems I was having at Ameritech's Chicago River West Directory Assistance Office was that I had to think like the managers.

There was a change in practices. That made it very difficult to use techniques I previously used in solving problem calls with customers. In fact, the so-called Optimization Techniques didn't optimize my productivity or work performance one iota. In fact, they had the opposite effect.

I would have Marjorie Scott as my regular Group Chief Operator. Although I committed NO errors, she wailed about my phraseology, excessive searching, and keystroke use. That made me recall the time that the Chicago Bears had beaten the Pittsburgh Steelers 20-0, while Ditka wailed: "This is not a very good team." From that point on, the Bears tanked!

What made my loggerheads with Ms. Scott so bad was that I could justify what I did, and why I did it, to send the customer away happy. The keying was particularly maddening. If I were to key just one letter for something on Belmont Avenue, I can assure you that I would bet something on Belle Plaine Avenue, Banks Court, Beaubien Court, and every other B street in the City of Chicago! Yet, when I put as little as "BEL" into my argument, I would be charged with over keying!

On the subject of single-state Area Codes, for instance, I developed the phrase: "The 302 Area Code services the entire state of Delaware!" However, Marjorie Scott flew off the handle at me for using that phrase. Ironically, I developed the phrase for the sake of speed, efficiency, and clarity.

Ducky #2, a manager who transferred from the Midway Drive Office, would cross-observe me on the boards one day. She, too, would have some issues with my work. She said, in a slow, prissy, but rambling voice:

"I was observing you and you were doing a lot of wild keying and phraseology, and yes you will be suspended for this. We can't have people just going off on their own like that. This isn't your company; this isn't my company. We have to work within the framework of a method-oriented format. "

I explicitly told Ducky: "I'm not trying to run the company.

That was the only way I could get these calls."

Ducky charged me with not paying attention to key details on one call. According to her, the correct tack for me to take would've been to refer that caller to an electronics repairman I just happened to have contact with. Instead, I just sent that caller to the main number of the major electronics supplier for that region.

While Ducky #2 was reading me the riot act, I started coughing violently. I pulled out an inhaler full of Vanceril and took it for relief of the attack. At that point, Ducky stopped, asked if I was OK, and did a post-mortem on one of my calls.

What Ducky #2 took issue with was a call in which I asked a customer if she was calling long-distance. I did that because I noticed that there was a Long-Distance indicator on my screen. Mark my word. Long-distance callers required a totally different way of guiding them through the listing and quoting the number. What made this call most difficult was that there was a familiar name on the listing. She had NO address. However, the customer provided me with a street that it was near. Now, I had something to go on. I scored a listing!

For Ducky # 2, that wasn't good enough. I showed her what I did and showed her all of the logic in why I keyed the way I keyed. However, Ducky #2 keyed in an atypical way and found another listing. However, that would've required me to spend inordinate amounts of time experimenting on how many characters I would've needed. By which time, I would've run into an inevitable customer confrontation and an unmanageable call. The database abbreviated the name of the listing, Ducky #2, found. That was supposed to be a no-no!

At that point, I was getting very annoyed. I told Ducky: "The trouble is, I always have to think the way the managers think."

I wasn't lying. I said it. I meant it. I felt that the only way to do the job was to think the way that the managers would think, given a similar situation. The trouble was that this system and database didn't even play by their own rules! Listings were duplicated. Cross references were nonexistent. Once again, I was criticized for questioning a customer for specific details, an issue raised from the past.

First, Ducky criticized me for negligence and failure to pay attention to details. Ironically, when I did detect a series of key details such as the long-distance caller, uncertain information, then a partial key detail on questioning, I am red flagged for that. This sample is how Ameritech Number Services did what I call flip-flops!

Ameritech eventually fired me for Practices and Procedures violations, allegedly. I appealed, and my decision contained this passage: ***"Rather, he was discharged because his performance over time failed to meet employer standards, expectations, or requirements, in a work environment where even reasonable employee latitude in the execution of tasks was deemed inimical to employer interests and a violation of procedures."***

Check what I've got marked in bold italics.

I made it very clear to the mid-office that I had reached a point where I had to think the way that the managers thought to be judged as being correct in my actions and decisions on the boards.

Nowhere was that inability to use "reasonable latitude" more evident than the time Ducky claimed that I used excessive questioning in helping to find a listing with a highly common name!

There was also another incident where, although none of the listings matched a customer's request, I turned up a listing that was within about fifty feet of the customer's desired location. I quoted that number. However, Ms. Scott charged me with failing to offer other alternative listings, even if those alternatives were irrelevant to what the customer wanted. I was suspended for that observation.

What Ms. Scott suggested that I do was in VIOLATION of the first practice of constantly checking, as given. In short, Ms. Scott did a flip-flop!

The listing I found was so close that it was a virtual match! I did, however, advise the customer that what I saw was not what the customer wanted.

That wouldn't be the only example of how Logic Errors would affect me. For instance: Another nightmare waiting to happen occurred on Thanksgiving morning, 1987. Mom was to be released from the Warren-Barr Pavilion of the former Michael Reese Hospital. She had sustained a Stroke that came perilously close to claiming her life. However, this was to be a ONE DAY RELEASE ONLY! She was to go back to Warren Barr that night.

Ted burst into my bedroom while I was still sleeping, yelled, screamed, and demanded that I clean the place up.

I told Ted: "I did clean the place up. I moved all of the stuff out of the living room and the kitchen and moved things around to make way for her."

But Ted said: "No, I'm bringing her in through the back. That way, it'll be easier for her to get in."

Since I cleaned the place up the day prior, I DID NOT KNOW WHAT TED WAS TALKING ABOUT. I did NOT know, nor was I told by Ted, that he intended to bring Mom in through the back door on the first floor, rather than the front.

This altercation I had with Ted raises another point. Part of my Glass Monolith was that it was always difficult, if not impossible, to see alternative ways of doing things. For instance, I never even conceived that Ted would even want to bring Mom in through the back door. True, it was the shortest way inside of the house. However, the flight of stairs was sharper, and involved having to get between a tight driveway, or limited space between building, driveway, and car.

The frustration I was experiencing on my job, as a Directory Assistance Operator, made me appreciate what Norman had in mind for me at or around the 1990 Super Bowl. That was our family holiday.

Our standard fare was to fix fried fish, usually Ocean Perch, and/or Buffalo, and my famous fried shrimp, plus some dessert. Then, Norman and, sometimes, Alverna, his wife, would come over and we would have ourselves a feast, and talk family hijinks, while watching the game.

It was at this time that Norman asked me to write down my ABCs. Since he was a Structural Draftsman, I knew he wanted me to make the letters the way a Draftsman would. Norman commended me for the way I wrote the letters, and soon, I would be subletting some of his work. The projects would be at home, and night after work. I would be getting some outside money for my efforts.

It was so peaceful doing the work that I found myself wishing that I could do it at Ameritech and junk the Directory Assistance Operator's job. Alas, it was NOT to be, for already, there were computerized formats of drafting being developed, such as AUTOCAD. These formats would slowly replace hand-drawn drawings. Norman also preferred that I learn to do the drawings by hand.

There were some issues with my work. For starters, I always thought that there was ONE AND ONLY ONE set of standards by which all drawings were to be made. Although Norman liked my lettering and the neatness of my drawings, my own naivete became an issue.

For instance, I used the standards set forth by the American National Standards Institute (ANSI). These standards were so strict that they set the minimum height for letters and numbers. During my ill-fated venture in engineering school, I learned about ANSI the hard way! I knew better when I tried Mechanical Drawing at Roosevelt University. Still, I misinterpreted my final project. I thought that I was supposed to dimension the test part. Therefore, I became quite surprised when Norman told me to make my "ws "straight up and down, in apparent violation of ANSI standards. However, making my letters "straight up and down" was in accordance with the AISC (American Institute for Steel Construction) Standards!

Norman also had some other wrinkles for me as I worked on some of his drawings. For instance, Norm told me to "get that 1/8 inch" out of my head about the heights of my lettering. According to ANSI, lettering and numerals could be no more than 1/8 inch high. In AISC, the standards could be a bit more liberal.

I used a device to keep my lettering and numerals uniform. That device, I affectionately referred to as Mr. Ames! It was the Ames Lettering Guide. The Ames Lettering Guide was a pocket-sized device that could be adjusted to any required lettering height. Once adjusted, any guidelines would also be spaced uniformly.

Norm didn't mind my use of Mr. Ames, but Norm preferred that I learn to hand-draw the letters without its use.

The wrinkles wouldn't stop there. For starters, during that ill-fated venture in engineering school, I was told to use H, 2H, 3H, and 4H leads. Come to find out, according to Norman, these leads were too hard to use for drafting. The linework would be too gray. When I took Engineering Graphics at Roosevelt University, I found out that the F, HB, and/or H leads were the absolute hardest I would use in the course. Then again, the teacher for Roosevelt University's Engineering Graphics was more acquiescent than the one at the University of Detroit.

Another wrinkle came when it came to the material I would work on. First, it would be Vellum, a piece of paper that was white with rust-colored lines and visible edges. My job was to trace over the vellum and transfer it onto white paper, at first, then eventually onto Mylar. Mylar, for the uninitiated, is effectively a plastic paper. That's fine for durability; however, Mylar can be problematic should a mistake be made. For instance, erasures required a special electric eraser, provided by Norman.

Since I was using Mylar, a different set of leads was indicated. Norm explained that these super soft leads, such as E1, E2, and E3, were necessary to keep the integrity of the lines. According to the Norm, the drawings would be run through a machine. That machine would wipe out the lines, unless I made them extra black and extra defined.

So, I decided that the use of white paper, as a scratch pad, was indicated first and foremost. I decided to show Norm my work before I advanced to the Mylar. Norm, however, thought that I could advance to the Mylar phase of the project without going through the scratch-pad phase. He had just that much confidence in my work.

There were two Glass Monoliths that I would run into during my short assignments with Norman. The first of these Glass Monoliths were semantics. For instance, I came home from work one evening, then gave Norm a progress report. I made the mistake of telling Norm that the project was "finished except for the lettering"

Little did Mom know that I liked to work in phases on drafting projects. First, I liked to start with my visible edges, or as Norm called them, "outlines". Next, I liked to put my hidden edges in. These were edges that are intended to show the person what cannot be seen. Next, I liked to put in other detail lines, such as center lines. That way, the project would be reduced to a "search and destroy" mission, and that I would be less likely to commit errors or omissions.

The second of my two Glass Monoliths, that I would run into while I was working with Norman, was what I called workstyle.

I liked to take no more than two pencils out at a time, two on the left for my detail lines. I would have two more for my hidden edges. Then, I would have two more, on the right, for my visible edges and/or letters and numerals.

Norm, however, thought it better that I have the whole box of pencils out, sharpened, and ready to go, all at once. Norm told me, "You might think that this might be petty, but that's what makes you able to get the work out faster."

What got me unnerved was that Norm was already bringing in some more work before I could get his stamp of approval on a project in progress. Norm explained that the object of the game was to make money. The quicker I could do the projects, the more money I could make. I capitulated.

Little did I know that with AISC and Norman's work style, I needed to adjust, but I failed to do so. I made a series of mistakes on one project. That proved unsettling to both mom and Norm.

No matter how you might slice it, I'd commit a whopper of a Logic Error in March 2001.

My former co-worker, Martha Case, from the Chicago Franklin Directory Assistance office, would keep in touch with me. Ms. Case was extremely cross with me for not coming to the phone on the day that Chicago's Blizzard of 2000 hit. Even when I explained to her that I was still stuck at the Metra Northbrook Lake-Cook station until past the dinner hour, Ms. Case explained that she felt the way she felt because she thought I had either abandoned or betrayed her.

Between the Blizzard of 2000 and the middle of March 2001, I heard positively nothing from Ms. Case. There were no phone calls or letters. Mom admonished me NOT to telephone Ms. Case, and I was inclined to agree with her this time. Ms. Case was a private person, and downright moody to boot. I allowed it, for I, too, had moments of privacy and moodiness. I oftentimes thought that Ms. Case and I were 1 2/3 of a kind!

At first, I sent a letter to Ms. Case. In that letter, I wondered why she was so cross with me for not answering the phone immediately. I reiterated that I was still stuck in Northbrook.

I was concerned about Ms. Case because, for reasons that will remain known ONLY to Ms. Case and This Author, I had reason to suspect that Ms. Case could've been at risk for some form of catastrophic event. I was concerned that a catastrophic event might have consisted of foul play, a catastrophic illness, or an event. She did live alone.

One of the reasons why I was worried about Ms. Case was that she lived in an unincorporated area of Lockport Township. Couple that with my other fears, and the unprecedented, and unexpected anger she had towards me, and I'd figure that something was not right!

HERE IS THE LOGIC ERROR!

During a break at work, I telephoned the authorities in the area of Lockport and asked them if they do what is commonly known as a "Wellness Check", a "Well-Being Check", or a "Welfare Check". The authorities assured me that they did. I then told the authorities why I suspected that something was amiss with Ms. Case.

My plan seemed simple enough. If I didn't hear anything from Ms. Case after making the check, I'd assume she was all right. If she were alright, I'd not contact her again unless she wanted to contact me. If something were amiss, the authorities most likely would've told me that something was amiss.

I expected the authorities to send out a single Police Officer and maybe, a single car, or perhaps, even a welfare worker to do the check on Ms. Case. Little did I know that the authorities went out to Ms. Case's residence-Blazing Saddles and all!

Obviously, Ms. Case was embarrassed by what transpired. Ms. Case was also livid with me!

I found out what happened that evening after I got home from work. I had finished eating. Mom had called Ted to the kitchen table to serve

111

as a witness. Mom then told me what happened with Ms. Case. Ms. Case told Mom to tell me not to call her, or to visit her, "ever in life!"

Even Ted understood that my intentions were honorable. However, he was concerned that if Ms. Case were to meet with foul play, I would make the perfect patsy! According to Ted, throughout history, White people had a propensity towards "turning on" Blacks where there was a long standing history or friendship. I'd hear stories about White women crying "rape" whenever they got sick and tired of a Black person that they might be dating.

Meanwhile, I went through a gamut of emotions. I was angry with Ms. Case, for not realizing that after the years she and I had known each other, the last thing I would intend to do would've been to KNOWINGLY cause the type of embarrassment I caused. I was also angry with the authorities for the way that they went out in Blazing Saddles! I was also disappointed with myself because everything went wrong.

Mom felt responsible for what went wrong because she asked me not to telephone Ms. Case. Mom acknowledged me for complying with her request. Mom did declare, however, that I did overstep my bounds!

Two days later, I got a letter from Ms. Case. It was a very nasty letter! That letter reiterated what Mom told me in regard to telephoning Ms. Case.

I wrote to the authorities in Lockport Township. I told them that what occurred was NOT what I intended and that the end result was that my friendship with Ms. Case was ruined. I also wrote to Ms. Case with a letter of apology. I complied with Ms. Case's request not to telephone her, as I worried about existing stalking laws.

To this very writing, I wish that I could meet face-to-face with Martha Case to apologize to her. Although my intentions were honorable, the fact of the matter was that I hurt Ms. Case. In 20-20 hindsight, it would've been significantly better to write a letter to the authorities and to explain to them that Ms. Case was a very private person. It would also have been better for me to instruct the authorities to conduct the "Welfare Check" in a very discrete fashion.

On the other hand, Ms. Case was NOT in a forgiving mood. It would be folly of me to think that she would want to even listen to anything I had to say. You have to want to forgive.

Author's Side Note:

This Author has also had a lifelong propensity to "CHASE THE RIGHT CAT UP THE WRONG TREE!" For instance, one of the things that I worried might have happened to Martha Case ACTUALLY did happen to Jazz/R&B-Soul/General Popular Music singer Luther Vandross! For the uninitiated, Luther Vandross suffered a Stroke, then lay where he fell for a whopping EIGHT HOURS BEFORE HELP ARRIVED!

Also, recall that had it not been for a Split Shift, I was working at Ameritech/South Suburban Remote #1, I would not have had an idea that Mom was in the throes of a Stroke! She, too, would've lain for several hours.

This Author finds it a miracle that either of these persons would survive their Strokes at all!

Before I could get myself a Mini-Cooper, or any other car that I liked, I had first to get a job. There was also a stark difference in opinion as to why I was striking out in my job searches. For instance, Lisa Leander thought that I lacked self-confidence. My position was that self-confidence was NEVER an issue. I had plenty of it, and it was still getting me nothing!

Ms. Leander countered that it was simply my confidence that told me that I had sufficient self-confidence if the reader can understand that concept.

To that end, Ms. Leander proposed having me participate in a Mock Interview session.

Christ Hospital's Vocational Services Unit occasionally had visiting professionals who would come in to conduct Mock Interviews with Job Club members. These visiting professionals would come from various walks of life. They would engage in role-playing, then evaluate the person being interviewed. These visiting professionals would provide WRITTEN feedback to the participant. Sometimes, Ms. Leander or Melissa would provide follow-up feedback on the Mock Interview.

Participants in the Mock Interview sessions were advised to dress as they would for ANY interview. Those participants were also advised to bring their most current copy of their resume.

My interviewer was a gentleman who was very dapper, upper-middle-aged, and White. He was about as tall as I was, if not slightly taller. He was gentle in his mannerisms. There was nothing about him that would cause me to be taken aback. Meanwhile, I was taking the interview as a real form of practice for an actual Technical Writing job. Therefore, I had to buckle down and key into the interviewer's questions and cues.

After the Mock Interview, here is what the interviewer had to say:

Jon Evans

THIS IS AN ACTUAL EMPLOYER'S EVALUATION FORM.

IT IS TYPICAL OF THOSE WHICH MOST INTERVIEWERS COMPLETE IMMEDIATELY FOLLOWING EVERY

INTERVIEW. HOW DO YOU THINK YOU WOULD BE

RATED IN EACH CATEGORY

FIRST IMPRESSION - As the applicant impresses you, so is he/she likely to impress others. A man's first impression can set the pattern for future effectiveness.

Outstanding _____ Good-x   Adequate____ Poor _____

PHYSICAL APPEARANCE - Was he/she neat and well-groomed? Was he/she dressed in good taste? Keep in mind he/she is trying to impress you favorably, and is trying to put his/her best foot forward.

Outstanding _____ Good-x   Adequate____ Poor _____

VOICE & SPEECH - Was his/her voice clear and easy to understand? Did you notice any annoying speech or voice habits?

Outstanding _____ Good _____   Adequate-x   Poor _____

EDUCATIONAL BACKGROUND - Is his/her educational level acceptable? What was his/her college average? Is he/she too well-educated for the job?

Outstanding _____ Good- x   Adequate____ Poor _____

POISE & SELF-CONFIDENCE - Was he/she at east during the interview? Did he/she seem to have a sound estimation of his/her abilities?

Outstanding _____ Good-x   Adequate____ Poor _____

AMBITION - What are his/her future goals? Are they realistic ones? Does he/she seem motivated for the job and eager to succeed?

Outstanding _____ Good -x   Adequate_____ Poor _____

INTELLIGENCE - Does he/she seem to grasp things quickly? Is he/she a good listener? Does he/she ask thoughtful and intelligent questions?

Outstanding _____ Good -x   Adequate_____ Poor _____

KNOWLEDGE OF OUR COMPANY - Did he/she know

anything about the company before the interview? Did he/she check with anyone about the company? Did he/she ask good questions about the company? Did he/she have a good concept of the job itself?

Outstanding _____ Good -x Adequate_____   Poor _____

OVERALL IMPRESSION - Is he/she the kind of person you would like to have work with you? What is your overall impression of him/her? Did he/she "sell" you?

Outstanding _____ Good -x Adequate_____   Poor _____

MATURITY - Do they impress you as a person whose overall personality is suitable for the job? Does he/she seem sufficiently mature in appearance and manner to deal effectively with the job?

Outstanding _____ Good -x Adequate_____   Poor _____

SCORING   EVALUATION

Outstanding _____ each 3 points   25 - 30 Excellent

Applicant

Good _____ each 2 points   20-24 Very   Good

Applicant

Adequate _____ each 1 point 15 - 19 Average Applicant

116

Poor _____ each 0 points   10 - 14 Marginal

Applicant

Below 10   Poor Applicant

ADDITIONAL

COMMENTS: Jon comes across as very articulate and a deep thinker. During the interview, he should be a bit less intense. This document was scanned and converted into Microsoft Word for compatibility and format. Therefore, I was not able to show that the interviewer circled the "good" range. The bottom line was that he liked me as an interviewee, and a potential candidate as well.

I had to bring something to the table as well. In 1997, I went through a "Mock" Interview through the Illinois Institute of Technology's Placement Center. The "Mock" Interview was conducted by a dapper, articulated chap by the name of Edward Byars. Byars, was Black.

Byars' comments ranged from outright ripping, to conciliatory, to supportive. His was the quintessential "tough love" kind of interviewer. What he ripped me most, was on my choice of suit for the interview; in my case, it was a 3-piece denim suit that I graduated from high school with. He also disliked my choice of socks, even though it matched the denim. He was most supportive and conciliatory of my conduct, tone, and preparation during the interview.

Now it was 2002. I thought that the most prudent thing to do was to remember the lessons of my "Mock" Interview in 1997. To that end, I used a more conservative suit and kept in mind that I wanted to fuse my interest in Science with my proven verbal abilities. That was why I chose Technical Communications in the first place! Once I conveyed that to the interviewer, I would be at least in the running to fare well this time around.

Although the plan worked, it wasn't to Ms. Leander's satisfaction. Laquinda Phelps, from DORS, scheduled a "staffing" session at Christ Vocational. It was there that Lisa, Laquinda, and I discussed my progress. It was also there that Lisa expressed concern about the "Mock" interviewer's comments. She feared that I was putting people off by being as intense as I seemed. As Lisa expressed her concerns, Laquinda also cast a jaundiced eye on me.

I had to defend myself somewhat. Could you imagine me going into that interview, being all "loosey-goosey," and using Polluted English? I had enough trouble being businesslike as it was! I expressed that issue to Lisa and Laquinda. In fact, I expressed that concern to Tomilee Jones when I first entered the DORS system back in the Summer of 1982!

I had to make one concession to Lisa and Laquinda. Given their reaction and given the overall comments on the "Mock" Interview, I could now understand why Tomilee Jones thought that I "came off as being obnoxious". I was either in the "On" position or the "Off" position. There was no "in between".

Lisa and Laquinda had another concern as well. In their mind, my scope of job searches was too narrow for either of them. In their mind, they thought that I should've been looking for jobs in State Government, and/or City Government as well as among the Federal Government. However, news reports indicated that with a new administration coming, cutbacks and hiring freezes in state government were virtually certain. Remember! I was not the type of quarterback who would knowingly throw into heavy coverage and risk an interception! If the reader does not understand that concept, I will say that I was not the type of person who would vie for a job knowing that the most probable outcome would be rejection.

Another example of a Logic Error, and my propensity for it, occurred shortly after I had surprised a co-worker of mine for her birthday. She was more beautiful than she gave herself credit for, and she was a grandmother on top of that. After I surprised her, this assignment in my Technical Writing class came up. I thought that it was relevant, since I did go shopping. Come to find out, it was NOT of the caliber of what Professor Amato was looking for. After I surprised Bunny, I got my first Technical Writing assignment that was to be scored, and here it was:

Assignment 1 (4 PP. typed, double-spaced):

Due 14 September

Background

Some areas of everyday experience are so ordinary, so practical, that we never think of questioning them. And when such everyday activities are made the subject of writing, most writers are surprised to find that they are more complex—and much less mundane—than they initially seemed.

Now, I assume that we all go grocery shopping, probably on a weekly basis...

Assignment

This assignment is, in fact, an assignment in basic technical report writing. I have taken the required format of the final report, as well as a few insights into the process of composing such a report, from J. C. Mathes and Dwight XV. Stevenson, Designing Technical Reports: Writing for Audiences in Organizations, 2nd. Ed. (Macmillan, 1991), pp. 203-239.

A report has a pattern. Mathes and Stevenson indicate that patterns have four basic principles: they "create and fulfill expectations," they "move from general to particular," they "present selected information," and "they have clear cues of content and format to hem hurried readers." (Consider yours truly a "hurried reader.")

.1   -

The problem is, patterns do more than this. They also restrict writing style (sometimes a bad thing); reproduce and reinforce existing institutional norms (often a bad thing); and inhibit creative approaches to problem solving (always a bad thing). Naturally, they can contribute to creativity, but conformity to patterns is generally enforced in ways that tend to work against creative impulses. (And creative assignments like this one. Ha.)

To Mathes and Stevenson's credit, they DO explore in a footnote at the bottom of page 239 the "exploratory" nature of patterns. That is, they can be used in traditional rhetoric as a guide to explore solutions, as a means of discovery. All too often, however, they become "containers" into which final solutions are to be "poured." For the sake of this assignment, this is precisely how I'd like you to use them. (We'll be getting away from the container metaphor as we go along...)

Now, here's the question that I'd like each of you to address:

WHAT FACTORS INFLUENCE WHY YOU PURCHASE WHAT YOU PURCHASE?

This suggests a cause/effect pattern: What factors cause person A to buy product Y? (Note the implication that we are, in effect, forced to buy as a result of such factors.)

This question could suggest a comparison! contrast pattern: Why is product X better than product Y? However, I asked not what, but why you purchase what, and this might be a function not of the product per se—that is, of how it stacks up against other such products—but of habit, familiarity, etc. Some products might be purchased out of need, others as a luxury. I am not asking for an itemized breakdown of how each product compares with its rivals.

Similarly, this could suggest a persuasive pattern: Why should person A buy product Y? Yet I asked not why you should or shouldn't buy a product, but why you do buy a product. To ask why one should or shouldn't is to invoke a measure of judgement, an evaluation of factors as better or worse; again, not what I'm looking for,

And this could even fit into a problem! Solution pattern: How should person A buy (generic) product Y? This would involve using the various factors as a basis for discussing how to go about employing them while grocery shopping. That is, first you'd have to identify the relevant factors, which is precisely why I'm asking you to employ a cause! Effect pattern.

Here's how I'd like you to go about addressing this question.

1.   Go grocery shopping. Bring a notepad with you.

2.   Record your reasons for selecting ten (10) of the items you've purchased. (Save your receipts!).

3.   Try to determine which general factors (habit, brand, commercials, packaging, quality, coupons, need, etc., etc., etc.) motivated each of your ten choices. Make a list of factors and generalize these. Pick the SIX most prevalent factors.

4.   Write an (approx.) three (3) page cause/effect report (What factors caused me to purchase these items?) using the following standard format:

Issue:

Statement of the issue and statement of your conclusion. Be concise and specific. Eliminate ALL personal pronouns. Use passive construction as necessary. ("A case study was undertaken to determine which of the following factors contribute to food product purchase.... It was determined that.

Causes (factors): Analysis of each factor, arranged in descending order of importance. Explain how each factor shapes your decision to buy.

Alternative factors: Which factors didn't influence you, but might have?

Summary: Restate the conclusion.

5. Attach a one-page memo to the front of your report addressed as follows:

From: Y. Name

To: J. Amato Re: Assignment 1

Date:

Explain in three paragraphs.

1)   whether and why you found this pattern to be useful (not at all, moderately, very much so);

2)   whether and why you found that this assignment required you to be analytical (not at all, moderately, very much so); and

3)   whether and why you found that this assignment required you to be creative (not at all, moderately, very much so).

Good luck! & I hope it's FUN!

After I read the assignment, I thought to myself that my foray into Bloomingdale's, a few days earlier, qualified closely enough to use it in this assignment. I still had my receipts or could get my credit card statements according to the assignment's parameters. At that point, I decided to go for it; that is, if I could get permission from Amato to use my birthday foray for Bunny for the assignment. I got that permission with nary a problem.

When all was said and done, however, I would hit an unexpected Glass Monolith, and here it was:

Jon, what struck me initially in reading through your paper was the very non-professional, non-technical form of address and format you employed in detailing your birthday present analysis. I tried to convey in the overview of the assignment that I was looking for a formal, research-style analysis of an everyday event. Instead, what you've given me amounts to a somewhat stuffy, somewhat archaic discussion of fashion aesthetics and personal judgment, all unwittingly gendered because of your assumptions pertaining to the "petite," "beautiful" "lady" in question. You do provide some nice insights, such as why you chose a particular shoe, etc.. Still, these are couched in a rhetoric that details not simply those factors that influenced your purchases, but the effect the purchases will have on this woman's appearance. The hair clip will clip her "perfect length" hair to "augment" her look, ever so

subtly" IF she uses the clip as you suggest. So, the factor at work here in your decision to purchase the hair clip, simplicity or subtlety of function, constitutes more of an assumption as to how beauty will be enhanced than a wish, desire, or hope that the item will have the intended effect (and be appreciated accordingly).

Sorry to sound a bit harsh. This is definitely not what I anticipated. And had I expected this, I would have insisted that you go grocery shopping and write about this latter—because this affects, first and foremost, YOU. But the basic problem evident in this piece of writing would, to some extent, have surfaced, I think, even had you written about grocery factors. Let me spell out precisely what I mean by looking at a few specific examples: "If my reader wants a real challenge... This is the "Dear Reader" form of address that characterized so much of the 18th-century English literature (and a good deal of 19th-century prose, as well). Your imperative to the reader to "Remember" (you do so twice) is also an example of this stylistic flourish. It is surely a far cry from the language I suggest—one that is concise and specific, that treats the subject in clinical terms (recall my phrasing, "A case study was undertaken," etc.) And note that to use the possessive my is to violate one of the guidelines of the assignment (viz., "Eliminate ALL personal pronouns" in your intro., by which I meant to take yourself out of this description). "Rest assured" is also an example of this rhetorical style—in effect, it anticipates an emotional state on the part of your reader. To reiterate: I was looking for a cause/effect analysis, composed in accordance with the following conceptual categories:

Issue

Causes (factors)

Alternative factors

Summary

"Another problem lay that this particular lady (of Spanish Extraction).."

Problems don't generally "lay," "lady" is no longer current usage (woman is correct), "of Spanish Extraction" is antique (and precious—and why the uppercase E?), and it remains unclear throughout what this observation adds to your statement of the issue. You are making aesthetic judgments even as you presume to detail the problem ("wonderful woman," "frumpy"), and this has the effect of alienating me somewhat, because I may not share your sentiments. That is, throughout your piece, it seemed you were intent on justifying your aesthetic choices, rather than simply presenting the factors that contributed to your purchases. "Her usual affair" is vague, almost absurdly polite, and in the next paragraph, you write "her usual fare" (incorrect usage here). And your next paragraph is much too short to stand on its own (as a paragraph).

"So how do you give someone a makeover without violating [sic] that person's belief in simplicity?"

The question, as stated, is highly... questionable! To "give someone a makeover," again, would seem to presume upon the woman in question as an object to be 'made over' ~ la My Fair Lady. Jon, I risk a judgment of you as narrator here when I say that you have objectified this gal as somehow at the mercy of your fashion insights, as though she were incapable of making the same judgments herself (her beauty, in your eyes, is "hiding under clothes"). There would seem to be an agenda buried under the weight of your prose (which is, at times, purple as hell). Perhaps it is your unstated but tacit attraction to this woman that results in your more oblique and presumptuous remarks (such as "To our birthday subject's credit" etc.)—and this in spite of your stated commitment to matching her form of dress (i.e., simplicity). I would rather that you refrained from rendering evaluations as to "sex bombs" and the like; though I imagine that you regard this latter as an "alternative factor," it is in actuality more an alternative mindset as you have expressed same.

To put it bluntly: whether this woman likes your gifts or not, the factor you are busy elucidating here—simplicity—requires, to be a factor, only your belief that this is what she likes, nothing more and nothing less. If she doesn't like your gift, it matters little how you conceive of its contribution to her wardrobe. And if you care more about your sense of, say, beauty than hers, the primary factor underlying your purchase is better stated expressly as a function of your fashion values. Note how redundant the following sentences are—their net effect is to suggest you need to justify your fashion decisions (and they occur in three separate paragraphs): As she intimated, she did not believe in overdressing to go to work. [Did she "intimate" this, or did she actually indicate it?]

So, the decision was made to use her own mode of dress to make the makeover possible. ["made," "make," and "makeover" do not read well when used in one sentence; the passive construction is O.K. here]

The question came as to how to augment the very mode of dress best that this particular lady prefers. [passive construction again, and "augment the very mode" is obscure]

More examples: 'Adding to the difficulty of the process was her dimensions." "... a trip to one of the more upscale stores ... was indicated." Should be "were her dimensions," and "was indicated."

I could go on and on and on. Note how awkward the following: "Asking such a question risked puzzlement on her part to the researcher."

It's unclear in the above just who is "puzzled" (primarily because of the tacked-on "to the researcher"). And your automotive digression again presumes upon the reader with a rhetorical question (sans the necessary question mark) as to "How many would dare" etc.—much as though I (the reader) would not appreciate the mighty six-cylinder blah blah blah. Jon, I was driving souped-up cars twenty years ago.

Note "been," "would've"—you need to read more carefully and write more professionally.

If you wish to revise this paper, I'm willing to give you that chance. But I'll want a complete rewrite of this assignment, starting with your trip to the grocery store. And I think it's fair to say that you're going to have to spend some time with the folks at the Writing Center. In any case, see me at break. It may be best for you to move on to the next assignment and put this assignment behind you, as it were— and as I've asked others in the class who didn't fare too well on this first paper, grade-wise.

In any case, please accept my response to this paper as bearing not on you as a flesh & blood being, but on the "you" you've offered me through your writing.

Paper Grade: C

I blew what should've been easy pickings! There were fundamental mistakes in my grammar. However, I was learning how to use a word processor. Even more insidiously, Microsoft Works lacked the types of spell-checking features that Microsoft Word would have. I had never even known about Microsoft Word, but I used it!

What hurt me the most was that I had this assignment format in front of me as I wrote it. Yet, Amato still accused me of failing to follow the format.

When I asked Amato about my paper, I found out that I had let myself get bogged down in the legalese of writing. For instance, I was under the impression that the word after a proper noun ALWAYS had to be capitalized. That was not the case.

I took NO comfort in knowing that only five people in the entire class met the assignment's parameters enough to get a good grade. Although all of us brought our shopping receipts, Amato didn't want them, even though he had specified that we bring them to document our work. Instead, he laughed and said to the class, "You guys are so anal!"

After I earned my Post-Baccalaureate, I decided to embark on a freelance research project.

The subject of my freelance research project would deal with why some people can get a job as readily as they can put on a pair of socks. Other people, on the other hand, are unemployable, regardless of their background. There seemed to be a caste system within the working world. I began to narrow it down to a few factors. I then formed a theory.

Every theory needs to be validated. To that end, I decided that I would interview a few people who were in the know about the question of employability. To that end, I decided that my first interview would be with John Challenger of the fabled consulting firm, Challenger, Gray, and Christmas.

It was here that I would commit a logic error.

I figured that I would need to set up an appointment to see such a busy man. To that end, I telephoned his office and set up the appointment myself. To my utter surprise, I had John Challenger on the line himself! That put me in the awkward position of scrambling to get a notepad and to jot down information on the points that would be germane to the issue of employability. Despite such a miscalculation on my part, John Challenger proved more than helpful as my first interview subject.

It just so happened that I remembered what Statistical Tabulating Company's (STAT-TAB'S) Patricia Doherty said about "Logic Errors"

Remember! Patricia (Trish) Doherty was disabled. Yet, she was more than capable of delivering a concept about programming that some able-bodied or able-minded persons could not.

The concept of a Logic Error stuck in my mind like Eastman 910 Adhesive, though in ways not immediately apparent to me. Now, it seemed that I was committing "Logic Errors" in the course of my work as a Technical Correspondent at Underwriters Laboratories in 2000.

For instance, some issues were coming up that Rich expected me to think about that I didn't know about-not out of volition, but because I didn't expect them. Also remember. After that incident with the emails, it seemed better for me NOT to do any thinking at all.

When I brought up the subject of the "Logic Errors" with Rich, he assured me that he was also aware of them. However, he merely told me that we would talk about those "Logic Errors" later. Little did I know just how much the "Logic Errors" were turning into a Glass Monolith-yet!

Errors and Omissions are death to Technical Writers-period! Therefore, the onus was on me to develop a systematic method for controlling and/or eliminating the errors and omissions. It was with those thoughts in mind that one weekend in mid-October 2000, I developed what I called EOCS (pronounced E-Ox).

My first step in the process of developing EOCS was to draw a flowchart. Although I had no computer program at that time, I did have plenty of notebook paper. Then, I considered issues such as directions, references, notations, data entry, and whether it was a Windows-based program or not. If it were, then I could use spell checker. If not, then I would have to go over the program line by line.

I put a "Decision Box" on the end of the flowchart and asked: "Does Document Pass Cross-Check?" If yes, I was in business. If not, then it was up to me to take remedial action.

Once I finished the flowchart, I transferred it to the office's Microsoft PowerPoint, a presentation graphics program that allowed me to put EOCS on a computer, and subsequently, a floppy disk.

I was also thinking in terms of sharing EOCS with other departments since their work could very easily involve the production of technical documents.

The very first thing I did that Monday morning was to share EOCS with Rich, and, as it turned out, a very curious Vella!

Vella was very fascinated with my use of PowerPoint. However, she had some concerns about EOCS. For instance, I used a "Decision Box" at the end of the flowchart. However, Vella's concern was that there could be "hundreds of those Decision Boxes in a single project!"

Not only did Rich concur with Vella, he added: "The problem I have with your flowchart is that it's like a boy playing baseball. He's got to figure out how fast to run in order to field the ball. There might be a host of variables in that. I'm also concerned that you might even get bogged down in a whole lot of paperwork with that flowchart of yours."

Although I hit a Glass Monolith in my presentation of EOCS to Rich, a very curious Vella popped back inside my office again. She asked me about some of the functions of PowerPoint and asked me to duplicate them. For that matter, so did Rich. At first, I fumbled and stumbled. Eventually, I was able to get it right. Meanwhile, Rich was taking mental notes of all these events.

The Logic Error would NOT only affect me on the job, but also in the arena of interpersonal relations. Most insidiously, some people would term me rude, even when I would not think about doing the types of things that I would be accused of. Some people would term me a lout! For instance, at East Midway Drive, there was a mirror where Operators could straighten or comb their hair while putting on a headset. However, there was a seat below that mirror. One day, my supervisor called me off the boards to clean up the seat. It was claimed that my hair was falling out onto the seat. I had no idea this was happening until I was called out.

Is there any other area affected by the Logic Error? See the next chapter!

Interpersonal Relations-
Outside of the Family

Before Marciea left Chicago to relocate to Seattle, she said it in the most succinct manner. She said: "Jon, you've always been a victim of what other people think of you!" During the Very' Early Autumn of 1992, I visited Maree, in Oakland California, three months after she gave birth to Baby Nicki. We spent a very poignant afternoon together, as opposed to a previous visit with her when she was a trial to be with. I mentioned the trying times l was having at Midway Drive. It was then that I mentioned: "I had turned up this problem in the system, in which I couldn't find this area of the United States. I reported it to the bosses. So, the time came around for an Open Forum meeting. They had the big men from downtown on it. I told them what happened. I got an answer within about two minutes! So, about a few months ago, I had another problem turn up, and I wrote the Manager of Number Services about it, and my supervisors got mad with me."

Marciea said, "Back then, that was because the meeting was an 'Open Forum' meeting. But this time, you were going over somebody's head, and they see that as being a threat to them."

I picked up on the word "threat" and said: "That's another thing. A lot of people think that I am a threat to them. I can tell you right now. I don't have enough brains to be a threat to anybody. If I did, I'd have long had their jobs by now!"

Marciea retorted: "That's where you're wrong! People see you as a threat to them because they don't know how to deal with you. They have to deal with you on a different level, and that bothers them."

Marciea's mind harkened back momentarily. Then she said: "I work with the public myself, and sometimes, you've got to kill 'em with kindness."

It was as if people had their minds made up about me before I had a chance to say nary a word. That may be the reason why I was having these types of problems with my customers and with my supervisors on the job. Perceptions of me might even have been the reason why I was having the kinds of career problems I was having.

I need to let my readers in on another secret. I always saw criticism as a form of punishment!

I had 20 years of criticism starting with roughly the end of second grade and continuing to the end of college. The worst of it came when I was in seventh grade. I popped four A's, one B, and a C in Math. You'd think my parents would be happy. Instead, I got criticism from my parents, teacher, and principal for not being independent, for not working with my hands, for not getting along with people. I even got heat for not wanting to attend an after-school party hosted by the same classmates who would bully me! And when Ted yelled at me for correcting a teacher, I completely lost it. I never did that well in school again.

 Shortly after I graduated from Roosevelt University, I knew that I would need Vocational Rehabilitation after the nightmare that was my Undergraduate. To that end, I was sent from Intake to an office on Stony Island Avenue, where I had my first meeting with my Counselor. She was a Black woman who reminded me of the late actress Madge Sinclair, of Trapper John, MD fame.

That first meeting seemed placid enough. However, we had a second meeting a couple of weeks later that bordered on a flat-out insult.

Ms. Jones said, "One concern that I have is that you should 'tone down!'"

I asked: "Was I too loud?"

Ms. Jones said, "I don't know. When I first talked to you over the phone, I hung up and thought to myself: "What an obnoxious person." I don't know what it is about you, except you've got to tone down."

I said, "I was a Directory Assistance Operator until I went to Engineering school, and I would constantly get complaints from my co-workers about my voice. The trouble is, the last thing I would think about doing is to talk loudly, that's why I had to ask."

Ms. Jones said, "One of the things you will need to do before we can provide you with services is that you seek some form of counseling. I don't know. Have you sought counseling before?"

I said: "Oh yes. I did that right after I was fired from the W.F. Hall Printing Company. In 1980."

"What happened there? "Asked Ms. Jones.

I replied: I was a Lab Technician. I would check books, coversheets, varnishes, adhesives, and other materials. Anyway, whenever there was something wrong, I'd write up discrepancy reports on them. Anyhow, they said that I was crying "wolf too much, and causing too much embarrassment to the company, so that's why they fired me."

Tomilee said, "It seems that you were trying to be too much of a crusader. For instance, I was on the bus one day, and there was this person who was picking a man's pocket. I just sat there and watched. I didn't say anything. You still could've been working there today."

"I've had two jobs ever since then," I said.

"That's two too many." Said Tomilee

"Hey! They were temporary jobs." I said.

Tomilee then asked: "Do you have friends?"

I said: "Very few. The trouble is that Black people, in particular, accuse me of being…"

"Homosexual?" completed Tomilee.

"Exactly." I said, and continued: "I'm not too high on Black people at all."

"Well, it is true that Black people can be a bit petty, but still! I don't know. You've just got to tone down." Said Tomilee.

I stumbled and stuttered momentarily, then made the mistake of telling Tomilee that I sometimes had trouble putting a thought together. That's when she told me, "You should think before you speak."

I was, by this time, getting a little testy. I responded: "Boy, you're ripping me apart. First, you say that I'm obnoxious. Then you say that

I was at fault for W.F. Hall, now you tell me that I don't think before I speak."

Tomilee said, "If I wanted to rip you apart, you'd know it. I did not say you're obnoxious."

I responded: "You just told me..."

"I said you come off as being obnoxious. "You see, sometimes, people have these defense mechanisms inside them that kick in. Sometimes, those defense mechanisms can screen out that warm person underneath."

I was quite cowardly. I tolerated the situation rather than lodging a complaint against her or responding more forcefully. I was afraid that she would react by cutting off any assistance I was looking to get.

But if Tomilee Jones was out of line for her assault on my character, she also gave me insight into what Black American women felt about me in general. The only difference was that Tomilee Jones came out with it. Other Black women would not. Instead, to many women, I would either be a novelty item, an eccentric, a nerd, or simply not macho enough for their tastes. The only time a Black woman showed interest in me, except for my novelty status sometimes, was if she wanted me to do something for her, or to provide her with some money. For instance, a former co-worker of mine wanted nothing to do with me after I told her that I didn't have a credit card. I had my friends back at the phone company, but only within my department. I had a few acquaintances from outside my department, such as Frames and Housekeeping, but that was it.

One of my pet peeves with my fellow Black Americans had always been that they NEVER wanted anything to do with me unless they wanted something from me! Here is a case in point. In 1988, as I was about to conclude my day at Chicago Southwest

#1, a Black woman ran behind me at a feverish pace, shouting: "Mr. Evans?" I thought she was one of the Group Chief Operators. Instead, she was just an Operator like me. She claimed that she was having an attendance problem, but couldn't get off on an upcoming Saturday without running the risk of being put on Probation. The upshot was that I would not get a rare Saturday off this time. Instead, I would get a Friday off! I let myself get sucked into that situation.

Back in 1982, I got a call from Tomilee. She would have me go down to the Jewish Vocational Services downtown. There, I would meet with someone named Ros Finch. Ms. Finch was White, perhaps Jewish, but young. She wore platform shoes that skidded across the floor as she stepped. Here, I would put my foot in my own mouth because I arrived late for the appointment. That didn't sit very well with her. Rightfully, Ros said that the best thing for me to do would've been to leave my home an extra hour or so early and, in her words, "camp out"

After I introduced myself to her and explained my situation to her, Ros said: "Well, unfortunately, that's just the way it is in the working world. They're not going to hold your hand. They want someone who can get in there and do the work, or they're going to find someone that can."

Ros then asked: "Have you ever done cold canvases?"

I said: "No. Oftentimes, I don't know what a company has in terms of jobs unless I see an opening. I wouldn't even know what types of workers a company uses. I've had ideas about what fields I would like to get into, but I don't know which way in."

Ros said, "You expect a company to tell you about the types of people that they hire? No! They're going to send you to the Public Library.

Tell you what. What I want you to do is to give me a list of jobs that you have had. Separate this list into two categories: Personality and Performance. Then I want you to provide me with a list of all the college courses you took, and what grades did you get on them? Again, concentrate on Personality and Performance. Then, I want to see you next week."

With that, I left, then went to the Main Branch of the Chicago Public Library to see just what it was that Ros Finch was talking about.

At the Library, I found a large book of occupations. I also found a possible field for someone with my background to get into. It was an Insurance Underwriter. From the description of the field, I had enough already to get myself a start. Considering my interest in Automobiles and health, I thought that I could concentrate on insurers dealing in these areas.

I spent that weekend slaving at my typewriter. I wrote the report per the parameters that Ms. Finch specified. Nevertheless, Ms. Finch was shocked when I submitted the written report to her.

When Finch got to the two courses in which I did get As, towards the end of my Undergraduate, she commented: "Well, here you got pretty hot."

After Ros Finch reviewed my report, she showered me with a lot of negativity and non-advice. She started by saying: "Somebody should've sat you down and said: 'College is not for you."

Then Ms. Finch asked: "Are you an only child?"

I was highly insulted by that question or comment because the implication was that I was some out-of-phase "wimp", "nerd", "geek," or "dingbat." Furthermore, people who are, indeed, only children should feel just as insulted as I was if they were to read this book. Only children tend to be stereotyped in this manner. Once I set Finch straight, she correctly surmised that I was one of the first persons in my family to have completed college.

It didn't do any good to mention the success I had at Science Research Associates either, at least as far as Ros Finch was concerned. She said, "So what are you going to do? Spend several months down at Control Data? That costs money!"

I replied: "I'm pretty sure that if I enter a training program, I'd have a better go at it than I did in college because…"

"You finally got the monkey off your back?" asked Finch.

"Exactly," I said.

I telephoned Tomilee at DORS after my second meeting with Ros Finch. I then told her how disappointing the meetings went. Tomilee admonished me against becoming frustrated. I didn't use the term "Glass Monolith." To describe my experience with Ros back then. However, that was the crux of my feelings about my meetings with her. I got no answers; no guidance; no suggestions; no job leads either-just a lot of criticism.

I arrived at Tomilee's office. Once there, Tomilee telephoned Ros Finch to get a read on what did or didn't go on. After Tomilee's phone conversation with Finch, it was Tomilee's turn to take more pot-shots at me, saying: "In all my eight years I have had here, I have never had such a negative person." "You come off as being very obnoxious. You have absolutely no self-esteem. You come off as being very obnoxious. You don't smile."

Meanwhile, I didn't think to ask what smiling had to do with anything, since I was trying to not only find work, but to establish a career.

Note: A Glass Monolith can consist of not knowing what the other person may be talking about or sending unintended impressions.

There was one point that Tomilee was correct in raising. To me, she said, "Ms. Finch told me that you arrived late for that first meeting. That indicates a lack of discipline. For instance, when I get up, I might put on a cup of coffee, then do my exercises, then get dressed to come to work. When I get here, I might glance at my paper for a few minutes, then get ready to start."

And in truth, I had given up on trying to get somewhere on time, since I was using mass transit and had no car. Come to find out, that was, indeed, the improper thing to do.

I was starting to become very worried about my inadvertent negative impressions. Not only did I rub Tomilee Jones the wrong way, but I also found out that I rubbed my new counselor at Catholic Charities the wrong way.

I did not know what I could do about the inadvertent negative impressions I was causing people to get. I told both Tomilee Jones and my counselor that I would seek ways to adjust. That left Tomilee Jones very delighted. As for my counselor, he conceded that his behavior failed to consider the difficulty of the Black experience. Although I found his response a bit simplistic, I also thought: "Well, at least he's not hostile towards me. anymore."

Hertz had a Distribution Manager named Frank Farmer. He was long-haired, classic White, and, as he would reveal to me, an ex-programmer. I left my folio over to him so that I wouldn't have so much to carry while I hiked cars. One day, Frank told me: "You might get into a situation where somebody is going to hand you a sheet or a big strip of paper and simply tell you: 'Program This'-and that's all they will tell you."

My relationship with Frank was problematic. He tolerated no mistakes. He had a propensity to swear at his subordinates. He made no allowances for foul-ups beyond my control. In one case, I got some profanity sent my way because a car I was delivering to Kinzie Street conked out on Lower Wacker Drive. I left it in a nook that was out of traffic and reported the incident to the Station Manager at Kinzie Street. I wouldn't find out later that the car was out of fuel.

My relationship with his assistant was not much better. I would be introduced to Connie Roberson, his apparent assistant in Distribution. Ms. Roberson was Black, petite, stocky, and carried a somewhat booming voice. Frank explicitly said, "Please treat her like a lady. If you don't, we will have further words!"

Since I addressed all superiors as Mr., Ms., or Mrs., I had no problem in complying. Nevertheless, Connie Roberson hated my guts! For instance, one time, I reported for work at the trailer, and Connie spontaneously said to me, with a smile on her face, "You'd mess up a two-car funeral!" I made no mistakes at that time, and was not long in knowing her. Nevertheless, she said this to me out of a clear blue sky. Had our roles been reversed, she would've blabbed to Frank, and I probably would've been issued some profane epithets, as well as a pink slip!

I only wish that the ribbing and razzing I got would've ended with the Hertz Clowns. It didn't. It was about May of 1983. I had just approached the corner of 119th and Princeton to catch my bus for work. As I waited at my stop, a young, relatively tall, about 5'10" Black male of about eighteen years of age pulled up on a bicycle. He asked me: "Hey! I got a transfer."

I told him, "I don't need it."

That should've ended the conversation right there. It didn't. He said: "You gettin on the bus ain't you?"

"I've got that covered." I said

This teenager went inside a store behind me. As my bus rolled up, this teenager came out of the store with a few friends. He then yelled to me: "You got a bus pass?"

I said "Yep!" and climbed aboard my bus. Meanwhile, this punk and two other of his friends would have themselves a belly laugh.

In another incident, he would get another rise out of asking me about my bus pass later, in front of one of his friends.

My relationship with Connie Roberson would serve as a backdrop for a serious situation that would come up between late April and mid-May. It was a weekday. However, traffic on the Kennedy Expressway was brisk, and volume was jam-packed. There were eight hikers and one Ford Fairmont sedan to be shuttled back to O'Hare base. The car was crowded. I sat in the middle of the front seat between two white males. The driver, whose name was Fat Dave, was quite obese.

Although the driving conditions were tolerable, the crew's actions were not. Fat Dave and a few of the others were passing a Marijuana Cigarette around between them. I explicitly told the crew that if the Police were to stop us, the entire crew would go to jail; that is, if we all weren't killed first! The crew continued passing the joint around, while saying: "No, we're not!"

The crew stopped off for a break on Belmont Avenue, just east of Kimball Avenue. At that point, I had enough. Fat Dave asked if I was going back with the crew. I told him I'd see him later. What I did was to jump on the Northwest Side Subway at Belmont and Kimball and took the train back to O'Hare. Once there, I took a Hertz shuttle back to the base station.

There was someone at Distribution who divided her time between being a lead hiker and helping Ms. Roberson. Her name was Nkema. Nkema was Black, college-aged, or just over it, a little taller than Ms. Roberson, and very enraged with me. As I reached the counter, Nkema yelled: "You! You don't just leave a crew like that! If there's something that ain't right, you wait until you get back and then you complain."

"Fine! So in the meantime, I get killed!" I said.

Before I could open my mouth, Nkema interrupted: "I know they were smoking pot! One joint ain't gonna hurt nothing!"

Nkema, you are dead wrong! It is because of you and your callous, casual, cavalier attitude towards drugs and/or alcohol that there is such carnage in and on our nation's highways, waterways, industries, schools, homes, and, in this case, workplaces. You say that "One joint is not going to hurt anything."

The fact of the matter is that "One joint" will exacerbate Driver Inattention! Driver Inattention is the number one cause of carnage on our nation's highways today. Alcohol is a major subset of Driver Inattention!

Even more insidiously, there are too many Nkemas out there. Had I not left the crew and reported the Marijuana smoking, I stood a very good chance of becoming another Richard Ramey!

In the Richard Ramey affair, a Chicago Transit Authority rider, by the name of Richard Ramey, was illegally smoking on the Rapid Transit train. The Chicago Police arrested him. Some time during his arrest, he was beaten to death! Richard Ramey was Black!

If the "Motor Marijuana" incident weren't bad enough, I would have yet another. There was a young, maybe 20–23-year-old, college-aged, Black Male who would hang out with two other friends. His name was Kevin Burch. I never spoke with him or with two of his other friends. Unfortunately, Kevin and I would meet, and it would not be friendly.

As we were about to leave the Evanston location, Kevin threw a spitball through one of the rent-a-car's windows, hitting me with it as he passed on the way to one of his cars. When I confronted him about the spitball, I showed it to him and ordered him to "cease, immediately."

The whole thing was a joke to Kevin. His response was to tell me to "Get the (bleep) out of his face before I (meaning he) would kick my (donkey). At that point, it turned into a shouting match. Meanwhile, the whole thing was downright funny to a bunch of onlookers, who were Black.

Goodkind was White but also thought that the harassment directed at me was a joke! I heard his voice, yelling "Sweet Pea! Sweet Pea!" as if he were yelling soo-ee! Meanwhile, I sat in the company lunchroom with a bus driver named Mr. Winsted and another driver. Goodkind walked over to me and handed me a trip ticket, which was used whenever a car was being transported from one station to the next.

Most insidiously of all, Goodkind put his arm around my shoulder and said: "I call him Sweet Pea cause he is my friend!"

I had had enough and told Goodkind: "Get your hands off of me! You are not my friend."

Goodkind jumped, then turned to Winsted and company and said: Are you my friend?"

They nodded in agreement.

Goodkind then turned to me and said, "If I were to kiss you, would you be my friend?"

I explicitly told Goodkind: "If you were to kiss me, I'd kick every one of your teeth down your throat!"

I stormed out of the lunchroom to look for the car that was supposed to be shuttled.

The next day, I telephoned Distribution to report the incident. Frank, the manager, was not interested in anything I had to say. In fact, Frank told me, "It's just like with a woman.

If she doesn't want anything to do with you, she ain't gonna have sex with you. No, it's that voice of yours."

Meanwhile, one day, Ms. Roberson instructed me to summon Kevin Burch. He would be in the lunchroom. I went to the lunchroom, saw Burch, and said to him: "Kevin, Ms. Roberson wants you."

Burch responded: "Who"?

I responded: "Ms. Roberson-Connie."

An enraged, belligerent Kevin Burch yelled: "Well, say that! (Bleep) it! Stay the (bleep) out of my way!"

Burch stormed out of the lunchroom with his friend in tow. I wasn't too far behind either. When I lodged a complaint against Kevin for his tirade, Connie Roberson also launched a tirade at me, saying. "I can't have any personality conflicts."

I replied: "I'm not causing the personality conflict."

"I realize that, but I'm still not having any personality conflicts." Said Roberson.

First, Roberson instructs me to summon someone. I summoned that person without comment or debate. Then the person I summoned swore at me, as if he wanted to start a fight with me. I would've obliged. Then, when I complained to that person, Roberson reprimanded me for what she termed a "personality conflict." This was the thanks I got for following the directive of Frank, the Distribution Manager.

These incidents I experienced occurred in 1983; yet Black on Black inhumanity and incivility remains so pervasive today, that it rivals the racism that Whites would subject Blacks to in the years between Reconstruction and Emmitt Till's Murder!

You can make a case for this being a Glass Monolith.

I had enough. I refused even to work that day, knowing that I had to ride with Kevin Burch as the lead hiker. As I waited for the Hertz shuttle to take me back to the Terminal and Rapid Transit. Burch yelled from a shuttle car:

"Hey! You riding with us?"

When I said "No", Kevin laughed and mocked: "Noooo!"

Ironically, there would be another day in which Kevin would lead a hike. While we were at Midway, Kevin had the nerve to ask to borrow money from me! I refused.

I also take issue with what Black Americans value. For instance, one day, at Kinzie Street, we waited for the shuttle van to take us back to O'Hare. While I was waiting, one Black co-worker asked, "How are you doing?" I responded in the customary civil manner.

His response was: "Well, you can't be alright if you're wearing that tie."

I wore a clip-on tie that was a solid rust color. It was wide. However, that's what people were wearing in those days.

My point is that Black Americans value style, trends, being hip, being in the clique, fronting, and other superficial nonsense more than substance. Although I was never a fan of The Bar Kays, the best song they ever cut, bar none, was his song "Smiling, Styling, and Profiling." This song is, again, actual of Black Americans.

Our crew picked up Fat Dave. All the while, the name-calling and derision continued. When Fat Dave joined in on the catcalls and hazing, I promptly told the crew: "I'm going to put a .22 up one of you clowns' (donkey) in a minute."

The crew was enraged. They asked: "Where do you get off threatening people?"

"If you can't take what you dish, then don't dish," I said.

Please notice here that victims of abuse oftentimes become vilified whenever, and if ever, they strike back against their abusers. Some people who strike back against their abusers are even referred to as troublemakers!

Fat Dave said: "I'll call you whatever I wanna call you. I'll call you "Butt (plug)! How would you like it if I were to put a .357 up your (donkey)? You'd probably get turned on by it."

He then turned towards the rest of the crew and said: He was the one who told Connie about us smoking a joint."

The entire group sneered at me, and for the moment, I thought that I might not reach O'Hare alive. Then I said: "I didn't tell on any person. All I said was that they were smoking reefer behind the wheel. If the cops had stopped us, we all would've gone to jail." I said.

After we got another run, the lead hiker, Mosely, said that there was a potential error in the way I filled out my trip ticket. He told the crew. The crew started hazing me again. They would say to me things like: "Look! You give us $10.00 and we'll tighten you up", or "If Frank finds out, he's gonna get you."

All the while, telling the Hertz clowns to bug off would continue to do no good. The bantering, teasing, and razzing would continue.

Finally, once we got back from Kinzie, and our shuttle van emptied, Mosely said to me: "Those guys! They were (bleeping) with you, that's all."

Think about it-playing; teasing; razzing; ribbing; signifying; hazing, practical jokes, or in Mr. Mosely's words: (bleeping) with people-namely me! Isn't that what led to the recent hazing incident at Northbrook's Glenbrook North High School?

Even more significantly, doesn't playing, razzing, ribbing, hazing, etc., escalate into acts of bullying, even sexual abuse?

Let us also not forget, it was the so-called playing, razzing, ribbing, and teasing students engaged in that eventually led to the massacre at Littlefield, Colorado's Columbine High School.

Playing, teasing, razzing, ribbing, signifying, practical jokes, or in Mr. Mosely's words: (bleeping) with people should end with graduation day from high school. Unfortunately, it sometimes doesn't, and many of these seemingly benign acts are highly dangerous!

Speaking of the Hertz Clowns, Kevin Burch proved to be the Clown Prince of Audacity. Even more insidiously, I set myself up for one of his pranks. On this occasion, I was in the van. Kevin touched me on my knee and asked: "How the hell are you?

I replied: "I'm fine."

I naively thought that after I stood up to Fat Dave and after Dondy and I at least established diplomatic relations, what I was going through was merely part of "becoming one of the boys" at last. I thought that maybe Dondy had somehow gotten to Kevin to tell him that I wasn't like what people were saying.

I should've known better.

Kevin then told me, "Why don't you get out of the van, so it'll make the group more live!" Then, he laughed.

He continued: "No. Really. There's another run that's looking for some drivers."

I replied: "You're just one person-What about the others? If you want me out, then vote me out!"

Kevin then turned towards the others in the van and yelled: "Yo! Y'all want him out of the van? "

At that point, a steady chorus of Out! Out! Out! Ensued.

With that, I said: "Well, I'm not going to stay where I'm not wanted."

I could tolerate Kevin Burch's point-blank sneers, verbal abuse, and insults. For him, that's par for the course. However, when one fakes burying the hatchet as a ruse for another prank, that is a sin that I find unforgivable.

As I may have mentioned, Kevin Burch was not the sole reason why I despised my own people. However, Kevin Burch was a quintessential reason why I despised my own people at that time.

When I mentioned how I was put out of the van by the crew, Connie flew into a rage at me! She yelled: "Get with the crew!" She also repeated her tirade about not having any "personality conflicts". Roberson was forced to reassign me when the van I was kicked out of had already left.

An incident the following week was almost as bad. A crew was forming, and I was the first to process my trip ticket and board a van. Then, the other crew members started to assemble. Meanwhile, I was in the far back of the van below the seats, out of immediate sight. Finally, a 25–28-year-old Black crew member with what looked like street tattoos on his arms, looked towards me and said to the lead driver: "Yo! We got us a fish back here!" He was referring to me!

Luckily, another crew was forming. Rather than getting into a potential fight with this person, I think that all concerned were happy to see me with a more receptive crew. I went with that crew instead.

In the six months I worked at Hertz as a hiker, I was subjected to physical assault, sexual abuse, mockery, derision, public ridicule, insults, bullying, and 101 other messages that let me know that I never did, and never would fit in as a Hertz hiker.

Management was no better. Jody Mackey, who was an older Black man, was the only manager I got along with. However, he had his ways. I ultimately submitted my resignation letter to Hertz at the end of September 1983.

I had a job at the Internal Revenue Service, so I no longer needed Hertz. What I didn't have was grace in dealing with virtually all women co-workers, case in point:

I preferred to speak, or to greet people, only if spoken to. I thought that if I were to speak in a predominantly female environment, the result might have been the perception that I was womanizing, flirting, coming on to women, or engaging in otherwise sexually abusive behavior.

Since most of the women were Tax Examiners, a hello might break their concentration, and subject them to serious errors!

Mrs. H. had an earful for me when I responded to Merissa without speaking to her. She flew off the handle, saying: "Jon! Please don't speak to Merissa or me.

Earlean also had a serious issue with my withholding a greeting until I was spoken to. She came up to me and said: "Listen! When you walk into a room, you're supposed to speak. Don't just walk in and not say anything to anyone."

In my defense, however, I would, on many an occasion, give a nod or a short bow, or a signal, just to let the other person feel welcomed. Mark my word. The last thing I ever intended by withholding my greeting, or not speaking, was to be rude, boorish, or loutish. It was just in my nature not to.

It would continue not to be uncommon for me to project unintended negative perceptions of me. Yes, it would be another component of the Glass Monolith I would face.

In fact, I sometimes got wrapped up in my work that I sometimes blotted out the ambient, as I did at the former Illinois Bell. That caused me to break in on a conversation between Barbara C and Mrs. H and did Barbara C let me have it for my miscue!

In 1988, a more serious incident occurred. I got off my South Suburban bus at 119th and Halsted and walked eastward from Halsted on 119th. At that point, I was just five blocks west of home. As I walked, there was a group of Black teenage girls walking westbound on 119th near Eggleston Avenue. It was between 10:30 and 11:30 at night.

As I passed the group of girls, one of them spat in my face for positively NO reason at all! I was immediately enraged and gave chase to the girl.

Although she zigzagged and feinted, I bided my time until I eventually caught her. As I loaded up to hit this p-tailed gal, she screamed! I froze. Was this a set-up? Certainly, if I told anyone that a teenage Black girl attacked me, who would believe me, especially in a neighborhood known for the opposite form of attacks? That was the only reason why I stopped my counterattack.

This p-tailed teenager ran off screaming into the night! Meanwhile, one of her friends was screaming at me to leave them, even though I was the victim! Again! When victims of assault fight back or counterattack, they can and do get vilified.

Once I got home a few minutes later, I had to report this incredible incident to the Chicago Police! They came promptly. When I described the incident to the policewoman on the scene, I noted the policewoman's hair was matted down, just like my attacker's. Therefore, I said: "Her hair was matted down, just like yours."

That didn't sit too well with Mom, who promptly groaned and scolded me for being as blunt as I was.

The next day, I was still reeling from this attack. However, I would start some controversy before the day was done. For starters, I told Ron, "They would not have even thought of doing that (Sugar In My Tea) to you because they'd probably feel a big, husky dude like you would try to rape them!

Ron laughed and asked me, as well as the rest of the group: "Do I look like a rapist?"

I made some denigrating comments about my fellow Black Americans during this conversation. I was also sickened by an incident in which a Black woman left her daughter inside a building that was about to be torn down! That daughter, in turn, would lose her feet to frostbite

152

injuries! I felt at that time, and still feel, that if you are too poor to have children, you must not have children-even if it means refraining from sex! Otherwise, any subsequent children would invariably suffer! Couple that with Black customers who spoke broken English, and you now had an operator who was very provoked.

Lady Ditka caught wind of my comments about my so-called Black brethren and reprimanded me for them under the provisions of the company's Code of Business Conduct. Princess explicitly told me that she was offended by my comments, even though I told her I intended my comments for those who commit such unspeakable acts, not the people of the telephone company.

I found Princess's reaction to me weird. She would come down on me hard for saying what I said about Black Americans, then admonish: "You still don't talk about them." Then, she would ask me: "Why do you do that?"

I was feeling the heat from Lady Ditka. I was this close to a suspension or a firing for a Code of Business Conduct charge. I decided to write and distribute a written letter of apology for my comments. I gave the letter to Lady Ditka and left it to her to distribute the letter to the parties I offended.

This incident had a bitter irony to it; for just as I submitted my letter of apology for offending my co-workers, one of my coworkers lost her daughter to a Black-on-Black home invasion/murder!

You'd think that such negative perceptions about me would end there. You'd also forget why I call this book, in part, The Glass Monolith! For instance, Milton would throw another housewarming. This one involved all of Milton's neighbors, friends, relatives, and people from all around. I was off work and was therefore able to attend this housewarming, unlike the more private one Milton had.

What I found so strange was how Milton's guests received me. Those guests who were White or of other ethnic groups would actually come over to me and introduce themselves to me. Some of them were quite warm in the way they introduced themselves to me. They would say things such as: "Hi! Aren't you Milt's brother?"

The Black guests, particularly Linda's friends, wanted nothing to do with me! There were two exceptions. The Black guests did respond when Milton introduced me to them. Meanwhile, Linda's friends were also selling African garb at the housewarming. One of Linda's friends turned towards me and asked me, "Would you like to look at our things?"

DRY ICE COULD NOT HAVE BEEN ANY COLDER! I thought to myself: "Was that all I was good for to these people, just somebody they could sell something to?" I graciously passed.

Little did I know that part of my Glass Monolith was that even my own people would think that I was from another world!

Given that I have been having such negative perceptions of me by my own people, I should NOT have been surprised by the reaction of Milton's Black guests at the housewarming.

However, I didn't have to do anything, say anything, or even speak. Black people generally found me repulsive. There was no two ways about it. Some of my fellow Black brethren don't even want me near them, unless I can provide them with money, favors, or a ride in my car.

For instance, there was one bizarre incident on a CTA bus. I was riding on the Jeffery, northbound, approaching 71st, when a Black woman I was sitting next to, spontaneously asked me: "Can I get you to do me a favor? Could you move up there?"

Like an idiot, I never asked why she wanted me away from her. I hadn't even looked at this woman, anywhere else that would draw her ire or disdain for me. Yet, I was being ostracized in such a manner.

When I started out at Midway Drive, I had a good relationship with my co-workers. Unfortunately, that would change, in a very insidious way. On about the very first day of May 1990, I was working in the back, or the most remote part of the office. Unfortunately, there were stand-up pods at the back part of the office that the Operators liked to use; that included a co-worker by the name of Al-Marie.

Al-Marie, though Black, was tall, full-figured, and attractive, with butterscotch colored skin. Oddly, she also detested me. On this occasion, early that morning, Al-Marie sneered at me, indicating that my voice was too loud. The next morning, I asked: "Al-Marie, I would like to take just two minutes of your time."

Al-Marie looked down upon and sneered at me, as if I were dirt under her feet, and said: "I haven't got two minutes." I said nothing further.

The two minutes I wanted with Al-Marie were to apologize to her for getting loud. I tried to assure her, as I did all of my other co-workers, that I had better things to do with my time than to purposely talk loudly to offend other people in the office. I was very hurt that Al-Marie did NOT give me that chance to apologize to her, especially since I had nothing against Al-Marie whatsoever prior to this incident.

Before the day was over, I would face yet another, even more insidious incident. There was yet another moderately tall, attractive Black woman with butterscotch colored skin. Her figure was not as full as Al-Marie's. However, not even Al-Marie was as much of a bully as this woman was becoming. For that reason, and the fact that I like hot cars, I'll call her Shellie Cobra!

155

Shellie liked to trump up charges against other co-workers, claiming abuse. This time, it was, unfortunately, my turn. As I put my pizza into the oven, I almost smacked dead into her. I excused myself.

Shellie accused me of saying something disparaging about her. She threatened to report me to the front office. I was shocked and angered. Since I have had a history of people who accused me of things I never did, I decided to beat her to the punch and report her. For a while, that quieted Shellie. However, word spread throughout the office like wildfire about what happened.

Author's Side Note:

Coral Snakes rank among the most beautiful animals but are highly venomous!

Another irony to the problem is that I was having issues with my ex-locker partner because I wouldn't speak when walking into a room. As a result, she and I got into an argument. I got a separate locker because I got tired of her complaining to me about things I was supposedly doing. I didn't even know she was there until I got occasional notes from her complaining about what I was supposedly doing.

Life for me wasn't getting any better on the boards either. For instance, I had an incident with a customer who ordered something. However, the address didn't immediately indicate that it was in Chicago. It was. Understandably, this customer was upset with me.

Al Bennett was the only Group Chief Operator who survived the Great Purge of late 1992! Al would also be my Group Chief Operator.

Al Bennett and I got along better in terms of work performance issues, although she too had issues with my long-winded style of working with my customers. She was also more concerned about my health than the other Group Chief Operators. That concern came to focus when newer, more menacing issues came up.

One such issue came up because fellow Operators were complaining about me blowing my nose at the boards. Ms. Bennett called me to her desk one morning and told me about it. I tried to keep my nose-blowing short, rather than long like a foghorn. Still, the complaints mounted to the point that Al called me to the carpet on it. I telephoned the EEO Office to discuss the complaint. Come to find out, I had the legal right to take a special (time-out) period if my nose was dripping as heavily as it was. This, I didn't know. Otherwise, I would've stepped inside the Conference room, if empty, blew my nose, and resumed working.

The nose-blowing complaint came early one morning. I would get another one that afternoon. This time, Operators were complaining that there were hair fragments on a seat as a result of me combing my hair! Al prompted me to clean the hair from the seat, and gave me disinfectant to wipe it.

What I failed to understand is why someone would want to put a seat directly below a mirror where operators would stop to comb their hair. I didn't have the presence of mind to ask. All I was thinking about was to comb my hair before starting, not deliberately fouling up the commons as some coworkers were suggesting that I was doing.

I didn't resent being told what was going on by Al. What I did resent was that there were elements within Midway Drive that were portraying me as a common lout! Mark my word. I had no time for willfully or vindictively engaging in boorish behavior. My relationship with people was becoming, once again, my Glass Monolith!

There was also one last Open Forum Meeting with executives of Ameritech. This time, questions had to be prepared in advance, unlike in previous times. I posted some questions relating to that bogus suspension handed down to me a/la Ernestine Horton. However, Al intercepted my list of questions and told me to consider quitting the company. In her words, the company was not going to change. Since Mychael was on duty at the time I submitted my questions, I surmised that it had to be him.

Run Out of Town

Back at work, I'd pay a visit to South Suburban Remote #2. There, I would run into some former co-workers from South Suburban Remote #1. I would also run into some transferees from Midway Drive. This was a special conference that emphasized the importance of customer service in our jobs. Since I had worked out at South Suburban Remote #2, many of the people who were there remembered me as well. Once I returned from that conference, I would once again face a menacing issue-Shellie.

Once again, Shellie deliberately and purposely occupied a position adjoining me, even though there were several other positions or workstations available for her use. This time, however, Mychael, the Group Chief Operator, saw what she was doing and was more than aware of the problem. He was livid.

Although Mychael assured me that the situation would see a resolution, I was NOT going to take any chances. I wrote another letter of

158

complaint to the mid-office. I toned down the venom in this written complaint.

While all of that was going on, I would get a new Group Chief Operator named Marjorie L. Scott. She was White, tall, and full-figured. She was a transferee from Chicago-Northwest and had just been promoted from Service Assistant. She wore brightly colored dresses most of the time. However, she had a demeanor that was pleasant on the outside, and Ditka-like on the inside. Her standards for the correct execution of a job were tough.

Ms. Williams, Ms. Scott, and I would meet concerning the complaint I had written. It was at that point that I was given an offer I would've been unwise to refuse.

Ms. Williams told me that the tone of my original complaint was so venomous that I was still eligible for dismissal under the Code of Business Conduct statutes. However, Ms. Williams offered to give me an early transfer out of Midway Drive, since Midway Drive was scheduled to close at or around the early Autumn of 1993. I preferred South Water, which was Downtown, and close to my weekly allergy shots and other doctor's appointments.

It was settled. I would leave Midway Drive-in late July 1993.

A couple of my co-workers were livid about the early transfer.

Their view was that Shellie should've been removed, not me. Peaches, whom I kept in touch with, was stoned livid!

I posted a note telling my co-workers that I was leaving Midway Drive. In that typewritten note, I would apologize for any problems my voice might have caused. I also included the nose-blowing problem as well.

The problem was that Ms. Scott intercepted my note. In her mind, she thought that it was inappropriate and over the top. Instead, she felt that I should've been more informal in presenting my issues. Nevertheless, I would end my run at Midway Drive with a hug from Lee.

Although South Water wasn't as rugged as Chicago Southwest #1, nor South Suburban Remote #1, South Water had its moments. For instance, there was one incident in which I attempted to synchronize my watch with the official clock in the office. This clock was in a computer room behind the SA's console. There were two ladies named Laura. One was White and diminutive. The other Laura was Black, full-figured, and businesslike in her demeanor. She was not too happy to see me in that computer room.

As I worked, there would be a discrepancy between the clock inside the computer room and my watch, which I had synchronized with the clock. So when the more diminutive Laura signaled my position to chastise me for being tardy returning from my break, I flew into a rage! That's how I met Lue Robinson, one of the Group Chief Operators at South Water.

Lue explained that Operators were not allowed in the back computer room because several items had been stolen. As for the changes in clock synchronization, a Central Access Group was necessary to manage the flow of business and control that function. Lue did allow me to resynchronize my watch, however.

I always synchronized my watch to the clock in the computer rooms at Midway Drive without a single issue. South Suburban Remote #1 had a clock that sat atop the Service Assistant's console. Everyone was expected to follow it. I used that clock to synchronize my watch. Therefore, I was highly surprised when South Water made a big deal about me syncing up with the office computer. Anyhow, whatever happened to the single standard clock that everyone was supposed to sync up to?

This discrepancy in clock times also put me at odds with another Service Assistant, whom I will call Snaggletooth!

Snaggletooth was an upper-middle-aged, Black Service Assistant. She was shorter than I was, frequently wore jeans and a blouse or T-shirt, and wore her hair very short, almost boyishly so. Snaggletooth did NOT look bad, except for the missing tooth on the left side of her mouth. However, let this be said. Snaggletooth was very overbearing! For instance, she would come to my position and tell me a line such as: "I need my experienced Operators to work faster."

One afternoon, Snaggletooth accused me of leaving my position too early. Again, I had my watch synchronized with the office, which should've eliminated the problem. When Snaggletooth came up to me with that mess, I went up to David Sons, the Traffic Manager at South Water. However, Sons was conducting a meeting. So once again, I had to work with Lue, who gave me a pass on the incident.

Let this be said about Snaggletooth. She was as much of a cutthroat as Midway Drive's Ernestine Horton! Ironically, Snaggletooth, nor any of the other Service Assistants, had any managerial or disciplinary authority.

Between the people problems I had at both Midway Drive and South Water, I was now plenty motivated to transfer out of Number Services as soon as I could pass a test and an opening could occur. In truth, I was not a people person. Instead, I was a thing person. Please put me in front of a car magazine or a consumer electronics journal, and I am in my element.

I picked up a pair of dress shoes that my podiatrist recommended, then, unfortunately, faced another unusual experience brought to me courtesy of my so-called Black Brethren.

There was a Black male who looked like Larry "Grandmama" Johnson who needed some change for the dollar bills he had to get on the bus, or so I thought! As I made the change for him, he turned and walked towards the front of the bus, without a word. When I asked him, "Aren't you going to give me my change, he responded: "(Bleep) You-Punk (Bleeper-Bleeper)!"

He kept walking towards the front of the bus. However, I was enraged. I just happened to have some hardware that I used for personal security. I pulled out the hardware and yelled: "DROP THE MONEY-NOW!"

This reprobate dutifully, but begrudgingly, extended the two dollars towards me that he had tried to con me out of just seconds before and handed them to me. He then was swearing at me, saying, "You don't pull that (bleep) on me. Don't you know I will kill you!"

I had already made my point. I got my money back. However, this punk was still selling woof tickets. Meanwhile, my fellow passengers were so frightened that the bus ultimately cleared out.

I made my point. I ultimately got off the bus I needed to get from NU Medical to Metra Electric Station in time to catch the 5:11 Express. Amazingly, I still managed to walk away without drawing the attention of the constabulary.

When I got home, Ted told me that what I experienced was one of the oldest con games in the book. People ride the buses all the time, looking for someone to pull that on.

Author's Side Note:

As I write this book, I find myself torn. Yes, I am, as you can tell, highly concerned about minority health issues.

Let me state, and go on record as saying, that the reason why I despised my own ethnic group was NOT solely due to our violence or crimes against each other. Instead, my reasons for my distaste for my own people included incivility, rudeness, callousness, belligerence, deceptiveness, pettiness, sarcasm, and destructive behaviors towards each other.

We Black Americans also have a propensity to impose upon each other. For instance, what I find even more insidious is that my fellow Black Americans rarely wanted anything to do with me unless they felt they could get money, favors, or rides from me, or to try to use me in some other way.

Then, some try to convert me to their religious mindset, again, mostly Black Americans. Not only do I find such persons downright offensive, they, in truth, are just as bad as the so-called heathens or hellions they try to convert!

It is fair to say that we Black Americans erect our own Glass Monoliths!

Having the views that I have had over the years about my fellow Black Americans would invariably cause the innocent among us to be offended, despite my best intentions.

I compared my feelings to NAPALM, which does not discriminate. Just ask that innocent Vietnamese girl, whose clothes were completely burned off by the Napalm!

As for the gangbangers, dope dealers, teen hooligans, and other reprobates in the Black American community, I don't care if I offend you or not!

Let's shift gears and go to 1994. I was now working on my post-baccalaureate and taking my first Technical Writing course. Amato was a staunch advocate of peer grading. I feared peer grading because the criteria for grading have nothing to do with a student's performance. Instead, it all depended on whether that student fit into his or her clique!

I let my feelings be known to Amato. However, he continued with a few peer-grading sessions.

Amato was slick about the way he had students grade each other's papers. He had the class eliminate the student's name to eliminate bias. He then had students pass papers to other students at random. Then, that student read the other student's paper in a fairly, but not completely, unbiased manner.

Fortunately for the students' papers that were handed to me, I was the most liberal grader in the class. Basically, if you used an EXPLICIT thesis statement, and you got to the point within the first two paragraphs of your paper, I gave you the benefit of the doubt.

However, if I had to read on to nearly the end of the paper before that student got to the thesis statement, that student was dead meat! The reason was that I felt that I was taught to get to the point! There was an assignment in which we were to describe the computer as an object, a device, or an appliance. However, there was a Korean student who rambled on about the CPU, the RAM, and its functions. He didn't answer the basic question or treatise of the assignment until later in the paper, if at all.

I knew that if I did what this student did, I would've been raked over the coals, so that's what I did to this student! Amato had to caution me to give him the minimum grade he was to allow! In my mind, he didn't even deserve that-nothing personal, mind you, but he failed to get to the point!

Meanwhile, I had compared a computer system to the stereo system I was already familiar with. That was either a love-it or hate-it proposition.

For instance, I compared the CPU in a computer system to the preamplifier of a stereo system. One student commented: "CPU does NOT contain CPU"! Even Amato found that comment very strange. Meanwhile, most students who evaluated my paper found my comparison between the computer and the stereo brilliant. As a result, Amato chipped in his two cents, and I was still in the running to get a decent grade out of the course.

Dr. Feinberg's class was diametrically the opposite. It was large, and long. We met on Tuesday and Thursday nights from 6 PM to 9:30 PM. There were all types of students from Engineering students to Technical Writing students, such as Yours Truly, to Law students, to other students looking to satisfy an elective or miscellaneous prerequisite. In fact, its size was like Amato's Class of the semester prior.

Speaking of Joe Amato, there were four expatriates from that class. First off, Elias from Verbal and Visual Communications would be one of them. Jerry Roach, who wowed Amato with his questioning style of writing, Mark Kopiec, who had himself one formidable Mitsubishi Eclipse Coupe, Carolyn Kucharz, who was the Michael (Formula One) Schumacher of Amato's class, and Yours Truly. As a result, I would muse that we were the Amato Five!

Dr. Feinberg presented us with her syllabus, then hit the ground running, unlike Professor Irving. She also presented us with plenty of material that she wanted us to work with. One such book was about Attila the Hun. He had a style of dealing with people that attracted Feinberg's eye.

Speaking of dealing with people, one of the most prominent areas that Feinberg stressed was the concept of Corporate Culture. This wasn't a completely foreign concept to me. However, as a Technical Writer, Feinberg seemed to imply that the idea of Corporate Culture would be one of the most critical concepts to pick up.

After I earned my Post-Baccalaureate Certificate, I embarked on a futile search for work in my field. I got very little solace at a job fair at the Marriott in September or October 1996. At one booth, the representative laughed at me when I told him that I knew Microsoft Works, rather than Microsoft Word. I did not have Microsoft Word on my computer.

At that same fair, I saw a potential opportunity. During my training at Technical Communications, my class visited a very prestigious firm downtown called Whittman-Hart. This company hired Technical Writers in many capacities. However, there was a group of Black Generation X males who were at that booth. They took a look at my resume, then handed it back to me, claiming: "You haven't got enough experience!"

Considering my history with my fellow so-called Black Brethren, I should not have been surprised by their reaction to me. However, I was. As far as I was concerned, my people resented me just as much as Whites did-if not more so!

Another area that Marciea couldn't deprogram herself from was her insistence that I have myself evaluated for Autism! I tried to explain to

166

Marce that one could not just self-diagnose something like that. It had to be done by way of a complete neuropsychiatric evaluation. If Autism comes up, it comes up. If not, it could be something else, or it could be nothing. Even so, before I could have any kind of neurological evaluation, I had to have a steady income first. That meant a job. That was what I was working on.

I was also hitting a Glass Monolith when I reached another agency. I interviewed with someone by the name of Elizabeth Banzhaaf. This time, I arrived on time and dressed appropriately. However, Ms. Banzhaaf rejected me for lack of an Information Technology background. With that, she asked me: "What do you think Technical Writing is, anyway?" She seemed to imply that I had no business in Technical Writing Training or not.

I had attended numerous Job Fairs over the time that I had left Ameritech, and especially after I got my post-baccalaureate. However, responses were very sporadic. I would submit resumes via the information I gleaned from the fairs. Sometimes, I would get acknowledgement letters and cards. Sometimes, I would get rejection letters within a matter of hours or days after I submitted my resume. Sometimes, the representatives would reject me on the spot! Rarely would I get an actual interview because of a Job Fair.

With all the rejections that I got from jobs, professions such as Engineering or allied sciences, and even my community in general, I was long wondering whether I should even be in society at all! The answer I was frequently coming up with was "no!"

Considering that I had already been out of work between 1996 and 1999, and still counting, there had to be some credibility to what Marce said about my being a victim of what people thought of me.

A Short Digression As a child, I didn't have enough sense to realize that it would've been better to walk away and go off by myself, rather than to try to convince other people to accept me. For instance, when I was 12, my day camp counselor told me that I would not be playing in a softball game, I simply should've quit the day camp. Instead, I continued begging, pleading, and ultimately crying for him to change his mind and allow me to play.

I got some revenge. I pulled for the rival day camp in a softball game to beat my day camp and got my wish!

However, as an adult, I still needed to support myself. That meant that I was dependent on the same society that was rejecting me. Besides that, my biggest motivation of all was that I did NOT want to spend the rest of my life as a Ghetto Geek! That was the conundrum I faced.

Author's Side Note:

The term "Ghetto Geek" was my new term I am introducing to describe the Black underclass. Suffice it to say that I considered the onus on me twice. The first onus was on me to break the Glass Monolith called poverty. The second onus was to break the types of stereotypes that caused me to coin the term in the first place.

In the Summer of 2000, I got a referral from Manpower Temporaries for a Technical Writing job. Ironically, I was sent to Ameritech's office in the Northwest Suburbs by Interstate 90. When I got to Ameritech, I was met by a svelte, petite, perky White lady by the name of Kristi. She had her assistant show me the facility. This facility was light years from the "boiler room" and "jungle music" type of atmosphere that was my job at Ameritech's South Suburban Remote, Midway Drive, and River West offices. There was even a fountain in the central atrium because it was found that the "white noise" that was generated was more beneficial than other types of noise.

There was another irony. As I was shown a typical workstation, one woman at that workstation recognized me. She was from the Society for Technical Communication. Therefore, she knew me from a few meetings I attended.

After the tour of the facility, Kristi's assistant gave me a test sample for me to edit. I was to phone the assistant when I was ready. If I had any questions, that same number also applied.

It was a highly peaceful environment in which I did my work. I did the best I could with it as far as making the edits were concerned. I concentrated on every element I could think of. Then, I handed over my test and hit another one of my now-famous Glass Monoliths.

In Kristi's mind, I was more of a "Creative Writer" than a hard-core Technical Editor. It was for that reason that I was turned down.

I had more luck when I arrived at Underwriters Laboratories later that morning, to early afternoon. I took my time and was as thorough about filling out my application and paperwork. Then, I took the typing test.

The copy and my actual work were directly above each other. That led to some issues in where to best place my attention. Nevertheless, although I was slower than I would've been if the copy were in a more typical position, I still eclipsed the minimum typing speed requirement for the job.

I met with the same lady that I met at Oakton College's Job Fair, and was told that I would be eligible for an interview.

The next day, I telephoned Manpower Temporaries about the Glass Monolith I hit during Ameritech's Technical Editing test.

I told Manpower about the bitter breakup that I had with Ameritech, when I was at River West in 1996. Given that, I surmised that they found out about me and rejected me.

Manpower scoffed at that theory. In their mind, Ameritech was looking to take on the Temp on a permanent basis. However, there were issues concerning the payment of a fee for services. In Manpower's mind, Ameritech was very picky about who they wanted. According to Manpower, it was for that reason, and not any bad blood from previous work at Ameritech, that I was rejected.

I got another inspection of my Glass Monolith after I was furloughed from Underwriters Laboratories. I got a referral from my neurologist to a Vocational Psychologist by the name of Julius March. After I gave a short job history, Dr. March responded: "There's something in your makeup that predisposes you to rub people the wrong way." The consultant then asked what I hoped to accomplish with this meeting. To that, I responded: "I need to take this evaluation, balance it against what I tested out on at the IETC, and compare it with employment guidelines for people with Autism so I can come up with a consensus as to what kind of training I should get into, and do it over the next two weeks or so."

To that, March said: "That's impossible!"

Speaking of encounters, I would have a more menacing encounter at or around this period of time. For instance, the 95th Street Rapid Transit Terminal was perpetually busy. One cloudy afternoon, I waited to board the West 95th Street bus. However, I noticed that there was a husky, Black male who would've backed into me had I continued walking down the narrow walk towards my bus. So I stopped. I never came any closer than about six feet from him, and never even touched him. This person looked like a cross between boxer Mike Tyson and Bryan Cox, a former middle linebacker for the Chicago Bears!

Oddly, he turned to me and said: "What the (fornication) are you doing-coming up on me like that? I'll kick your (so and so)!"

I excused myself, then collected myself. I thought to myself: "No-no! I'm not going to let someone intimidate me like that."

Once I collected myself, I went back into the Terminal and consulted one of the many Chicago Policemen who were inside the terminal for one reason or another. When I told him what had happened, even he found it bizarre, unusual, and profound, until I took him to this testosterone-crazed person, who was not backing down one iota! Even when the officer told him that he could NOT go around threatening people. Even when I told him that I had NO interest in doing any harm to him, such as maybe picking his pocket, he still went on.

The police officer had to stay with me until I boarded my bus while he boarded his.

Part of my Glass Monolith was that I sent unintended negative signals to other human beings. The 95th Street Terminal Incident was one example. Another one was the results of my second "Mock" Interview at Christ. Here it was:

Jon

THIS IS AN ACTUAL EMPLOYER'S EVALUATION FORM.

IT IS TYPICAL OF THOSE WHICH MOST INTERVIEWERS COMPLETE IMMEDIATELY FOLLOWING EVERY INTERVIEW. HOW DO YOU THINK YOU WOULD BE RATED IN EACH CATEGORY?

171

FIRST IMPRESSION - As the applicant impresses you, so is he/she likely to impress others. A man's first impression can set that pattern for future effectiveness.

Outstanding___Good__-x Adequate_____ Poor

PHYSICAL APPEARANCE - Was he/she neat and well-groomed? Was he/she dressed in good taste? Keep in mind that he/she is trying to impress you favorably, and is trying to put his/her best foot forward.

Outstanding__ Good__-x Adequate____ Poor____

VOICE & SPEECH - Was his/her voice clear and easy to understand? Did you notice any annoying speech or voice habits?-unique __

Outstanding_____ Good ___Adequate_____ Poor_____

EDUCATIONAL BACKGROUND - Is his/her educational level acceptable? What was his/her college average? Is he/she too well-educated for the job?

POISE & SELF-CONFIDENCE - Was he/she at ease during the interview? Did he/she seem to have a sound estimation of his/her abilities?

Outstanding____ Good___-x Adequate____ Poor____

AMBITION: What are his/her future goals? Are they realistic ones? Does he/she seem motivated for the job and eager to succeed?

Outstanding____ Good____ Adequate_-x__ Poor____

INTELLIGENCE - Does he/she seem to grasp things easily? Is he/she a good listener? Does he/she ask thoughtful and intelligent questions?

Outstanding___Good___-x Adequate_____ Poor

KNOWLEDGE OF OUR COMPANY - Did he/she know anything about the company before the interview? Did he/she check with anyone about the company? Did he/she ask good questions about the company? Did he/she have a good concept of the job itself?

Outstanding_____ Good_____ Adequate_____ Poor_____

Page 2

OVERALL IMPRESSION - Is he/she the kind of person you would like to have work with you? What is your overall impression of him/her? Did he/she "sell" you? (Fooler)

Outstanding_____ Good_____ Adequate_____ Poor_____

MATURITY - Does he/she impress you as a person whose overall personality is suitable for the job? Does he/she seem sufficiently mature in appearance and manner to deal effectively with the job? (Fooler)

Outstanding_____ Good_____ Adequate_____ Poor_____

SCORING   EVALUATION

Outstanding_____ each 3 points 25- 30 Excellent Applicant

Good_____ each 2 points 20-24 Very Good Applicant

Adequate_____ each 1 point 15 - 19 Average Applicant

Poor_____ each 0 points 10- 14 Marginal Applicant

Below 10 Poor Applicant

ADDITIONAL COMMENTS:

Just as with the first interview, this is the actual evaluation sheet that I saved, scanned, and translated into Microsoft Word. If you think that I would cast a jaundiced eye over the first interview, this one would be a duress!

For instance, Lisa asserted that I was embellishing my background!

Because I had been cutting my resumes to the absolute bone, in order to get rid of such embellishments, I was crushed. Because I had a fit when the firm, Challenger, Gray and Christmas was telling me to put the embellishments in, I was crushed. Since I had been reading in various newspapers NOT to use such adjectives, I was crushed. Remember! Unless I went into a forum where I expected criticism, any form of criticism was always, to me, an indictment of my character, personality, or morals.

When this interviewer asserted that I was a "fooler", I got the impression that I was trying to surreptitiously try to put one over on someone-namely the interviewer. That interviewer might as well have called me a charlatan; a flimflam man; a con artist, a snake oil salesman or even most insidiously, a fraud. Therefore, I was crushed.

I was very hurt that I would be put in the same company as Louis "Fraud-A-Con"! The irony of the matter was that I didn't have the intelligence, much less the ability to do what this interviewer accused me of doing during the "Mock" Interview. He didn't even make any entries in some of the sections of the evaluation sheet, nor did he even give me an overall score.

For instance, whenever someone, or an agency documents that you can type at a certain typing speed, you could use that typing speed in a resume, and/or interpret that as being a form of certification; but not so fast! For instance, Lisa exclaimed: "In your resume, you say, "certified". That gives someone the impression that you went through this long, drawn-out process of going through some type of exhaustive training, and someone graduated you with this type of typing speed. That's what might be interpreted as "embellished".

Melissa not only agreed with Lisa on that "Mock" Interview #2, she also believed that I was taking the results of that interview much too personally. Melissa also believed that it was perfectly permissible to put adjectives into a resume per the guidelines of Challenger, Gray, and Christmas. Ironically, she thought that such adjectives did NOT constitute embellishing the resume.

For instance, during a Job Club session, Melissa asserted:

"Don't you think that you're courteous?"

I replied: "Of course."

Melissa responded: "In fact, you're the only one that calls me Ms. Bos."

For business formats and environments, I actually liked referring to superiors, higher-ups, luminaries, and other so-called "muckymucks" as Mr., Mrs., or Ms. There are even times when the formal salutation has a better ring to it than the informal salutation. For instance, I even referred to my former mechanic as Mr. Cirese, rather than Jim. It simply had a better ring to it and constituted more respect for that person. Fortunately, Mr. Cirese understood, as did Lisa and Melissa. There is one exception. I found it downright awkward to address someone as Mr., Mrs., or Ms, and then use the first name. Instead, I preferred to use the formal salutation and the LAST name of that person.

Some published reports, This Author has read, have indicated that people with Asperger's Syndrome may be predisposed to being viewed with a negative image. Even getting picked on or being hazed was not that out of the ordinary for someone with Asperger's. Remember. There was a huge gap between the time I got my Undergraduate and the time

I finally learned that I had Asperger's Autism. Then again, it is nuances such as these samples that always made up my Glass Monolith.

That begs the question:

Does someone with Asperger's Syndrome generate an aura that causes people to react in an adverse way? Bob Ewing mentioned the aura that I was generating.

If you raise the possibility of auras, then you raise the possibility of Asperger's Syndrome being a SOCIAL DISEASE! If that is, indeed, the case, how do you cure a social disease when there are only symptoms evident in behaviors, rather than in physical characteristics?

Interpersonal Relations-My Speaking Voice

I also take issue with what Black Americans value. For instance, one day, at Kinzie Street, we waited for the shuttle van to take us back to O'Hare. While I was waiting, one Black co-worker asked, "How are you doing?" I responded in the customary civil manner.

His response was: "Well, you can't be alright if you're wearing that tie."

I wore a clip-on tie that was a solid rust color. It was wide. However, that's what people were wearing in those days.

My point is that Black Americans value style, trends, being hip, being in the clique, fronting, and other superficial nonsense more than substance. Although I was never a fan of the Bar Kays the best song they ever cut, bar none, was the song "Smiling, Styling, and Profiling." This song is, again, true of Black Americans.

Ironically, this clown had the nerve to talk about the importance of knowing words and word power. He asked me to use the word "deride" in a sentence I made the mistake of saying: "I was derided because of my voice."

Then, the entire crew started a feeding frenzy. For instance, one of Kevin Burch's friends, Pip Squeak Todd was riding with this particular crew. He was Black, with dark skin, and short-more so than I was. He was not a dwarf, but he was a pip-squeak.

Todd sneered at me and said: "Look man! If you're gonna talk to us, you got to get rid a that accent!"

Confused, I asked: "What accent? I don't have any accent?"

"That's a lie. You sound like you come from joy, see," said Pip Squeak Todd "I'm from right here in Chicago," I said "Well, you better talk like you're from Chicago." Someone else said.

"You bet not go up in the Bronx talkin' like that," said Pip Squeak Todd "What does the Bronx have anything to do with this?" I asked. "Why is it that everybody is so worried about my voice, but nobody says anything whenever Prince (a pop-rock-soul music artist) goes dancing around in his bikini drawers, poses naked, and sings: 'I'm gonna be your lover? His voice is just like mine, supposedly."

"That's different. People like that are entertainers." Said Pip Squeak Todd. Goodkind wasn't finished with me either. I heard his voice, yelling "Sweet Pea! Sweet Pea!" as if he were yelling soo-ee!

Meanwhile, I sat in the company lunchroom with a bus driver named Mr. Winsted and another driver. Goodkind walked over to me and handed me a trip ticket, which was used whenever a car was being transported from one station to the next.

Most insidiously of all, Goodkind put his arm around my shoulder and said: "I call him Sweet Pea cause he is my friend!"

I had enough and told Goodkind, "Get your hands off of me! You are not my friend."

Goodkind jumped, then turned to Winsted and company and said: Are you my friend?"

They nodded in agreement. Goodkind then turned to me and said, "If I were to kiss you, would you be my friend?"

I explicitly told Goodkind: "If you were to kiss me, I'd kick every one of your teeth down your throat!"

I stormed out of the lunchroom to look for the car that was supposed to be shuttled.

The next day, I telephoned Distribution to report the incident. Frank, the manager, was not interested in anything I had to say. In fact, Frank told me, "It's just like with a woman. If she doesn't want anything to do with you, she ain't gonna have sex with you. No! It's that voice of yours!"

I had chronic diarrhea during this period. As a result, I needed to see a proctologist. He was so thorough that he conducted the complete physical examination, and I was scrambling around trying to get away. That included a Medical History. I told him about the flak I was getting at Hertz because of my voice. A couple of weeks later, my specialist gave me his report, along with permission to go back to my usual diet.

He also admonished me to consider taking voice lessons. I declined to take my proctologist up on his suggestion because I thought that taking voice lessons would've been tantamount to changing my ways for other people.

Most of those who criticized me because of my voice were Black. If there were a bona-fide medical problem, rather than somebody's cultural bias, I would've considered my doctor's suggestion.

Some people at the Internal Revenue Service, Black and White alike, loved my voice! The same thing occurred with my customers at Illinois Bell when I was an Operator! At Roosevelt University, in the Career Placement Center, a retiring gentleman commented: "You speak the King's English!" That's how I learned that the term "King's English" is still in use today.

That retiring gentleman was White!

In the case of the Hertz Clowns, the use of the King's English was tantamount to being from another planet! For instance, I was talking about the then-new, and upcoming 300 ZX Nissan with an amateur boxer and his friend. He interrupted the conversation to talk about the way I was saying Z. He thought that I could've put some bass in that Z.

In the meantime, Pip Squeak Todd would mock me when I asked Ms. Roberson whether she was cracking down on the picture IDs. It was becoming evident to me that she was.

I turned around and left the Distribution trailer, never working that day. It was during my ride home that I made my decision.

Although I could have derived an ID from my IRS badge, I was wondering: Why? I needed two jobs badly, but at what price? In the six months I worked at Hertz as a hiker, I was subjected to physical assault, sexual assault, mockery, derision, public ridicule, insults, bullying, and

101 other messages that let me know that I never did. I never would fit in as a Hertz hiker. Management was no better, and for what? My voice!

There seemed to be an unwritten law that you ran the risk of ostracism in the Black community if you used the King's English. In truth, I allowed my language to be polluted by Black English, or Ebonics, just not enough!

By the way, Ebonics is Polluted English!

My co-workers at the Internal Revenue Service had some issues with my voice. To them, it was just plain loud. Bernardine even contended that I could do something about my voice. Oddly, she would ask me: "Why do you do that?" It was as if she thought that I had some control over it, and could exercise control over my voice, yet refused to do so.

One very warm November in 1983, I had a large lunch of a turkey sandwich, and I needed to walk it off fast. As I walked the area around the Federal Building, an old flame remembered me and called me. I thought that she forgot me-fat chance! It was Joy!

I had so much to talk about that I put the rest of it on a prerecorded cassette. That led to some interesting fireworks. For instance,

Joy had some choice words for me a few days later, when she telephoned me during my break! Fortunately for my butt, they were kind words. But first, Joy told me something only Mikey's ex-wife told me. Joy said:

"Jon, you have a very unusual voice. I don't know." "Your tape-I couldn't listen to it all. Your voice-it sounds so scary!

On Tuesday, 11 February 1987, I'd return to the Ameritech Illinois Bell Telephone Company. It would be two and a half years from the time I escaped Alpha Metals Corporation in late 1984.

Once I arrived at South Suburban Remote # 1, I was met by an upper-middle-aged White woman named Ruth Anzuras. Ms. Anzuras was one of several forewomen, or Group Chief Operators, at South Suburban Remote #1. Ruth was quite friendly, and we chatted for a few minutes. I asked if we could go into the Conference Room because I was getting worried about my voice disturbing other operators. Ms. Anzuras agreed.

One issue I felt I needed to address before going out on the boards was the power of my voice. I advised Princess, Mark, Ms. Anzuras, and "Lady Ditka" that I had a propensity to get overly strong. I asked all four involved, as well as fellow operators, to signal me with a "Thumbs Down" if, for any reason, I got too loud. That would signal to me to lower my voice.

Princess put both of us out on the boards one last time before our training was completed. It was at that time that Mark, a fellow trainee, would indeed try out the "Thumbs Down" signal on me, but first, he whispered: "Hey Jon!"

Other operators with stronger voices than mine did NOT have the problems I was having. For instance, there was another operator, by the name of Bill Baker, who had a deep, resonant, booming voice that could be distinctly heard throughout the office. Ironically, no one complained about how loudly he talked.

Another issue that made me believe that I was being singled out for criticism about my voice was that there was an in-house speaker. This in-house speaker wasn't playing "muzak", but the local rock and popular music radio stations of the day. For instance, I liked Kenny G-a lot. However, in an environment like that of Air Traffic Controllers, it would be, or should be, inappropriate to have the G-Man playing while I am gleaning information from a customer. My complaint is a variant of Mom's adage that there is a time and a place for everything.

Unfortunately, Aurelia, a Group Chief Operator, didn't see it that way. When I complained about the music, her only response was that no one else had a problem with it.

Even more insidiously, I had a co-worker accuse me of bothering her when I showed her the "Thumbs Down" signal. Seconds later, she asked if I always asked people if I was being loud. I answered "Yes". Some co-workers would snap at me, rather than give the "Thumbs Down" signal.

If I didn't have to compete with the office jukebox, I would have to compete with blaring radios and jukeboxes from the customer's end. In one instance, I actually got a customer complaint from Lady Ditka that said that a customer said, in his words, that I "tried to take his ear off"! I told Lady Ditka: "I probably had to compete with Farley Jackmaster Funk (a local DJ that specialized in specialized mixes and/or "House Music")!

I didn't mind being asked to lower my voice at all. However, I was being made out to be a common lout by co-workers and superiors alike! Ironically, the last thing I ever intended, much less thought about doing, was to try willfully, vindictively, or consciously to conspire to talk loudly at the expense of my coworkers' rights. I had better things to do with my time!

Pat Schwartz was my one saving grace throughout all of this criticism. She told me not to let it get to me. Had it not been for her, I would've gone off on many a co-worker.

I was also having problems with my digestive tract again. There was also a co-worker there who was having the same digestive tract problems that I was.

It was at that point that I started to learn that maybe I did have a problem after all. I asked this co-worker about her progress on her health. Meanwhile, a very small White girl accompanied her grandmother. When this girl heard my voice, she responded by saying, "He talks funny"!

In the past, I had frequently been told that I "talked funny". However, my critics were usually Blacks who worshipped what I called "Polluted English." Therefore, I dismissed these criticisms as coming from those who wouldn't know the "King's English" from Kingston, Ontario!

This incident, however, seemed to give my critics a measure of credibility, and it scared me!

An unexpected example of how my speaking voice would leach into my life occurred on the day that Milt Three, my nephew, would graduate from high school. I got off at the Elgin Terminal, and there was a bus that awaited me. This bus would take me to Milton's apartment.

I was the sole person at Milton's apartment. Milton was out on a short errand, but not for long. Milton was surprised that I was able to come to the apartment without the aid of a car. Nevertheless, he was glad to have me.

In a twinkling, Milton had to step out again for yet another short errand. Meanwhile, there was a phone call. I answered the phone in the following manner.

"Milton Evans' residence, Jon Evans speaking." My understanding was that it is the preferred way to answer the telephone.

The caller paused, then stated his business. Afterward, I went about what Milton had me do and thought nothing further of it.

Milton returned from his errand. Not too long after that, people started coming. One such person was a friend of Milton's named Les. I opened the door, then spoke. Les, however, loudly refrained: "That's the voice!"

I was very put off by the way Les spoke. I found his conduct very insulting. However, I was too cowardly to strike back.

Instead, I had to wonder: Why was it that people thought that my voice was so different? I used Standard Prestige Dialect in addressing callers on the phone. What I did was no different from the way that I addressed Mikey's callers when I was in Hawaii. Ironically, no one in Hawaii made an issue out of my speaking voice at all!

Yet, I was always the one pegged as being odd, or different in the way that I did things. I found it all very unnerving.

But first, I would go on loan to Chicago Southwest #1 for a couple of weeks!

When one of the new Operators found out about my going on loan, her response would be in her Black Dialect: "Omma kill you! I can jog from my house to over there!"

Meanwhile, this woman had a friend named Robin. For some reason, she was prompted to ask me: "Do you always talk like that?"

My last day at South Suburban Remote #1 would be spent with an admonishment from Stac not to talk too loudly. My first day as a transferee to the Midway Drive office brought the issue of my voice up again, unexpectedly. The Queen Bee quashed my "Thumbs Down" idea even before I thought about bringing it up in our conversation! Therefore, she knew about the

"Thumbs Down" idea LONG before my transfer to Midway Drive took place! This facet of my Glass Monolith shows that I always had little or no persuasive ability! People were going to believe whatever they wanted to think about me, and there was NO changing their minds when they did.

Ernestine Horton was starting to scream bloody murder about my voice! She was the only Group Chief Operator who complained about it at that time. I also received a note from one of my co-workers. However, I passed the note on to Ms. Cole, and the problem was taken care of.

Clues From Dr. Herzon

While all of this was going on, I was referred by my doctor to an otolaryngologist named Garrett Herzon, MD. Dr. Herzon was a technician, heart-first and foremost! That was NOT, however, to say

that there was no personability to the man. In fact, he looked pretty similar to former Cincinnati Redleg great Johnny Bench!

I also had a conversation with another co-worker that revealed another facet about my voice. To her, I sounded "spoiled!" Before she said that, she asked if I were an only child! I took that thought to Dr. Herzon. I also told Dr. Herzon about the flak I was getting about how loud my voice was allegedly being.

Herzon arranged to have a hearing test done. Not only did I pass the hearing test, but the technician also told me that I had hearing levels common to ten-year-old girls! As for the loudness, she did note that there was a powerful tone to my voice. The technician revealed that sometimes, she too had to speak loudly because she had to work with patients who had hearing difficulties. Therefore, it was a force of habit for her.

Herzon also arranged to have me consult a Speech Pathologist at Northwestern University's Institute of Speech Pathology. I had a Kenny G concert at the Star Plaza in Merrillville, Indiana, as my 35th birthday present on 3 January 1989; then, I made my appointment with Cathy Lazarus, a Speech Pathologist, two days later.

I prepared for this appointment by copying my old cassette tape of my radio program, Free Form Fusion, at Roosevelt University's WRBC Radio Station. For my meeting with Ms. Lazarus, I edited out the bulk of the music and emphasized my speech and mixes. As a result, a two-hour audiotape was cut down to a mere thirty minutes.

Lazarus, however, had a special audio tape recorder. With it, she was able to skip over the musical portions of the tape and concentrate on the portion where I spoke. Lazarus was able to discern the portions even though her tape recorder was on fast forward and at high speed. Therefore, she was able to analyze in less time than I expected.

Next, Lazarus had me do a series of voice tests that most people would find rather embarrassing; however, they'd give her an idea of where problems in my voice occurred. She also examined my throat and the mechanics of my vocal cords.

Finally, Lazarus had me lean back and close my eyes. Then, she touched the one area where I was known to be very sensitive to tickling-my throat. I jumped! Once Lazarus explained that she was doing a laryngeal massage, I calmed down enough to let her try again, and I found her touch quite pleasant. Lazarus attempted to get my voice down during the laryngeal massage; however, she could not.

Lazarus then came up with this verdict. According to her, I was straining my vocal cords. As a result, she found my voice very thin and strident. My speaking range was very high, compared to males of my age, and very limited. Lazarus also told me: "First of all, I had absolutely NO idea you were Black, and I at first thought you were a woman, and yes, I thought you were gay!"

I noted that there were other men with voices similar to mine, such as sportscaster Al Michaels, of ABC Monday Night Football, Bobby Kennedy, and the "Miracle on Ice" announcer. However, Lazarus thought that those voices were altogether different.

Lazarus' diagnosis was what I thought was: Functional Hypertensive Dysphasia. However, Lazarus hand-wrote her diagnosis. She recommended that I have regular speech therapy sessions and practice home exercises regularly. Even then, her prognosis was very guarded, due to her inability to change the pattern of my voice during testing.

Lazarus's diagnosis presented a problem. If I were going to follow the doctor's orders and undergo regular testing, I would need to schedule regular time off from work. That meant that I had to see the Queen Bee first.

Unfortunately, the Queen Bee could not guarantee regular time off for such speech therapy sessions. Even more insidiously, those speech therapy sessions were NOT covered under my company health insurance policy. I was screwed before I even got out of the gate! I did get one consolation, however. The Queen Bee told me of a similar situation to mine in her extended family. Therefore, she could identify with the issues I faced.

Mom was NOT too happy to learn that Lazarus told me that she "had no idea I was Black." I knew Lazarus meant no harm, since Blacks often had deeper voices than Whites on average. But to someone who came up through the so-called REB-TIME, any reference to my being Black would be bound to be inflammatory, regardless of intent.

Shortly after my visit to see Cathy Lazarus, I did a follow-up appointment with Dr. Herzon. There, I discussed Cathy's diagnosis of what I thought was Functional Hypertensive Dysphasia. Come to find out, it was actually Functional Hypertensive **Dysphonia**. He then gave me a hard copy of Cathy's report for my records.

Herzon also had an explanation that I thought was more plausible. He asked where my parents were from. I explained to him that my mother was born in New Orleans, Louisiana, while my father was born in Farrell, Mississippi. I also told Herzon that My Grandparents and maternal great-grandparents were all from parts of Louisiana, while my paternal Grandmother was from a place called Piker Peak Parish, Louisiana.

At that point, Dr. Herzon theorized that I might have been carrying a highly dominant Cajun/Creole trait to my speech!

Herzon also noted that my voice would get sharper and stronger if, and/or when, I was to get excited in any way. Nevertheless, the point was made. I was NOT just being an obnoxious lout. Instead, I had a bona fide voice disorder.

For a while, I corresponded with Cathy Lazarus. For instance, during the late 1980s and early 1990s, there was a Pop/Disco/Soul/R&B singer whose voice was super-strong, but only when she sang! Her speaking voice was like divers who breathed mixtures of Helium and Oxygen in diving vessels! Her name was Michele Le! Her biggest hit was No More Lies.

I asked Lazarus about Michele-Le. Lazarus replied that she didn't think that my voice compared to Michele Le's in any way. Instead, she felt that my voice was more unique than that. As far as the flak, she gave me her opinion on how I should measure various comments made about my voice.

For starters, I volunteered to go out on loan to the Customer's Name and Address Bureau. There, I would meet an interesting set of characters, starting with the lady who trained me in the art of working the Name and Address boards, Gerri Brown! My thoughts immediately went to composers John Lee and Jerry Brown, and their album, The Chaser! She was tall, Black, slightly full-figured, and nice. Oddly, she loved my voice! The Group Chief Operator, Lynn Long, however, thought my voice was sometimes strong. She was Black, tall, and thin, though muscular. She was, however, more civil to me than most Group Chief Operators who had issues with me about my voice.

I became anxious about my voice after an Open Forum Meeting with management. During the meeting, I presented the problem of a well-known listing that I thought should've been in the database and wasn't! As I met with Ms. Cole, Ms. Bennett informed me that John Corothers wanted to see me. I asked to meet with him away from the Operators, to prevent my speaking voice from disturbing others. Here, I'd hit a Glass Monolith.

When I started out at Midway Drive, I had a good relationship with my co-workers. Unfortunately, that would change, in a very insidious way. On about the very first day of May, 1990, I was working in the back, or the most remote part of the office. Unfortunately, there were stand-up pods at the back part of the office that the Operators liked to use; that included a co-worker by the name of Al-Marie.

Al-Marie, though Black, was tall, full-figured, and attractive, with butterscotch colored skin. Oddly, she also detested me. On this occasion, early that morning, Al-Marie sneered at me, indicating that my voice was too loud. The next morning, I asked: "Al-Marie, I would like to take just two minutes of your time."

Al-Marie looked down upon and sneered at me, as if I were dirt under her feet, and said: "I haven't got two minutes." I said nothing further.

The two minutes I wanted with Al-Marie were to apologize to her for getting loud. I tried to assure her, as I did all of my other co-workers, that I had better things to do with my time than to purposely talk loudly to intentionally offend other people in the office. I was very hurt that Al-Marie did not give me that chance to apologize to her, especially since I had nothing against Al-Marie whatsoever prior to this incident.

Another area where I was running into a Glass Monolith was in my relationship with my co-workers. For instance, I had another run-in with Al-Marie, a co-worker who sneered at me and blew me off when I attempted to apologize to her. On this late January 1991 day, she worked at a stand-up pod next to me. There were other boards available in the office. So why did she work next to me if she detested my voice and me so much? She interrupted her call and told me, "Customers are complaining about you?"

I became so annoyed with Al-Marie's complaints about my voice that I gave her a dressing down so loud that it bordered on a full-blown altercation! Minutes later, Hot-Rod, one of the supervisors, called me out just to cool off. He gave me the option of sitting out just to cool off, then going back on the boards. Option B was to simply call it a day.

I chose Option B! I had enough of people complaining about my voice for the following reasons:

1.   As I stated many times before, I had better things to do with my time than to talk loudly without any regard, willfully, purposely, or spitefully to my fellow co-workers. Yet, I was the one being vilified.

2.   I had to compete with a loud, blaring office radio!

3.   There were other people in the office with voices just as loud, if not louder than Your's Truly. Yet, I was the one being singled out and vilified!

I didn't just take what happened to me lying down. I took the Metra Electric Downtown from Midway Drive and took my complaint to Company Headquarters. Headquarters, in turn, authorized that I get paid for the first half of the day until noon, but I would be declared absent after that. Al-Marie would cost me perfect attendance lasting three years!

The next day, both Peaches and Lee tried to cool me off. That, they did do. As for Al-Marie, she made one complaint to a

Service Assistant, a few weeks later, then never bothered me again.

About four months after I went off on Al-Marie, I was suspended for allegedly sending a customer to automatic when he said NOT to. Keep in mind that I had done much worse than this, without drawing a suspension. You can blame Ernestine Horton for that.

The suspension was bad enough. However, just about a week after the suspension, a customer complained that I "talked like a computer!" Ducky subsequently reprimanded me for that complaint! It was one thing to have a Glass Monolith. It was another thing for someone to use a Glass Monolith against me! That was what Ducky #2 was doing. Her rationale for reprimanding me about the computer voice complaint was that the complaint was really an offshoot of her phraseology complaints.

I had to talk to the union steward about so outrageous a complaint. However, when I conferred with the steward, she denied that I was officially reprimanded and written up for the "computer" incident. Therefore, she felt that a grievance was not necessary.

It was now March 1993, and I would be faced with an even more insidious issue. That issue was Shellie, the office bully!

Shellie would make her rounds, instigating conflicts with coworkers by trumping up accusations, verbal abuse, or other forms of trying to cause trouble. This time, she attempted to engineer a conflict with me.

I was in the far back portion of the office. Meanwhile, there were plenty of vacant positions available, both a stand-up and seated variety. Shellie, however, chose to occupy a stand-up directly adjoining me. Since Shellie despised both my voice and me, I found it highly inconsistent that she would want to occupy a pod next to me-unless she wanted to start a conflict. That, she did.

It wasn't long before my first break that I got a complaint from the Service Assistant. Shellie had complained that I was talking too loudly. When I went up to the SA, he didn't want to hear it. He told me that Shellie and I had to work it out.

It was with those thoughts in mind that I telephoned the EEO Office. It was also with those thoughts in mind that I left a typewritten letter of complaint about Shellie's antics to the middle office.

I held that since Shellie had a history of conflicts with other coworkers, I was prompted to ask why the middle office was keeping her around. I also issued a stern warning to management. I told the middle office that if it did not take steps to curb Shellie, and she were to pull such a stunt again, I would curb her a/la Al-Marie, or worse!

The "or worse" part promptly scared the middle office. Since Shellie was on Mychael's team, he addressed the problem in the presence of the shop steward. He was worried but accommodating. Al Bennett, on the other hand, was in a reprimanding mood. She cautioned that my complaint bordered on a Code of Business Conduct Violation, and if I carried out any action against Shellie, I could lose my job.

We now had a new Traffic Manager by the name of Sally Williams. She was White, and not only tall, but of a stature that could play on the Ladies Professional Golf Association Circuit. She wasn't too happy about my written ultimatum to Shellie either. However, she held off on any action on it for the time being.

So serious was my written ultimatum that the Union President came down to Midway Drive for a visit. She and I conferred over lunch near Harper Court. She was quite accommodating as far as my redress of grievances. She also gave me her telephone number and admonished me that if I ever were to get to the point where I was going to blow up the way I was about to do, to call her.

During my return visit to the company-appointed Psychiatrist, she and I both agreed that the best tack to take would be to see the very Psychiatrist that Dr. Cheung recommended earlier.

194

I was now back at work. I'd pay a visit to South Suburban Remote #2. There, I would run into some former co-workers from South Suburban Remote #1. I would also run into some transferees from Midway Drive. This was a special conference that emphasized the importance of Customer Service in our jobs. Since I had worked out at South Suburban Remote #2, a lot of the people who were there remembered me as well. Once I returned from that conference, I would once again face a menacing issue-that issue being Shellie.

Once again, Shellie deliberately and purposely occupied a position adjoining me, even though there were several other positions or workstations available for her use. This time, however, Mychael, the Group Chief Operator, saw what she was doing and was more than aware of the problem. He was livid.

Although Mychael assured me that the situation would see a resolution, I was NOT going to take any chances. I wrote another letter of complaint to the mid-office. I toned down the venom in this written complaint.

While all of that was going on, I would get a new Group Chief Operator by the name of Marjorie L. Scott. She was White, tall, and full-figured. She was a transferee from Chicago-Northwest and had just been promoted from Service Assistant. She wore brightly colored dresses most of the time. However, she had a demeanor that was pleasant on the outside, and Ditka-like on the inside. Her standards for the correct execution of a job were tough.

Ms. Williams, Ms. Scott, and I would meet concerning the complaint I had written. It was at that point that I was given an offer I would've been unwise to refuse.

Ms. Williams told me that the tone of my original complaint was so venomous that I was still eligible for dismissal under the Code of

Business Conduct statutes. However, Ms. Williams offered to give me an early transfer out of Midway Drive, since Midway Drive was scheduled to close at or around the early Autumn of 1993. I preferred South Water, which was Downtown, and close to my weekly allergy shots and other doctors' appointments.

It was settled. I would leave Midway Drive-in late July 1993.

A couple of my co-workers were not happy about the early transfer. Their view was that Shellie should've been removed, not me. Peaches, whom I kept in touch with, was stoned livid!

I posted a note telling my co-workers that I was leaving Midway Drive. In that typewritten note, I would apologize for any problems my voice might have caused. I also included the nose-blowing problem as well.

The problem was that Ms. Scott intercepted my note. In her mind, she thought that it was inappropriate and over the top. Instead, she felt that I should've been more informal in presenting my issues. Nevertheless, I would end my run at Midway Drive with a hug from Lee.

The next day, I would start out at South Water. This would be a subterranean office. However, I would have plenty of shops in which to get a bite to eat. There would even be a Post Office next to my new job for my convenience. Most importantly, I was a hop, skip, and a jump from my doctor.

I was also a hop, skip, and a jump from Headquarters and their Medical Department, where, once again, I had to meet. The doctor knew that I had been transferred. She scoffed, however, when I told her I felt as if I was run out of town. The psychiatrist I would meet with also echoed those same sentiments.

In time, the South Water Office would eventually close, while a newer office at River West would open. There, I had to compete with the loudest radio in all the offices I worked at. Even more insidiously, that loud radio would have been playing the loudest hip-hop and rap music. Sundays were different. The only difference was that instead of a discotheque, River West would sound like Ebenezer Baptist Church!

There would be discord at work between me and an Operator and a Service Assistant. It was all over my voice.

Despite my best efforts at isolating myself from other Operators and despite putting myself in positions near columns, I was still getting flak. One morning, before my first break, I sat near a remote position by a column. Meanwhile, a Generation-X Operator was working at a cluster that I thought was off limits to Operators because of hanky-panky. This Operator came over to my position to complain that I was talking too loudly. Fortunately, that drew Lynn Long, a Group Chief Operator who had transferred over from the now-defunct Customer's Name and Address Bureau. Now she had reservations about my voice.

The worst was yet to come. On the morning of 23 August 1994, I sat at a remote workstation, right next to a pillar, no less. However, Kay, one of the Junior Service Assistants, sat at a workstation right next to me. There were scores of other workstations available between the front of the office, where the majority of Operators were, and the back of the office.

So why would Kay sit next to me? I noted her presence and made a conscious effort to watch my voice. Still, Kay stopped me and complained that I was talking too loudly!

I had enough. I had hit a Glass Monolith.

There was NO other Service Assistant on the floor at the time, and NO Group Chief Operator present. Therefore, I stormed out of the office without a word to anyone. As I boarded my elevator, Ms. Harris, and

Marjorie Scott from Midway Drive had just gotten off-no matter! I had spoken to them about the flak I was getting, and I was getting nowhere with them fast. So, I left River West and marched myself straight over to Headquarters and their EEO office.

I told the representative about the incident that occurred a few minutes prior. I also told the representative that these incidents about my voice have been ongoing. I also let EEO know that there were other operators with loud voices that wasn't getting the heat I was getting. So the question comes up. Was it my voice that was the problem, or was it something else?

If my voice was disturbing others, why would River West have hip-hop and rap music blaring at levels approaching that of a discotheque? If my voice was the problem, why would other operators, with prominent, booming voices, get off scot-free without any sort of flak at all? If my voice were the problem, why would some Operators prefer to sit with me, despite my warning them that I had a problem with the strength of my voice? If my voice were the problem, why would I pull down a couple of Customer Service commendations because of it?

I was singled out for harassment, plain and simple!

I posed these issues to the EEO Representative, and she promised to look into them. I left there with this admonition. "I'll give you one week, or it's war!"

I returned to River West after my conference. However, the controversy would not end there. Ms. Harris called me in for a meeting with David Sons, the Traffic Manager at River West, about why I left. It was then that I told him about Kay. I told him that I had an ongoing situation with being singled out for my voice.

Sons, however, wasn't buying any of it. He tried to imitate me to show that I could control my voice. He also noted my arms folded posture and called it a defensive posture. When I asked He asked him about putting up an isolated booth, and he also scoffed. In fact, he told me, "If you weren't the type of Operator you are, you'd be out of here right now!"

The only concession I got from Sons was that he would talk to Kay about it. And for a while, at least, Kay kept her distance.

One week later, I filed grievances with the Illinois Department of Human Rights and with the Federal Government. However, when I talked to the Feds, they didn't see a problem. The representative told me that if there was any problem, it might be in the content of what I was saying, rather than in my voice.

Meanwhile, Back at Class

Now that I had my satellite home theater up and running, I still had to deal with Amato. Fortunately, he divided his time between lecturing and trying out various phases of written assignments on fellow class members.

That led to a point of contention.

The discussion turned to my background, particularly my voice. The class knew about it. One Black co-ed replied: "At some point, you have to have thick skin!"

Amato then said: "Now Jon, I don't want you to take an AK-47 to work, but there are cases in which there are pressures that people are finding overwhelming. That makes people want to go out and do (Sugar-Tea) like that.

Amato, as I discussed, still had a weird side. For instance, someone had brought a Jack-O-Lantern to class. With that, Amato said: "Technology has come to the point that even teachers could soon be obsolete. For instance, we could have a pumpkin sitting in that chair, have a lecture piped in from some remote location, and then have Jon's voice come through it!"

After I started at Underwriters Laboratories in late 2000, I had a conference with the Chief Personnel Administrator, Richard O'Sullivan. It was bad enough that I was having adjustment problems that were brought to his attention. Then O'Sullivan told me of another complaint against me. This time, it was coming from the adjacent cubicles to me. My neighbors had been complaining that I was so loud on my telephone that they could not transact their business!

At first, I wanted to scoff at that complaint. However, in light of the severe charges that already were lodged against me, I considered myself in NO position to tell anyone where to go or what to do with those complaints. I had to lump it and listen to what O'Sullivan had to say. Meanwhile, John Haley merely told me to "zip it!"

For instance, I got a lead and an interview for a job testing emissions in Bedford Park, Illinois. Since there was a United Parcel Service in Bedford Park, and one in Hodgkins, a more distant suburb, I boarded Bus #395 at 95th Street and Western, and asked the driver if I was on the correct bus for Bedford Park. The driver was kind enough to let me off at 95th and Cicero continued to my interview.

As I questioned the driver, I was bombarded with insults from an all-Black ridership about the way I talked, the way I dressed, and even the fact that I was looking for a job. I got tired of it. I took umbrage at all of the insults and let the passengers know it.

Mom also believed that I could control my voice. We even had a big blowup about the issue on the morning of her 75th Birthday party. I thought that she was nitpicking.

The accusations that I faced may or may not have been related to that Glass Monolith I faced called Asperger's Syndrome. Not all Asperger's patients would have odd voices. In truth, I thought that some neurotypical people would have voices that were as odd or more so than mine.

But let's not mince words. I had a voice that people either loved or hated! Many people loved my speaking voice, and their love of my speaking voice would manifest itself in my earning several Customer Service commendations while I was at Ameritech/Illinois Bell. Even some co-workers at the Internal Revenue Service liked my speaking voice.

Milton thought that my not using the Ghetto Dialect was significant enough a difference to make people notice, even though I contended that I spoke no differently from other Blacks.

Then there were those who thought that I was some form of computer! Others thought that I wasn't even human. So, who was right?

Interpersonal Relations-
Sexuality

The sexuality part would rear its ugly head time and time again my adult life whether I chose to bring it up or not. Therefore, I need to state openly that I am an ECONOMIC ASEXUAL By that, I mean that my poverty and inability to establish a professional-level career dictated that I remain celibate.

As I write this, I must underscore an observation of mine.

Human Sexuality is nothing more than a con game for a man to get a woman to give up her body, or sometimes, to take advantage of even a child, sexually, OR as a vehicle by both sexes, for manipulating another human being for various purposes.

I couldn't even figure out why I had these types of feelings about sexuality until I had started watching the Maury Povich Show for a few years. There were plenty of men who were very astute in conning their women out of their bodies! Yet, these feelings about sexuality were always within me, me-primordially!

Tomilee Jones of the Illinois Department of Rehabilitation Services would indict my character when she and I met in the Summer of 1982. However, if she was out of line for her assault on my character, she also gave me insight into what Black American women felt about me in general. The only difference was that Tomilee Jones came out with it. Other Black women would not. Instead, to many women, I would either be a novelty item, an eccentric, a nerd, or simply not macho enough for their tastes.

During a joint conference between Tomilee Jones and Bess Robertson of the Center for the Training of the Disabled, I was getting an earful from both of the women over choosing a Clerical Training program. That happened in April 1983. At that point, I had enough and countered: "I meant to ask you something. You said I didn't smile. I figured that I had to be more businesslike around a woman."

Tomilee really went off the beaten path, saying to Bess, "I have to deal with this all the time. People see me as a kind of threat to them because I am a woman. You should see their behavior towards me. It's kind of cold sometimes. But I have to sometimes take the risk of being the heavy, and sometimes I run the risk of being referred to my supervisor."

I replied: "I wasn't even talking about that. What I was talking about was sexual abuse."

"Nonsense! That's not in you!" said Tomilee Bess interjected: "Yeah, Jon told me that he only had five dates in his entire life."

Bess was referring to that informal conversation we had after the evaluations were done. I told her I had a disdain for asking women out because I felt that most Black American men were womanizers. I still feel that way at the time of this writing. I felt most comfortable if I were the one being asked out by a woman. (On the rarest of occasions, that has happened in my life.)

I told Bess that I saw, and still see Black American men come off with lines like: "Hey Baby! What's Happenin Mama!" Bess countered that I could seek a woman without what she termed flirting. She did agree that the "Hey Baby" model I presented was an example of flirting.

Getting back to the confrontation, Bess said: "What you have to learn about is how to deal with women like the ones in Tomilee's age group, rather than like the ones in mine."

At Hertz, my relationship with an assistant named Frank Farmer was marginal. My relationship with his assistant was not much better. I would be introduced to Connie Roberson, his apparent assistant in Distribution. Ms. Roberson was Black, petite, stocky, and carried a somewhat booming voice. Frank explicitly said, "Please treat her like a lady. If you don't, we will have further words!"

Since I addressed all superiors as Mr., Ms., or Mrs., I had no problem in complying. Nevertheless, Connie Roberson hated my guts! For instance, one time, I reported for work at the trailer, and Connie spontaneously said to me, with a smile on her face, "You'd mess up a two-car funeral!" I made no mistakes at that time, and was not long in meeting her. Nevertheless, she said this to me out of a clear blue sky. Had our roles been reversed, she would've blabbed to Frank, and I probably would've been issued some profane epithets, as well as a pink slip!

I dismissed the incident as being a fluke. However, I couldn't dismiss what happened at Hertz. As I sat with a few other hikers in a shuttle van to await our next run, a Black man, about my age, turned towards me and said: "I heard the rumor!"

"What rumor?" I asked.

"I heard that you're gay!" said this person.

"So that's it! Well, I'm not," I said

The rumor mill had been churning vicious gossip about me. There were rumors flying around about my sexuality.

What this co-worker said to me brings up another reason why I totally despise Black Americans, even though I am a Black American myself-vicious gossip!

A Short Digression:

During my last job prior to putting up with the Hertz Clowns, I worked with a marketing student. One day, while we were working, this marketing student explicitly told me that soul singer Teddy Pendergrass had bisexual tendencies.

I explicitly told this marketing student that what he said was not true, since women were known to throw their panties at Teddy Pendergrass.

Come to find out, this marketing student was correct! Later that year, Teddy Pendergrass was involved in a crippling traffic accident. Inside the car was a female impersonator who had previous indictments on various sex charges!

In addition, if anyone told me that actor Rock Hudson did what he did, I also would NOT have believed that person.

I didn't even bother to attempt to tell the Hertz Clowns about why I feel the way I felt about my sexuality, other than my comparison to Prince. Nevertheless, I was becoming more and more offended that I had to field such outrageous allegations.

During my training at STAT-TAB, the subject of sexuality would again come up in a novel way. With only six terminals available to students at one time, there was a lot of downtime unless a lecture was to take place. The smart ones studied, but with all of that noise and banter, studying was quite daunting.

Part of that noise and banter would be classmates talking about everything from their sex lives to the most recent wild party. Admittedly, I was part of the banter on many an occasion! In the words of T.K. Motogusinile, he would say to me: "Man, I came here to learn about COBOL. But all I've been learning here is: "Just The Balls!"

Actually, T.K. was learning more than "Just the Balls!" He was the leading student in the class. Everyone would strive to catch him. My classmates, including me, would've had better luck trying to see Formula One Driver Michael Schumacher during his heyday.

On one night, I would provide a source of banter for the next day. I was coming home from Hertz via the South Michigan to 119th Street bus. As my bus was between 108th and 111th Street southbound on Michigan, there was a full-figured deep brown, Black woman who was walking north on Michigan. She bared her Black breasts, areolas, nipples, and all! Although she had on a black leather jacket, it was zippered only at the bottom. As a result, her bare breasts were emphasized. She was a prostitute! In addition, this prostitute had on striped hot pants! As a result, she looked not only fatter than she probably was but was a touch nasty to boot! Any policeman would have arrested her for whatever he felt like arresting her for, unless she was paying a street tax to the Vice Unit. That can and has been known to happen.

When I told my classmates about what I saw the next day, they dismissed her as being a Sunday school teacher, comparatively speaking! That did not mean that they didn't get a chuckle over the Michigan Avenue Hooker!

Once I left STAT-TAB for the Internal Revenue Service, I wound up working around a 90 percent female group of coworkers.

At this point, in compliance with the Secrecy of Communications Statutes of the United States Internal Revenue Service, I must restrict my discussion to the cast of characters that I would work with, rather than the individual job functions.

That cast of characters would be important, for they would provide many days full of hijinks that would serve to make my job less of a chore!

In addition to Ms. Wright, her supervisor, Ruth G. Harvey, sat in a cubicle just to the southern end of the office. She was tall, Black, with shoulder-length straight black hair. Ms. Harvey was regal in her mannerisms. She seemed almost prissy. In contrast with the country dialect that Ms. Wright spoke, Ms. Harvey spoke the King's English. Oh, there was a light touch of Black twang to her manner of speech; however, that was ironic because she was a touch younger than Ms. Wright.

The first of my co-workers I would work with was a fellow Control Clerk named Betty Acres. Betty was short, cute, and had the same "country" dialect that Ms. Wright had. However, Betty's voice was sharper than Ms. Wright's. Her hair was down to just above shoulder length and was also quite dark. You couldn't accuse Betty of wearing anything provocative. She frequently wore a midi-length dress. She always wore flats- never high-heeled shoes.

Next up was Shirley P. Shirley P was a grandmother with moderately long brown hair. She was also Black. However, her skin was lighter but not butterscotch. I would describe the tone as being more caramel in color. Her voice was a little deeper than Ms. Wright's. However, she had a comical/feisty/sapphire style in her mannerisms. Often, she wore pants, jazz oxfords, or gym shoes, Then there was Barbara C. She very closely resembled pop music singer Dionne Warwick, save for a much heavier voice than Warwick's. She was a cross between a sapphire and a pistol-packing mama! Fortunately, she, too, was very comical. She could and would talk about you given the appropriate impetus to do so.

Then there was June-Marie. She was full-figured and round. Her hair was short. Most of the time, she wore dark colors. She could get a little crazy, too.

Then there was Bridget C. She was of Polish American descent and lived near Midway Airport. She resembled, in terms of personality, the maid on the TV sitcom Different Strokes! She would provide the office with a lot of perspective about much of what was going on in the world at that time.

The second of two White women who worked for my group, was also the quietest. She was also the most respectful. It didn't matter if you were Black or White. In her eyes, you warranted respect unless you did something to un-warrant that respect. Her name was Livja (Lee) Kruse. She was from Latvia. Her hair was brassy platinum and very short. She was tall. She was slightly endowed at the bottom and did not dress provocatively at all. It was just basic slacks and oxfords for her.

Then there was Geraldine Goss. Because of her initials, I called her "GG" for short. GG was short. She was Black. She was svelte-more so than any of the other cast of characters in Special Processing Unit I. She, surprisingly, dressed in a delightfully conservative way. I would find her mode of dress one of the best of the bunch.

Then there was Rose Marie Seaberry. She was also svelte though not the way that GG was. I found out that her astrological sign was Capricorn. She too wore slacks and either sandals, gym shoes, or flats-no pumps. She was Black- with mocha brown skin. She was approximately my height. 5 feet 8 inches.

Next up was Earlean Young. She was very short, and very plump. She carried shopping bags a lot. Her voice was a touch lower, but not overly heavy. She too was Black. She too could get a little feisty in terms of humor, or if she had to admonish or dress someone down.

Then there was Rosemary Harris. She was also plump.

However, it was a sculpted plumpness that made her attractive. She wore hair the length of her shoulders. Unlike the others, Rosemary spoke the King's English. There was a sweetness about her. That sweetness was also evident whenever she dressed herself.

Then there was Deloris. Her voice was extremely heavy, and very deep. She was tall. Her hair was short and brown. She was endowed at the shoulders. She was Nubian tall. However, she too would prove to be quite a nice person Finally, to round out the cast of characters I would work with was Mrs. H. Mrs. H was both a mother and a grandmother. Her hair was long, and there were streaks of gray in her hair. She spoke, if I could quantify it, about 65% King's English, and 35% of the Black dialect-about what you would expect of Blacks coming from affluent, more settled Black districts. One of those communities was Chatham. That's where she was from I had gone from complete joblessness and borderline destitution to two jobs and lofty talk about seeing my second Olympics in eight years, in a matter of just two weeks. Unfortunately, my second job, as a Trip Hiker would give me little peace from sexual harassment i.e., being perceived gay!

Goodkind would cool it almost entirely, while Fat Dave would find something else to amuse himself-momentarily. However, the Black Trip Hikers would start on me. It didn't have to be in an overt manner. Instead, it would be more subtle.

Let me clear the air once and for all.

My readings indicate that penile-anal contact, oral-anal contact, and oral-genital contact, and even kissing, regardless of sexual orientation, all make excellent media for the spread of bacterial and viral infection and/or Oral Cancer! These infections include bladder infections. I had NO problem with Female Homosexuality. However, my disdain towards Male Homosexuality had always been due to sanitary reasons.

I thought that the only thing a man could do for me sexually is to stink and give me the Herp-AIDS!

I already mentioned that there were Black notables, such as entertainers, who never received close to the ostracism, rejection, and abuse that I was receiving. Never mind that their conduct is, and was, blatantly queer!

My accusers never saw me in bikini drawers, pointed-toe shoes, platform shoes, earrings, bracelets, socks as thin as women's hosiery, nor did my accusers smell any cologne on me. Some men even carried handbags. I did not. I never even wore a shirt with an unbuttoned top button. Fat Dave's car was a Cadillac!

Many of my accusers drove cars with automatic transmissions. Every car I owned between 1987 to 2003 has been equipped with the stick-shift, or manual transmission.

My literary staple has always been magazines such as Road and Track, Car and Driver, Home Mechanix, Sports Car, Radio and Electronics, Sound and Vision (formerly Stereo Review) During my boyhood, I played with cars and even built birdhouses and all the way live rocket! Rarely did I fool with my sister's dolls. If I did, I was attracted to the closing eyes mechanisms and the wetting system. During my early teens, I drew up sketches and various plans for rockets, cars, submarines, houses, mini-bikes, and even hovercraft!

As an adult, I picked up a very unusual hobby. I have seen several IMSA/American Le Mans, Sports Car Club of America, Indy Car and Formula One races in cities such as Detroit, New Orleans, Vancouver, Grand Rapids, and Miami-just to name a few cities. I'll call them Road Race Vacations for brevity's sake! Never mind that I also visited two Olympic Games!

Yet, I am supposedly the fag. I believe that pots are calling the kettles, Black!

There was another irony in my work situation at Hertz. I had no trouble with the women at Hertz, save for Kevin Burch's girlfriend, Nkema, and Connie Roberson, the Assistant Distribution Manager. Some women were indifferent towards me. Some were friendly towards me. It made no difference whether these women were Black or white. I could at least get along with these women.

I wonder what would've happened if I tried to come on to any of the women. My mind goes back to what STAT-TAB's Carole Ann said that shocked me.

According to her, a lot of problems stemmed because people didn't touch each other!

When she said that, I responded: "You'd better not touch, or these women will give you a great big swat!"

My COBOL class gasped when I said that. Ironically, Carole Ann was the type who could very easily swat someone and knock that person across the street! Remember! She was your classic sapphire type!

Generally, my attitude was to look, and even admire, but don't even think about touching! The price of touching, in my mind, and opinion, was much too high for me to pay.

There is a saying in the hood that "you've got to pay the cost to be the boss!" All I have ever said was that I could never pay the cost. Therefore, I could never be the boss. I believed, and still believe that the core of Black America's problems lie in poor persons getting into relationships.

When poor persons, of any ethnic group, get into relationships, and/or have children, the problem becomes much worse.

Now imagine me trying to convey this type of message to the Hertz Clowns. I would get laughed out of the company-even by management-truth or not. Although I talked a lot, this one belief, I kept to myself.

Mr. Husky continued: "All this (Sugar in my Tea) is all because folks think you're gay. Even if you are, that's cool, as long as you don't come this way with it. But let me tell you something. (A woman's pet cat) is the easiest thing in the world to get. (Negroes) don't have to go around making a big issue out of it."

I already mentioned the physical and sexual harassment in the last chapter, and that was, indeed the reason why I resigned Hertz Rent-a.Car's O'Hare division. In the weeks following my decision to leave Hertz, peace would come. I got along with my co-workers at the Internal Revenue Service-Black and White. Some of my co-workers, Black and White alike, even liked my speaking voice, in contrast to the Hertz Clowns, who didn't.

But some of my co-workers provided me with something to like about them as well. It was their mode of dress. Many of my women co-workers would refrain from dressing in cleavage or otherwise "putting their business into the street," as I called it.

GG figured out that the way to my heart was to wear a blouse with a high-necked collar. Although GG's observation was close to my feelings about what I found appealing, there was more to it than that. For instance, I told GG and Mrs. H. about an episode of Soundstage that starred soul singer Aretha Franklin at the Park West theater club in Chicago. Aretha looked like the 111th and Michigan Avenue Hooker!

There would be a change in Group Secretaries during that period. My first Group Secretary was someone by the name of Narnina. She was slightly taller than I was, Black, well-dressed, and well-mannered. Otherwise, she wasn't very colorful. I didn't get to know Narnina at length.

Narnina's replacement, Lourdes, was a slightly different story. Lourdes was Hispanic, with skin that was a bright tan. She was between Betty and me in terms of height. Her hair was straight. She, too, was well-mannered and well-dressed. Little did I know that Lourdes was also more observant than she let on. For instance, one morning, I stopped and paused to stretch myself at my desk.

Remember what I just said about Glass Monoliths enabling a person to see the result, but not the underlying reason behind the result. That can go both ways. Lourdes was seeing something in me that prompted her to ask if I was nervous. Otherwise, she would not have asked.

You would think that being gun-shy would prevent me from making a (donkey) out of myself. It didn't. There was another case in which I was to interview for a receptionist's job at the Metropolitan Correctional Center in Downtown Chicago. This facility was just one furlong south of the Internal Revenue Service, downtown! It was a Federal Prison! Ironically, it looked, for everything in the world, like a Downtown high-rise condominium!

Arriving on time for the interview would be the easy part. What was deceptively difficult, however, was a questionnaire I had to fill out about prisons and Federal inmates. One of the questions, for instance, asked me about my thoughts on working for a Federal prison. My reply was that for a facility like Metro Correctional, I had no problem with it. However, for a facility like Marion (the new Alcatraz) or Leavenworth Federal Penitentiary, I had a problem with it. I stated that Metro Correctional was a minimum-security facility!

Come to find out, Metro Correctional was a VERY HIGH security facility! Also, come to find out, Metro Correctional housed some genuine bad (donkeys)! Come to find out, Metro Correctional not only housed white collar criminals such as embezzlers, fraud convicts, tax cheats, and accountants who liked to cook the books creatively, but also people who would commit such crimes as dismembering their own mothers!

There was another issue. I would be required to undergo Federal Law Enforcement Firearms Training in the same manner as someone becoming an FBI Agent or a United States Marshal! Even that did not bother me. However, what bothered me was that sometimes, I would've been required to escort inmates who were being transferred either to or from Metro Correctional.

What really tore it was that I would've also have been required to conduct, or assist in, STRIP-SEARCHES!

I was already being accused of being gay! The last thing I needed, or desired to do, was to go looking, let alone poking up people's (donkeys)! For that, I would say get someone from Chicago's north end of Halsted Street, or from San Francisco's Castro Street and Buena Vista Park area to conduct strip searches and wish them all the jollies they could get!

I turned down any further discussion about this job. Given my responses on the questionnaire, I do not believe that I would've been offered the job anyway.

During this period, shortly after I left the Hertz Clowns, the weather would turn cold, then warm up again. It was during the period when the weather would slightly increase that the woman would take some interest in me. For instance, one day, while I ate at the Federal Employees' Cafeteria, I sat alone. I wouldn't be alone for long!

A very short, svelte, Black lady stopped at my table, noticed me, and inquired: "You're eating by yourself?"

This table was more than capable of accommodating her, me, and two other people. Therefore, I had no problem with allowing her to join me. I knew the place was crowded. For another, she was attractive.

There was an opera singer frequently featured in the former Stereo Review (now changed to Sound and Vision) Magazine. Otherwise, there was a beautiful and very capable newscaster by the name of Lyn Vaughan. In Lyn's early career, Ms. Vaughan at first had her hair rolled up into two buns, then just one.

Madame X, as I'll call this woman of mystery, looked like either one of these samples I mentioned. There is one qualifier. Madame X had the single bun.

Madame X was a touch darker than Lyn Vaughan and was about as dark as that opera singer, but only in the face! Her skin tones on the other parts of her body varied from cognac brown to butterscotch in some places! It was as if she were a human with one of those multi-hued paint jobs common to modified sports compact cars! She wore a gray or silver dress of midi length. She wore platform pumps. She wore no stockings on this occasion. Instead, her legs and the tops of her feet were oiled, with not a sign of ash anywhere on her body.

Madame X revealed that she was from New Orleans. She pronounced it "New or Leans!" She had a very low opinion of Chicago, and even more importantly, the people of Chicago. She found the people of Chicago very rude. According to her, even some friends she met from another country told her that they would have to meet in a city other than Chicago. Oddly, although Madame X only knew me a scant few minutes, she found me to be an exception.

What made Madame X's first impression of me so unique was that I NEVER asked her name. I felt that to do so would be coming on to her sexually. I never gave mine either. Oddly, I figured that this meeting was a one-off occurrence.

I figured wrong. About two weeks after meeting Madame X, I had to run down to the seventeenth floor to make copies of government documents. When I reached the copy room, Madame X saw me, smiled, and said: "Hi friend!"

The women of the Internal Revenue Service were like that, with maybe three exceptions. Some liked me because of my speaking voice. Some liked me because of my manners. In truth, my manners were nowhere near those of an IRS department executive by the name of Almond Dawson, or WVON Radio's late hostess Bernardine C. Washington. Some commented that I looked much younger than 29 years old at the time. Still others knew I had a college education. Some liked the way I complemented their mode of dress. Others liked the novelty of having a man around the department. There were more men on the seventeenth floor than on the 20th floor, where I worked.

It wouldn't end there. A couple of weeks later, Madame X was on the elevator again. This time, Madame X would tell me: "I like you! I really like you! You're so intelligent."

I tried to play what Madame X said, off, replying: "Oh, it's my wit" meaning my comical side.

"That's part of it." Said Madame X Madame X repeated: "I really like you." She then disappeared at her stop.

I am embarrassed to say this. However, I was shocked, honored, dumbfounded, stricken with disbelief, and was immediately steamed up!

I wouldn't see Madame X again for a little while. However, I would be left with one more reason for getting steamed up.

It was very shortly before Thanksgiving 1983. The weather was a delightful 68 Fahrenheit degrees, or about 20 degrees Centigrade. That made for an afternoon that was perfect for walking off a hefty lunch of turkey on sourdough bread. There was a shop along Dearborn Street that had some camera and small electronic equipment. I was window shopping at that shop when a voice yelled "Jon!"

I quickly whirled. It was Joy!

I met Joy through her attractive mother three years prior. Even then, it was as a result of her Mom giving me a ride from Roosevelt University. But Joy and I only spoke in passing. We never dated, nor even visited each other. I did keep in touch with her by proxy. Even then, only at the place she worked.

When I met Joy, she was a svelte, stealthy ballet dancer who was also into music.

This time, however, Joy had filled out-tremendously! She wore a black dress with a wide, rather than a plunging V cut. Nevertheless, her breasts seemed poised to leap out and attack me at any moment! She wore black ankle-strap pumps with a rounded covered toe, and a stiletto heel. The ankle straps seemed to fit very snugly around her. Her feet, legs, arms, and shoulders all appeared to be larger than when I last saw her.

Finally, she told me that she had, indeed, been putting on weight. Nevertheless, her skin was still a fluorescent butterscotch in color.

Joy was still precisely that to behold! A lecherous man would've referred to Joy as being very "juicy"!

I walked Joy to her office at the Continental National Assurance building where she worked. That way, she and I could make small talk about some of the things that were of mutual interest. For instance, Joy asked me if I would consider going back to school. But after the nightmare that was my undergraduate years, I had to tell her: "I doubt it."

One thing that struck me as odd was that although she was putting on a few pounds, she was munching on a bag of small chocolates! Joy pleaded no contest to that, but added that she wanted to splurge now, and buckle down later.

Joy did chide me for not keeping in touch with her-even if only by proxy. As I left her, I struggled to bring myself up to explain why I stopped.

In truth, Joy was one of the most attractive women I ever met when I met her. Although Joy had become quite chubby, she was still, nonetheless, attractive.

What attracted me most to Joy was not the way she filled out, nor was it the V-cut dress she wore. Instead, it was Joy's grace and impeccable use of the King's English, rather than that polluted English known as the "Black English", or Ebonics.

Therefore, I could imagine every man on the South Side of Chicago making a play for her in some way.

Deep inside, I knew that one of the best ways to disrespect a woman would've been to come on to her, and I was on the borderline of doing just that. I have always held that Black American men were, and still are, common womanizers. Do Black American men really care about the objects of their attention, or do these same Black American men merely want to con the objects of their attention out of their bodies?

Judging by skyrocketing illegitimate birth rates and skyrocketing numbers of deadbeat dads, I am, to this day, inclined to believe that Black American men merely wish to con the objects of their interest out of their bodies! The trouble is that whenever Black Americans run this con game on their objects of interest, those Black women who are decent, oftentimes suffer. They suffer abuse, neglect, embarrassment, ridicule, and themselves become the object of vicious gossip! Some Black women in this predicament become hardened. Once that happens, shame on the next person they have a relationship with!

To put it in simpler terms, Black American males practice Rape by Deception!

I didn't explain all of that when I made another audio letter that night and sent it to Joy. Instead, I said: "Let's give Joy a little space!"

Joy had some choice words for me a few days later, when she telephoned me during my break! Fortunately for my butt, they were kind words. But first, Joy told me something only Mikey's ex-wife told me. Joy said:

"Jon, you have a very unusual voice. I don't know." "Your tape, I couldn't listen to it all. Your voice-it sounds so scary! On the other hand, you cheer me up."

Joy also allayed my fears about coming on too strong since she had taken herself off the market for personal reasons anyway.

Still, she found it a delight that I would keep in touch with her. She encouraged me to continue to do so.

In all fairness, it was truly best that I limit Joy to a lovely fantasy. After all, to see a car such as the Porsche 962CR, even if it were only on satellite or home video, is to love the Porsche 962CR. However, only six Porsche 962 CR sports cars were ever manufactured! Therefore, the odds against my having a Porsche 962 CR in my driveway are astronomical! I didn't even mention how much a Porsche 962 CR would cost if I could have such a car!

I also have been enamored of the Ford GT-40. While there were considerably more of those on the street, in original and/or kit replica form, plus Ford's revival of the car, the odds against my having a Ford GT in my driveway are also astronomical.

Similarly, to know Joy always was to love Joy. Realistically, I had to stand in line with everyone else. Besides, Porsches, historically, have been high-maintenance cars. I always held that it would be better for me to be without a woman of any kind than to fail to do justice to a relationship with one.

I admit it! November 1983 was barely three weeks old, if that long, and already, Cupid put his foot up my (donkey)-twice! There was a common denominator to all of this-grace! I was a sucker for it; both Madame X and especially Joy had it. For that matter, Joy's mom also had it, so Joy would only microscopically be less than a chip off the old block!

Yet, for all my being attracted to women of grace, I couldn't define it. Yes, manners are important. However, there are some prissy women that I would not have wanted to touch with a ten-foot pole. Culture and refinement help considerably. However, that would be too simplistic to talk about in this context.

Can my relationship with women be part of my Glass Monolith? Yes and No! Unlike my main Glass Monolith, I knew what the problem was-Women Cost Money! I see no way that I, as a poor, underachieving person, could even hope to win a woman of quality. As I said before, I was an ECONOMIC ASEXUAL! If I wanted a 119th Street floosie, I could get one with the most tragic of ease!

Let it be said that my Glass Monolith gives rise to my having to do all the above. But at least I had something to talk to Bess Robertson about the following week or two later.

I would keep in touch with Bess Robertson during this period. I wrote her and she asked to see me. However, finding a meeting place suitable for the two of us would prove to be the most daunting. Ms. Robertson wanted to meet at Gladys' Lunchionette in the 40s on Indiana Avenue. I wanted us to meet at Water Tower Place. However, Bess was firm and adamant about wanting to meet on the South Side.

About the only place I knew of, on the South Side, that was safe enough for an after-work meeting was Harper Court. This was in a bustling, but integrated Hyde Park district of Chicago. Harper Court was also a hop, skip, and a jump from the University of Chicago Medical Center and the University of Chicago Campus. Bess Robertson agreed. Along with some work-related issues, I just happened to mention Madame X and Joy. At this point, Ms. Robertson thought that I should actively seek out women and relationships. As for my theory that my being poor and underachieving would gum up the works, Bess Robertson scoffed. Ms. Robertson also scoffed at my theory that a woman who wanted me badly enough would let me know in no uncertain terms. To that, she thought that women were inherently shy.

Ms. Robertson and I agreed on one thing: those god-awful dating services were to be avoided at all costs! Not only was their reliability in question, but there was a "creep factor" inherent in the dating services.

I had one idea. Since I liked specialty interest organizations, I thought that the Sports Car Club of America would be a place to meet people of quality, if I were lucky enough. Bess thought that I should've considered things like hayrides and church activities, since she was heavily into the Black church scene. Anyhow, it was good to keep in touch with her, and our meeting ended at the 53rd Street Metra Electric Line.

Meanwhile, back at the friendly confines of the IRS's 20th floor, there would be two more shakeups. Our unit will have a new secretary. Her name would be Merissa Topps.

Merissa would be dark Black, tall, svelte, and attractive. She was almost statuesque. Oddly, I was already old enough, at thirty, to be her older brother at least; it would NOT be outside the realm of possibility for me to be old enough to be her father! Her hair was long and straight. She wore stiletto pumps and often wore a variety of outfits that ranged from business conservative to a touch of naughtiness. Her speech was rapid, with even a touch of that dreadful Ebonics in it. However, I noticed the rapidity of her speech more than I saw the Ebonics in it.

Strangely, Merissa looked to me for answering many of her questions about how the job worked, where everything went, and even what to do. Oddly, we would strike up an odd sort of friendship. Let the truth be known, however, that Merissa already had herself a beau! I was way too old for her in any case!

The trouble with having a brother whose ex-girlfriend worked for the Internal Revenue Service became evident when I was working, I was at a set of files by the Special Processing Unit II. The files were very low to the floor. Since stooping for a long time, I decided to kneel rather than stoop. That drew the attention of Gladys, Ted's ex-girlfriend.

I heard someone ask: "Are you praying?" However, I was so wrapped up in doing my work that when Gladys came up behind me and touched me around the shoulder the way Hertz's Goodkind did, I was immediately startled. Some people would refer to it as a "panic attack".

I almost as immediately passed the incident off as a nondescript type of affair. However, I could not dismiss Mom and Ted's reaction to the incident when Gladys blabbed about it to them. I got terse reprimands from both Mom and Ted over the incident.

I purposely avoided Gladys to prevent putting Ted's "business in the street, so to speak. Mark my word. Ted always was someone who, if provoked, would become highly dangerous. That's what made Ted's reprimand of me especially painful.

I was not enamored of the fact that Gladys would "blab" to Ted and Mom either. As far as I was concerned, she may as well have been one of the Hertz Clowns.

Special Processing Unit I would get a new member. Her name was Philmania. Philmania lived near the area of 51st and King Drive. She was Black. Her hair was straight with a touch of gray. That same hair was neat and rolled into a bun. She was quite regal in her demeanor and mannerisms. She spoke more of the King's English than any of the other members of Special Processing Unit I. She was widowed.

Philmania had a bone to pick with me. When I told her that I was refraining from marriage or a relationship due to my poverty, Philmania contended that I was selfish. It was then that she told me she considered introducing me to her daughter, but had withdrawn the idea.

I just coined the phrase ECONOMIC ASEXUAL only recently. Therefore, there was positively no way I could tell Philmania that I was an economic asexual, I just had to endure the misconception that I was being selfish in refraining from relationships.

Some of the things that This Author sometimes thought of could get me into trouble! For instance, I entertained the idea of introducing Philmania to Ted. Little did I know that Gladys, Ted's ex-girlfriend, also knew Philmania! Therefore, I stood a good chance of getting lynched by either Gladys or Ted had I introduced Philmania to Ted!

I would wind up having lunch with Merissa. Merissa, in turn, would have two other friends along with us for lunch. One such person was Chari. Chari was Black. However, her skin was just slightly darker than butterscotch, but lighter than mocha. Chari was just a hair taller than I, and a little more developed about the shoulders. Then there was Gwendolyn Pettigrew. Gwen was taller, darker, and considerably feistier than all of us combined.

What made Chari and Gwen significant was that they would be joining us on the 20th floor. The only difference was that Gwen would be working in a unit next to us called "The Pipeline." Chari would be going back and forth between several units.

There was another feature that made my relationship with Chari and Gwen unique. One morning, Gwen asked me if I would join Chari and Merissa for lunch. That prompted me to ask Mrs. H if it were common or acceptable for women to ask men to lunch during the time that she was coming up. Mrs. H replied: "No. We might have only thought about it, but we had better not do it!"

Mrs. H and I did agree on one thing. The pick-up lines commonly used by Black American males, such as "Hey baby!" "What's happening, Mama?" were in Mrs. H's words, very insulting.

So, Merissa, Gwen, Chari, and I would form what I called "The Lunch Club." There was a movie called The Breakfast Club that prompted me to give my group this name. Chari was the most conservative of the club. She had a rambunctious son and had her hands full keeping up with him. Merissa was much more liberal. However, I was inclined to think: "What should I expect. She's young." Gwen was the kind of person who would "let it all hang out!" She was by far the feistiest of the bunch. No member of The Lunch Club was more conservative than I was. Neither of my fellow Lunch Club members took themselves too seriously.

There was an even more serious issue that came up. I preferred to speak, or to greet persons, only if spoken to. I thought that if I were to speak in an environment that was predominantly female, the result might have been the perception that I was womanizing, flirting, coming on to women, or engaging in otherwise sexually abusive behavior. Since most of the women were Tax Examiners, a hello might break their concentration, and subject them to serious errors!

Mrs. H. had an earful for me when I responded to Merissa without speaking to her. She flew off the handle, saying: "Jon! Don't speak to Merissa, and don't speak to me.

Earlean also had a serious issue with my withholding a greeting until I was spoken to. She came up to me and said: "Listen! When you walk into a room, you're supposed to speak. Don't just walk in and not say anything to anyone."

In my defense, however, I would, on many an occasion, give a nod or a short bow, or a signal, just to let the other person feel welcomed. Mark my word. The last thing I ever intended by withholding my greeting, or not speaking, was to be rude, boorish, or loutish. It was just in my nature not to.

Madame X also thought I was a bit peculiar. I was coming in from lunch when I was about to miss an elevator. Madame X was coming out as I attempted to get on the elevator. However, the elevator beat me. So, I thought I'd salvage the moment with a talk with Madame X. However, Madame X asked: "What's wrong with you?" When I explained that I attempted to catch the elevator, she said: "I thought you were having a fit!"

Later that afternoon, I rushed for another elevator, and this time, I made it. Madame X was on it. That prompted her to ask: "Again?"

While I was walking the scant three blocks or so from Federal Plaza to the Daley Civic Center, a figure with butterscotch colored skin glowed in the 85-degree (about 28 Centigrade) sun. She was wearing a black, polka dot dress, white, flat sandals, and nude hose. That figure bounded across from the east side of Dearborn Street to the west side of Dearborn, where it and I would run headlong into each other. That figure was none other than Joy herself.

Joy would glow even further when she saw me. Joy was as curious as a house cat. She impulsively saw my Identification Tag, touched it, and raised it up to her for a closer look. All the while, I told her that I was on my way to see the Olympic Flame pass to Walter Payton at the Daley Civic Center.

It was at that point that Joy would make a strange, eerie prediction. She said: "You will have many opportunities to travel-too see other places, and meet interesting people, and do interesting things." As she spoke, her voice was as angelic in tone, as she appeared to glow in that bright sunshine. She then sent me on my way lest I miss my objective.

One of the things I liked about De Brucio's was that there was a svelte, White waitress who was very endowed about her bottom.

She was no sex bomb. However, she was warm and caring. I would benefit from it. Before I ordered dessert, my favorite waitress cautioned me to forget about the menu. They had some new Italian Ices.

Having had Italian Ices before, I was stone skeptical. The Italian Ices I had were in a cup barely the size of the ones that doctors use to have patients in hospitals take pills with. My Favorite Waitress allayed my fears when she showed me a brandy snifter with Italian Ice in it. To that, I cried: "Formidable!" (That's French for Great, or Excellent!) She got a tip for that one.

I had a special plan for Monday, June 12, 1984. I called it Co-Worker Appreciation Day, and why not? This was the absolute first time I ever held a job for a period of one year outside of the former Illinois Bell Telephone Company!

I started that day off by taking the Metra Electric to the Randolph Street Station. A flower shop was located at the Randolph Street Station. I decided to get flowers for all my co-workers to wear in their hair if they so choose. I had a problem, though. Had I tried to buy roses for all of my coworkers, I would've gone bankrupt very easily; so, I made a compromise. I decided to get carnations for the rank and file, while I reserved the roses for the Department heads and bosses.

The plan worked. I would have more than enough money to get flowers for everyone. One of the customers asked me: "Can I be your co-worker for a day?'

Now all I had to do was get the flowers to work. I still made it on time, but Ms. Harvey would wind up a bit surprised at seeing someone carrying such a large bouquet. She originally intended for me to make one last sortie out to the satellite office. However, Ms. Harvey saw that I wanted to give my gift without a word being said. She had someone else substitute for me.

My first target was Modestine, the Manager of all of the Processing Sections. We chatted for a couple of minutes, then I moved on to my next target, Sharon Townsend. She was not at her desk. However, Ms. Bowie was. I hated that I forgot her in all of this. Next came Ms. Wright, Ms. Almond, and finally, Bernadine. Now that I had given the roses to all of the managers, my next step was to pass out my carnations to the rank and file.

G.G. told me that she purposely dressed herself in a conservative blouse and top just for me that morning. The others would shoot the breeze with me and wish me a fond farewell. I did some errands, and while I rode back up the elevator to the 20th floor, I saw Madame X one last time. No, I did not have anything left from my bouquet, and in truth, I saw Madame X so sporadically that I wondered if I would've even seen her that day. Besides, I still did NOT know her name!

I would receive a telephone call early that afternoon. It was Sharon Townsend. She revealed that she was overjoyed to find a rose on her desk. I told her that I did it in appreciation of all of my co-workers and managers.

At about 2 PM that afternoon, there was a sort of informal Closing Ceremony to my term at the United States Internal Revenue Service's Special Processing Units. I was working. At my desk, when all of the ladies would gather around my desk, including Ms. Harvey. I could surmise as to what it was about. Then, Ms. Harvey called me and said: "We're here to wish Jon good luck today. He's been with us, and we loved having him, but now his time just ran out. Maybe we could see you again someday. You never know."

With that, my co-workers broke into applause.

With that, I responded: "I thought about giving some long, drawn-out speech, but decided not to. Instead, I'll say: You're a better class of people."

At about 4 PM, 12 June 1984, I completed one last act as an employee of the Internal Revenue Service's Special Processing Unit I. I stopped at Ms. Wright's desk to turn in my ID card.

Ms. Wright had forgotten, but my visit to her jogged her memory. I got a card, but no money from the Special Processing Unit I. I did, however, get an admonishment to return to the office after the Olympics!

When I worked at Ameritech's South Suburban Remote #1

In the office, I started some fireworks.

During one such occasion, I spied a Fiero SE sports car. This one was all silver. It belonged to one of my co-workers' husbands. I asked about the car. Oddly, she described it as a dog (dew-do)! She did admit, however, that the car cornered like a train on rails in dry weather. In wet weather, it tended to aquaplane.

Sadly, Pontiac decided to drop the Fiero from production that year. That made Stac, the Senior Service Assistant there, very happy. Her complaint, when I talked about the car, was: "You can't put a family in that thing."

When I told Stac that I was not going to have a family, Stac blew her stack! She described me as being selfish and going against God! Stac's tirade uncovered another Glass Monolith cultural issue! Other than that episode, Stac and I still got along great.

There was another bonus when I transferred to the East Midway Drive Office in late 1988. During this period, I would meet some unusual co-workers. For starters, there was an Operator who was positively gorgeous. She was my height. She was Black, although her skin was butterscotch in color. That butterscotch-colored skin, plus the exemplary way she dressed, from head to toe, made her positively radiant. She wore thin dreadlocks at that time. As a result, there was a meeting of Operators in which my eyes were simply riveted on her. After the meeting, I had to fess up to her.

This woman had the right to have me lynched. Instead, she accepted my compliments, and we became friends. I'll call her Peaches because she was, indeed, that-a peach! It also helps me protect her privacy as well.

I would also meet another friend who was studying on her own. There was a local civil rights leader by the name of Al Raby. This woman was a former sister in-law to the late civil rights activist. Lee was from New Orleans. She was slightly shorter than myself. She spoke the King's English more than she spoke Polluted English. Her skin was deep brown, but with a very smooth texture and tone. Therefore, Lee was also quite attractive.

Lee was delighted to learn that my parents and grandparents were from the New Orleans area. She was even more delighted to learn that I enjoyed Creole cuisine. In turn, that led to a question that was a bit odd.

When I mentioned that I liked crayfish, Lee asked: "Do you suck heads?"

I responded: "Uhhhh!"

I recovered myself to realize that what Lee referred to was that some gourmets and gourmands, including Justin Wilson, the late Cajun Chef, actually ate the fatty brains of the crayfish! Happily, I did NOT eat the fatty brains of crayfish, or any other fatty portion of any seafood.

I admonished Lee about the possible sexual connotations of "sucking heads". For instance, I wondered what would happen if I asked someone that question on North Halsted Street in Chicago, or the Castro Street District in San Francisco! Lee, once I mentioned my concern, agreed! Nevertheless, Lee's question was downright funny!

Since the Customer's Name and Address Bureau was Downtown, I was closer to my weekly allergy shot at Northwestern. Speaking of those hijinks, I had two nurses that administered the weekly darts; that's what I called them-darts! Charmain, the nurse who hit a Glass Monolith when she tried to draw blood from me, was one of them. The other nurse was a beautiful, Black woman from Belize. She was short, svelte, and understandably, married! She spoke the King's English exclusively, with a lovely accent that was almost cockney. However, Dana, this nurse, very quickly pointed out that the prevailing language was Spanish.

Side Note: Belize was formerly British Honduras!

When both nurses learned that I was 35 and still single, they read me the Riot Act! I attempted to explain to them that the reason why I was still single was that I was still a poor, working-class paraprofessional at best. I also explained that such persons have a very high likelihood of a failed relationship. I also told them about the cost of raising just one child from the ages of zero to age eighteen.

Both Charmain and Dana thought I was out of my tree when I told them that I vowed NEVER to attempt to raise a family unless I was either a millionaire or a multimillionaire! Again, I countered with figures on the cost of raising a family. But more importantly than that, I am sick and tired of seeing so many poor people, fathering or bearing so many poor children, and setting off a chain of social problems that Tom and Tommetta Taxpayer are forced to clean up!

I'd challenge Dana to a debate on the subject: Should Poor People Have Children?

I so badly wanted to present the debate on some of the local talk shows of the day, such as Oprah, Sally Jessy-Raphael, etc. Dana, however, thought that she would win. Remember. My lack of persuasive ability was yet another facet of my Glass Monolith.

Another blessing came when I visited the Molson Indy Vancouver, or, as I called it, the Vancouver Grand Prix in the Pre-Autumn of 1993. That blessing was in the form of a waitress named Cori. Cori was White, very petite, angelic in facial look, and downright waifish! She dressed in black, except for the blouse she wore. That included her stockings and the flats she wore. Cori treated me as if I were a king from the moment I walked into the hotel's restaurant! For starters, Cori told me: "I thought you might want to read this!"

It was some news supplement that had updates and a wrap-up on the race I just concluded seeing! I don't know whether I had told her I just came from the race. It was still thoughtful of Cori.

My meal would consist of a boneless, skinless, grilled filet of Salmon, a bed of rice, a biscuit, and for dessert, I would have an apple pie. The Salmon tasted as if it were caught from the adjacent Fraser River just five minutes prior!

There was no question about it. I had to tip Cori. I decided to use the higher valued American currency, rather than Canada's 2/3 of the American Dollar, at that time (1993). There would be NO leaving her some cheap, chintzy little tip either. I decided to put my meal on my American Express and make a $10 tip for Cori!

But they didn't call it a tip in Vancouver, British Columbia! Instead, they call it "the gratuity", as Cori would say in a low, cockney voice. I found Cori's cockney dialect very seductive!

It should be said that you don't have to be a sex bomb to be the bomb! Cori was the bomb! Even more importantly, Cori would forever serve as the benchmark by which I would compare all customer service!

I returned to my room with the most lecherous of fantasies about Cori dancing wildly through my head! Fortunately, I came to my senses! I, instead, decided to write a letter to Choose Hotels

International, once I got back to Chicago. Not only did I tell them about Cori, I implored Choice Hotels International to give her the kind of pampering that ladies usually like to have, a massage, manicure, and pedicure, all at a spa that might be affiliated with them.

Cori, my benchmark waitress, brightened my mood when I stayed in Vancouver. Meanwhile, I would meet a new friend who would pick up where Midway Drive's Peaches would leave off. She was, like Cori, very petite, spoke the King's English, and, unlike Cori, she spoke Spanish as well.

When I worked at the Name and Address Bureau in early 1989, there was a very cute, perky lady of Spanish extraction. She dressed herself like a 1960s-style hippie sometimes. We never spoke during my time at the Name and Address Bureau. However, she was quite glowing in appearance.

This lady, like Vancouver's Cori, had a natural cuteness about her. In fact, I would find her more beautiful than she gave herself credit for. I would describe her as being a cross between a Cabbage Patch Doll and a bunny rabbit-a little Spanish bunny rabbit! Therefore, to protect her identity, I will call her Bunny!

What accentuated Bunny's cuteness was her sheer cheerfulness. For instance, she befriended me. She recognized me from my short stay at Customer's Name and Address Bureau. Although I did remember a pixie-like lady at CNAB, this one seemed a bit filled out by comparison, no matter. It was nice of her to remember me, let alone befriend me the way she did.

Bunny's usual outfit consisted of black slacks, a matching black blazer, and either a plain T-shirt or a white blouse. She was fully covered up on top. She wore jazz oxfords that were buckskin, either black or brown, and usually white socks. Sometimes, she wore stockings. Her alternative outfit was a complete blue denim outfit with the same white blouse and shoes. As a result, she would not prove to be a slave to fashion. There was even a counterculture look about her.

Bunny was also a grandmother! One Saturday afternoon, she brought two of her grandchildren, no more than eight years old, to work. She had an activity in mind for them.

It was a good thing that I had someone like Bunny. Although South Water wasn't as rugged as Chicago Southwest #1, nor South Suburban Remote #1, South Water had its moments.

Between Thanksgiving and Christmas, 1993, I drew a fairly good check and some flak from one of my co-workers.

Wilma noted my reaction to what I had on my paycheck before I could even say a word. Wilma also had a propensity to tease.

She said to me: "Alright! That means you can go out and get a family!"

I responded, in a cold, monotonic way: "No, because I don't have the hundreds of thousands of dollars necessary to raise a family!"

Another co-worker, Blanche, was absolutely incensed by what I told Wilma. She screamed, with fire and anger in her eyes: "You're the one who's got your new car and your satellite! Your trouble is, you're not grateful, and you're gonna have these things taken away from you! "Your trouble is, you're trying to get the 'big picture!" You can't do that!"

Blanche's outburst was completely unwarranted. For another thing, part of the reason why Black America has failed to advance since Dr. Martin Luther King lost his life is because we Black Americans have failed to "get the 'Big Picture'!" The next day, I produced a flowchart and showed her, in graphic detail, why I had to refrain from having a family at all costs.

Here is that flowchart!

Issue: Poverty, Children, Relationships, and Marriage; Why I WON'T Marry

Step 1. Lifetime Underachievement (This Author's Category)

Step 2. Lifetime Underachievers ALWAYS marry or engage in relationships, expecting a partner to compensate for a person's shortcomings.

Step 3.   That Always fails

Step 4.   Criticism of Spouse

Step 5.   Blaming the spouse for shortcomings.

Step 6.   Philandering, due to seeking another to fulfill Step 2.

Step 7.   Spousal Abuse

Step 8.   Child Abuse

Step 9.   Tertiary Results

(Murders of spouse, children, separation, divorce, or some other breakdown in relationship)

NOTE: Steps 4 through 9 can occur simultaneously So, what is the basis for the model I have presented?

It is my family history in relationships. Everyone in my family, and even my extended family, has flopped in relationships. Norm had the most success. But here, too, there were some problems. Given that, I believed that going into a relationship, without becoming successful, would be like racing a stock, air-cooled VW Beetle against a ZR-1 Corvette! It isn't always about money. Instead, it is about balance between money, success, emotional stability, health, education, and insight.

I am quick to tell the Michael Jordans, Oprahs, and John Johnsons to have as many children as they desire. But I must reiterate that it would be a sin for Jon Evans to father any child.

I showed my flowchart to Blanche and told her, "You got on my case yesterday for trying to get the 'big picture.' I hold you'd better try to get the 'big picture' or else these things will hit you like a ton of bricks!"

But Blanche stubbornly replied: "You've got the wrong idea about things."

Blanche was also wrong about me having my satellite. It hadn't come out yet!

Blanche wasn't the only one like that. For instance, J.C., the office jerk, and his friend were in the cafeteria. They saw me as I walked in, and said: "Jon, you need to go out this weekend and get yourself a couple of these women!"

I told them: "May I remind you that there's a 55% Illegitimacy rate in the Black Community!"

J.C. jumped up and retorted: "You're selfish! God said, be fruitful, and multiply."

I told J.C., "May I remind you that there are 6 billion people in the world already; half of whom are starving to death as it is!"

But J.C. countered: "The reason why they're starving to death is due to discrimination! Michael Jordan can come down right now and give somebody some money to feed some of these people!"

Fortunately, I had a younger relative of a former classmate. She got tired of the bull plop that J.C. was talking, and said: "Uh-Uh! Don't nobody out here owe anybody anything!"

At that point, I let them go at it while I went about my business.

However, a couple of points needed to be made.

For starters, why would J.C. quote the Bible about the "be fruitful and multiply" part, when he most likely would not observe the Bible on any other parts or interdictions?

Most importantly, This Author holds that the Holy Bible, the Holy Koran (sometimes spelled Quoran), and Karl Marx's writings on Communism have caused more trouble than any three or four books known to man! For instance, lives have been lost; wars have been fought, and people have been victimized, in one way or another, all because of these books!

What J.C. was doing was to use the Holy Bible as a subterfuge for being a "Buddy Love (The Nutty Professor) type of player! For instance, the next day, I corrected myself by saying that only one out of seven people in the world were starving to death! However, when I told him that, according to U.S. News and World Report, the earth could handle ten billion people, he came talking this smack: "The Bible says the earth can handle 100 billion people!"

Show me the passage, J.C., unless it is just another subterfuge of yours for your smack-talking, womanizing ways!

What I found heartening was that Bunny had no problem whatsoever with my voice. In fact, she liked working with and around me. Bunny told me that it was quite peaceful to work around me. I found Bunny's words as comforting as making love itself!

I picked up a few words of Spanish while I was on the job. Therefore, I was able to tell Spanish-speaking customers about Ameritech's Spanish Speaking Customer Service Bureau. Alas, I didn't know how to tell Spanish-speaking customers to hold for the number.

Bunny said "Aqui Para Numero Por Favor!"

I, at least, knew what the "Por Favor" meant. Thanks to Bunny, I now had a phrase I could use.

Sadao Watanabe would wipe me out when he played the Park West in September 1994!

I would also get the opportunity to wipe someone out! Bunny had a birthday during early September. During this time, I was plotting a surprise for her.

Bunny dressed informally, as I discussed. However, what if I could enhance the beautiful creature she was? Even better yet, what if I could enhance that beautiful creature by using the type of things she liked to wear herself!

So began my attempt to give Bunny a mini makeover! It was a Saturday, and I was off that day and the next day as well.

First off, I knew that Bunny's dimensions were quite diminutive. I was able to pump her for information on her shoe size. That was a big help. Next, I surmised that if I went to one of the neighborhood or mass-market stores such as K-Mart or Wal-Mart, I would have difficulty finding shoes in her size range.

Ipso-Facto, I chose Bloomingdale's at the 900 North Michigan Avenue Shopping Center! 900 North Michigan was an upscale collection of shops, with Bloomingdale's as the anchor store.

Once I was there, it was decision time. I knew that Bunny dressed either in blue jeans and a matching blue denim jacket, or in black slacks, with a matching black jacket. Since Bunny dressed in either a covered blouse or a T-shirt underneath, I decided to let that alone. Besides, I did not know her measurements anyway.

Now my choice was both a pair of blue denim clogs and matching navy-blue stockings, or a pair of black clogs and matching stockings. I thought, then agonized, then came to a decision. Some people, including actor Wesley Snipes in the movie Passenger 57, would say: "Always bet on the black!"

So, I bet on the black! I made sure that the heels were NO more than 1 inch high. I would never dream of buying a woman high or spiked heels, lest they'd break her feet! Then, I made sure that they matched her shoe size. Now that I had the clogs, I needed some black stockings to go along with them. I knew that the "one size fits all" concept was a myth. Fortunately, I found some knee-high black cable stockings in her size range.

I came directly from Bloomingdale's to River West, added a black beret that Keith gave me, then slithered onto the floor. I then gave the "big brown bag" to Anita and instructed her to give it to Bunny. I then scurried away!

Bunny was beaming when she returned to work that Tuesday. She told me that my sneaky little birthday makeover prompted her family to give her a few goodies as well. Bunny revealed that I hit the nail on the head with the stockings. They fit perfectly.

Not everything went as I drew it up, however. For instance, the clogs were very comfortable and fit perfectly. There was one problem. Clogs or slides required a whole different way of walking that took some getting used to. Bunny revealed that as she was walking down some steps, one of her clogs slipped off her foot!

I groaned in disappointment. As for the hat, Bunny revealed that she didn't wear hats, as I discovered when she gave the hat back to me before I left my workstation. So, for a while, I was stuck with a hat that Keith tainted.

Still, my birthday surprise had another effect. Anita, one of the Service Assistants I could get along with, had become jealous. She told me that her birthday was on 13 June and hinted that I should keep that in mind.

Anita got her wish sooner than that! She was a family woman and proud of it. That included loyalty to her husband. Therefore, I got his permission to get Anita an item that would help the couple enjoy "the world's oldest sport!" The idea was a hit.

Therefore, the result of my mini-makeover was a mixed bag. I would term it successful, with some qualifiers. Bunny cautioned that she never liked, nor did her doctor recommended high-heeled shoes. Considering that I never believed in buying a woman a pair of high-heeled shoes, I had already listened to her before she warned me!

At least shopping for Bunny would be easier than shopping for the one thing that I needed for the course, no ifs, ands, or buts, a word processor!

For my second presentation, back in Verbal and Visual Communications, we were supposed to take a position of advocacy. Since Welfare Reform was becoming a hot-button issue of the day, I thought to myself: "You're not going to make a dent in the problem of Welfare Reform unless you attack one of the major reasons why people go on Welfare in the first place: Illegitimacy!

My position was that unless strong sanctions against those who bear illegitimate children are taken, any talk about Welfare Reform would be just that-talk! To support it, I heavily armed myself with several articles from Time, Newsweek, and a book called Birth Control and Conscience that I just happened to have in paperback form.

My position on attacking Illegitimacy consisted of the following three features:

1. Making it a Class Four Felony to father ANY illegitimate child. I took this position because more often than not, illegitimate fathers deny, rather than accept, and care for their offspring. Therefore, who pays? Tom and Tommeta Taxpayer!

Author's Side Note:

In Illinois, the commission of a Class Four Felony is/punishable by at least 21/2 years in prison. I believed that those who would capriciously get a woman pregnant are just as bad as those who commit the crime of rape itself. In fact, during my presentation, I even referred to Illegitimate Fathering as Rape by Deception! If Theft by Deception is classified as a felony, then should the theft of a woman's body also be classified as a felony?

2. Enacting a 20 % Income Tax Surcharge on ANY person, father or mother of two or more illegitimate children. My rationale here was that such persons were taking up the bulk of the health, welfare, and/or

human services dollars in taxes. Therefore, such people should shoulder the greatest responsibility for supporting the health, welfare, and/or human services systems that were or are already in place.

3.　　　Enacting a 10% Income Tax Rebate to anyone who decides to have a Vasectomy or a Tubal Ligation done on themselves. My reasoning here was simply a positive incentive NOT to place a burden on the health, welfare, or human services systems in the country. It is a sacrifice to refrain from having children, and such persons who would go through this radical step should be acknowledged accordingly.

But there was still that Glass Monolith!

When I introduced my presentation, I made the mistake of quoting Mick Jagger's song Some Girls. I cited that controversial passage about his lyrics pertaining to Black women to show how Illegitimate Fathering has caused negative stereotyping in the Black American community.

Unfortunately, my classmates did NOT get it! Two of the five students in my class were Black Women, and they wanted to "keel" me, even though I specifically stated that I was after Illegitimate Fathers and wanted them to pay for their crimes. I also had trouble with some of the non-Black students in my audience. For instance, Elias thought that additional jails would be necessary and that more money would be wasted in building those extra jails.

Anita Georgees was about the most civil critic of the bunch. She liked my idea of having a 10% income tax rebate but felt tax penalties and even jail time for illegitimate fathers would hurt the same children that I would've been trying to help.

One of the Black students, Trina, tried to be slick! She posed the hypothetical case of sperm banks and sperm donors to break down the concept of using coercion to curb illegitimate fathering. She almost succeeded in cornering me. However, I had a way out. I told her that I would separate "Brave New World" scenarios, such as what she was talking about, from straight-ahead legislation of responsibility. Meanwhile, there was another student whom I will call "Jazzy Jam" in order to protect her identity. She wanted to hang me.

Both Black students thought that illegitimacy was no big deal. Their response was, "You have sex, you get pregnant, you take care of the baby. That's it." They also tried to accuse me of centering on abstinence over staying on the subject of illegitimacy. I countered that they were really the same, especially if you look at the problem from a big-picture perspective.

I ended my presentation by saying, as I will say now: "You can't legislate morality, and you can't legislate common sense, but you can sure as shooting legislate responsibility."

Trina took that cue to give her presentation, and ironically, hers was on the subject of why Sex Education was failing. Trina gave a variety of reasons for that failure but continued to advocate for Sex Education. Given my presentation, I wasn't so sure. Once Trina's speech ended, she and I got into a donnybrook about our positions.

What was Professor Irving's position in all of this?

According to him, I offended the audience. I didn't persuade; I antagonized. As a result, my grade was relegated to a C.

Professor Irving also took issue with my use of the terms "Mack Daddy players" and "hot little mamas" as being derogatory.

As the next Verbal and Visual Communications class started, Jazzy Jam saw me and said to me, "You realize that was just your opinion!"

That report would say that the incidence of non-marital Childbearing among Blacks in America would run as high as 70.2 percent! I quoted the figure I cited from the Parade Intelligence Report, which cited a 55 percent Illegitimacy rate among Black Americans back in the 1980s! Even in the year 2000. The Illegitimacy rate among Blacks, according to the National Vital Statistics Report, was 68.7 percent throughout the entire United States!

Even more alarming were the figures for the State of Illinois, my home state. Here, the Illegitimacy rate among Blacks was a whopping 76.5 percent! Only Wisconsin was worse.

Jazzy Jam, I would also like for you to tell me that this Associated Press article is "just my opinion."

This article was as recent as May 2004.

This judge got tired of this couple that consistently had a track record of child neglect, that same neglect that stems from Illegitimate parenting, as well as other forms of dysfunction.

Since I had a tape of my presentation on illegitimacy, I made a copy and played it back. I didn't like the way I slouched or gave the presentation. What I did like was the content. In fact, one of my co-workers, Wilma, was more than a little interested in what I had to say about the subject of illegitimacy. Once she viewed the video, she had no problem with it. Another one of my co-workers stated that they should merely make the man pay for the child, nothing more.

Mom, however, was NOT happy with my presentation at all. She strictly admonished me against giving a presentation like that again.

In all fairness, I made the mistake of mentioning what Mick Jagger said in his song, Some Girls. Once I did that, I shifted the focus from the general problem of illegitimacy to Black Illegitimacy. I inadvertently led my audience off on a tangent, although a couple of people still did get it.

If my example is a typical indication, people with complex Neurological/Social Functioning disorders, such as Asperger's, can be dragged into controversies, such as Sexuality, without even knowing it. Or, they can engage in it, and, because they don't know how to manage such a complex part of life as this, be dragged into the mess.

Interpersonal Relations-
Within the Family

I would be wrong of me to say that Dad was all villain. In truth, at least with me, he was well-intentioned-even if some of his ways with me and the statements he made about me would sometimes be inappropriate.

However, I could say that generational, background, philosophical, ethical, and perceptual differences between Dad and me would serve to form another Glass Monolith.

However, perceived lack of common sense aside, Dad termed me as being "educated", even before I started college. Here's why!

Dad was reared in the hard-core poor South (Farrell, Mississippi, where people didn't suffer from the effects of racism. Instead, they suffered, what I am calling: "In-Your-Face-ism"!"

I am coining a new word here. I describe In-Your-Face-ism as the most flagrant, point-blank, overt, and blatant form of hatred, prejudice, and racism that one can have towards another ethnic group of any kind! The fact is that In-Your-Face-ism has resulted in church bombings, lynchings of Blacks, assassinations, poll taxes, the "dead time" jail periods that blues singer Riley "B.B." King spoke out against, and on and on.

Dad left home at a very early age and came to Chicago. He only went as far as his freshman year at Dunbar Vocational High School before dropping out. Remember! There was very little incentive back in those days for Black Males to complete school, so they didn't. In fact, he saw the military as a potential source of solace. So, Dad lived by his wits. Hence, he valued "street wisdom" over anything else because he had to. I would term Dad's background as being strictly "Chitterling Circuit."

Unfortunately, Dad insisted on smoking whenever he came in, despite my having Asthma, and even despite Mom's now having Asthma. He lit up while I was chatting with him. I made the mistake of telling him, "If I don't get down into the basement within the next few minutes, I'll start coughing."

That sent Dad into a rage. He insisted that my problem was "nothing but a cold," and that all I had to do was to take a teaspoonful of honey and a teaspoonful of Mineral Oil.

One of the problems I had with Dad was that some of the things he would suggest that I should do, or should have done, risked life, limb, and/or even machine. Here are some cases in point. For instance, Milton had brought in a 1973 Subaru Sedan with a manual transmission. Although it was a four-door sedan, I still wanted to see how the car rode, just in case I were to run across a GL coupe. So when

Dad, who had come in from Detroit, wanted to go out to the store to get some liquid libation, I offered to drive him.

What I found so weird was that while I started the Subaru up and was giving it the proper rpm necessary to get underway, Dad insisted that I put the car into second, rather than into first. His reasoning was that I wouldn't have so many gears to shift. I didn't argue with him, but all the while, I was thinking that starting out in second gear was an excellent way to lug, and subsequently destroy, an engine.

We never made it to the store. As I rounded 120th Street westbound, I noticed an idiot light. It was the oil pressure. I promptly circled the block and headed back home.

"Where are you going?" Dad asked.

"I just got an Oil light coming on," I said.

"So, what! Go ahead." Said Dad.

"No. I've got to get this thing back home now." I said.

I got the car back. However, when I reported the incident to Milton, the strangest thing occurred. Milton said, in a nonchalant manner, "It's supposed to cut on." Meanwhile, Mom was reprimanding me for my body language, or in her words, "having all those knots in my face."

In the meantime, I became enraged with Dad over the next day. He always contended that I did not know how to drive or would otherwise depict me as being a functionally incompetent dingbat, someone less than capable of being an adult, conducting business affairs, or otherwise conducting myself as an adult. His bossiness while I was driving him was just a subset of that behavior. I let him know about it the next day.

Dad would get more moving violations in eight months than I would in the eight years I had my license. Save for the accident that I had and the fender bender I was a victim of, I had a perfect driving record. Yet Dad insisted that I didn't know how to drive! Even more insidiously, he told me that I was not qualified to drive a motorcycle, even though I took and completed an approved Motorcycle Driver Education program at Northeastern Illinois University, one of the premier Motorcycle Driver Education programs in the country!

Then, there were still Dad's occasional criticisms. He came in from Detroit one time. This time, he insisted that I was NOT trying hard enough to look for work, and that I should even be kicked out. He would tell several people, from friends to relatives, that I was not trying hard enough to look for work.

Also, in a drunken episode, he continued to say to me: "I don't know about you", after experiencing one of my coughing spells, then referred to me as a "mama's boy"! I should've had him thrown out right then and there. Fortunately, Mom knew better.

Dad would telephone the house from Detroit that night, and I would make the mistake of telling him the news that I had the "Twitchy Lung Disease" plus Bronchitis.

Dad said: "Now here's what you do, and I want you to listen to me good. You take a teaspoon full of honey. Then you take you a teaspoon full of Mineral Oil. Then you take that every day. Don't miss any days. What'll happen is that you will feel a lump in your throat, and you'll want to spit that stuff up."

I only said "Yes."

Dad continued: "Now don't come telling me 'Yes,' and don't do it.

What you do is to keep on taking it every day. It'll clear that up."

I must confess that I had positively NO INTENTION of taking a teaspoon of honey and a teaspoon of Mineral Oil for my condition. The reason why I was so solidly opposed to what Dad was talking about could be summed up in two words: FOLK MEDICINE or STREET MEDICINE! The kind of medicine that Dad was talking about bordered on sheer medical quackery!

In some cases, the type of medicine that Dad talked about was sheer quackery, plain and simple. As a child, I read a very large medical book that described such things as copper bracelets to cure arthritis, various herbs, dimple makers, etc.

Even worse, my late maternal grandmother would occasionally smoke Asthmador Cigarettes for her Asthma! These cigarettes smelled exactly like Marijuana, or as I called it, Devil Weed! I am told that they may have been made from Jimson Weed! I believe it! The stench from Asthmador Cigarettes was just as strong and as acrid as Devil Weed! In the end, my grandmother would die of complications stemming from Asthma, as I stated.

Dad's justification for the use of Home Remedies was that Blacks, at the time that he was coming up, did NOT have access to ANY medical care at all. So, we had to come up with some things that would help us.

In all fairness, my grandmother on my father's side would make salves that both Dad and I used to relieve chronic itching and breakouts. Also, in all fairness, you can determine whether a person is ill by the way they smell! It doesn't necessarily have to be about the Gastrointestinal tract either.

However, temporary relief of itching was one thing; treating Asthma was altogether different. Even more brazenly, Dad referred to his treatment for Asthma as a cure.

Let the truth be known about a teaspoon of honey and a teaspoon of Mineral Oil. It's a cure alright-A QUACK CURE! At best, such "cures" may indeed make a person feel better for a while. However, home remedies and folklore cures can mask symptoms of more serious, if not life-threatening, medical problems. Eventually, those problems come back to bite the person using a folklore cure in the most insidious of ways, if not the most fatal.

Another GRAVE DANGER in cures such as the ones Dad sometimes suggested can be found in this article I have lifted from the Chicago Sun Times!

CHICAGO SUN-TIMES • TUESDAY, AUGUST 20, 2003.

Death of an 8-year-old at church-ruled a homicide Milwaukee police arrest minister who led healing service BY TOOD RICHMOND MILWAUKEE—. -An autistic 8-year-old boy who died after he was wrapped in sheets during a prayer service suffocated, the medical examiner's office said Monday. The death was ruled a homicide. Terrance Cottrell Jr. died because his chest was somehow restricted and ¬could not expand, according to ¬a statement issued by the office of the Milwaukee County Coroner.

"Air was not able to get in or out," said Eileen Weller, the office's administrative manager.

A man has been arrested in connection with the death, which occurred Friday night at a run-down strip mall.

Police have not identified him, but David Hemphill Sr., bishop of the Faith Temple Church of the Apostolic Faith, said the man is his brother, Ray, another minister who led Friday's service. Ray Hemphill remained in jail Monday, according to the Mil¬waukee County Sheriff's Depart¬ment. Milwaukee County District Attorney E. Michael

McCann said he hasn't decided on charges yet and planned to meet today with the head of his office's homicide division to study the case further.

The mother had been taking her son to the church three times a week for the last three weeks in hopes of curing his autism, David Hemphill said.

It was after more than an hour of prayer that a parishioner noticed the boy was no longer moving and called emergency workers, Hemphill said.

"We were asking God to take this spirit that was tormenting this little boy to death," Hemphill said. "We were praying that hard, but not to kill."

Hemphill said he has not talked to his brother or the boy's mother, Patricia Cooper, since Friday night. Hemphill said church members had wrapped the boy in sheets to keep him from scratching himself and others, but he was allowed to sit "any way that he feels comfortable."

David Hemphill started the independent church in 1997. - It meets twice a week and has a congregation of six families.

AP Another problem with folklore cures is that they can sometimes involve the use of caustic, if not outright dangerous, materials. For instance, I read, in a Sunday newspaper, about a folklore cure commonly used in the Hispanic community to treat upset stomachs and other gastrointestinal problems. That folklore cure involved the use of Mercury, one of the most toxic substances known to man!

Dad would leave for other relatives on the West Side. However, Mom had to hear his ranting. She told me: "You should've heard your daddy after you went downstairs. He went on: "I've been smokin around the nigger all my life, and now he comes up tellin me that the smoke was gonna bother him. He was going on about "being a man," about how "he needs to mix with other people," and bull (plop) like that. I was getting sick of him."

I also heard Dad tell someone, "Jon does NOT know Street Life!" That statement could be about the "naïve" or "lacking knowledge of social rules."

One weekend, Dad came in again. As far as I know, that weekend was uneventful.

A scant couple of days later, I tested for a job on the North Side. I aced the reading and even the typing test, but had my application set aside for future considerations due to a lack of telemarketing experience!

I took the L-Subway and Ho-Chi Minh Trail back home immediately after that interview and test, turned the key to my door, and entered the beginning of a shocking story.

Mom was holding a registered letter in her hand. Dad had filed suit for a divorce against Mom! According to the suit, Dad was also after some of the interest in my old boyhood home! The divorce papers were forged. They had Mom's name on it, which she never signed!

What made me very livid with Dad wasn't the suit for divorce at all. Whenever Mom and Dad were together, they fought so much and so hard that it was hypocritical of them to chastise my siblings and me for fighting. However, Dad was with Mom the weekend before, and just a few days before this service. Of course, he was doing what comes naturally.

Dad could've told Mom of his intentions then, rather than to "hit and run" the way that he did. Dad's conduct, to me, belonged in the "Lowdown Hall of Fame"!

Mom commented: "If he wanted a divorce, I'd have given it to him. He didn't have to come out of a bag like this."

That night, I spoke of Dad in language so vile that Ted thought I was out of line, complete with barnyard epithets! In Ted's mind, he was still my father. I contemplated not even attending his funeral when he eventually met his demise.

The sanctions I did impose on Dad were that I vowed NEVER to visit him at his house. If it were a neutral site, such as a cousin's house, fine. However, I would NOT set foot in his house-ever! I also insisted that Dad be barred from the Southfork, our home, forever!

I wrote Dad, what Mom termed, "a smoking letter!" In it, I stated the sanctions I would impose on him. I expected him to honor my request NOT to set foot inside the Southfork again, for that matter. While I was at it, I also responded to his many pet peeves about me.

For instance, on the mixing, I told him that I had the right to determine when I would mix with people, where I would mix with people, and with whom I would mix.

The battle lines were drawn. Mom was very supportive of the sanctions I imposed on Dad, as well as the letter I wrote him. Mom also revealed, on the day he sued her, that Dad was to "never lecture Jon about being a man again!"

Norman and Ted enthusiastically backed my sanctions against Dad, and Milton was also at least warm to the idea. Marciea and Dwight were vehemently opposed. Mikey was neutral. Norman even insisted that Mom throw out a 19-inch television set that Dad bought her on a previous trip to Chicago.

All of this wrangling and strife was over a woman Dad had met and was in a relationship with. The story went that Dad was stringing her along, so she called his bluff.

Oddly, while Dad declared war, Mom was only interested in defending the property she worked so hard to redeem, NOT to counterattack Dad in any way. She wanted NO alimony from him; no punitive damages; none of that-just the divorce that he sued her for. That strong religious upbringing was definitely at work here.

With Mom, it was different. She kept me on a very short leash. She would nitpick. She would be bossy. She would tell me how to drive, despite NEVER having driven in her life. She would even regulate how much food to put in my mouth.

I believe that Mom was the way she was out of revenge. She also faced what I call "IN YOUR FACE-ISM!" That included the segregated signs for riding streetcars and buses in New Orleans, and the fact that positively NO Blacks could ride the old Panama Limited. Even when we Blacks were allowed to ride the City of New Orleans, Blacks were restricted to a baggage car!

In Chicago, there were even hospitals and some parks where Blacks could NOT go, such as the Birdcage at South Shore Country Club. In fact, the primary reason why the 47th Street shopping district thrived was that Blacks were NOT permitted to shop at most downtown stores!

Now, Mom, having been controlled all her life, was doing the controlling!

However, there was still that horrid cough, and this time, Mom would nag me about taking my medication; that she didn't have to do. I was taking it four times daily.

Mom still insisted that I consider taking the cough syrup. However, since I was on medication, I did NOT want to run the risk of crossing over-the-counter medicines with prescription medicines without consulting Dr. Grasser.

Mom was also putting pressure on me to go to the Cook County Hospital for help. That was even worse than what Dr. Grasser proposed! Weeks earlier, Dwight was in a traffic accident so nasty that it put him in the hospital. When it was discovered that he had no health insurance, he was sent from Mercy Hospital to County Hospital.

Ted and I had to go to take him some clothes. Mom coerced me into letting him borrow some slacks since Dwight had a habit of permanently borrowing my clothes!

My situation was now so bad that I decided to boycott Thanksgiving! That meant no grace at the table. Mom would have none of that because she thought that the only ones in the family who really suffered were Ted, Norman, and Raymond.

Mom was involved in a relationship that was abusive and loaded with neglect. As a result, the older brothers went for a considerable time without a meal. At that time, there were no social service organizations or groups that could help the hungry, as there are now.

I must, at least, counter that anytime you cannot support yourself, and don't know why, that's misery plain and simple. To be thankful for running into numerous Glass Monoliths, in my case, be it inability to get funding for school or impotence in the job/career arena, amounts to nothing more than a façade, and I was having NO part of it!

It seemed illogical for Illinois Bell to ask me to fill out an application, only to reject me shortly after I completed the application. When I went to their Personnel Office, they explained that anytime a resume was included with an application, that application was immediately referred to Management Personnel, where there were NO openings whatsoever.

I gave up in disgust as I stormed out of the door. However, once I got home, I received another call from Ms. Godmond. Mom took the message and passed it along to me.

When Mom told me that Ms. Godmond called, I told Mom that was "bull (plop)"! I told Mom what happened when I went down to Illinois Bell and how they told me that they never had anything.

Mom was NOT the type of person to hear of giving up in a case like this. When she was growing up, and even for the better part of her adulthood, she had many a door slammed in her face. Her life philosophy was to tolerate these issues and to "pray over it". In her mind, this spot of difficulty I was experiencing was the system's way of attempting to "break somebody's spirit". In her mind, I was NOT going through anything that she didn't go through.

Therefore, she effectively told me to climb back on the horse that I had been thrown from. Mom insisted that I return Ms. Godmond's phone call, despite what I was told, and what I was going through.

This time, I was able to get in touch with Ms. Godmond, and with that, I learned I was to come in for processing, including a Medical on February 10.

Eight months later, Mom would suffer a stroke. I fortunately came in time to notice her in the throes of the stroke. Therefore, I was able to get Mom to the hospital in time to save her life.

The only one fresh from the fight was Mom herself! I was exhausted. I saw that circumstantial gift from Officer Miazga as an opportunity to get some rest, but would I?

About two days after Mom's release, she wanted to get her hair done. Even more insidiously, she wanted to go to one of the local beauty shops. Even more insidiously, it was biting cold, though not yet subzero.

I could see an already weakened Mom attempting to negotiate glare-ice-laden sidewalks. Then, I insisted: "NO!"

Mom begged and pleaded, insisting that she would be all right. I was just as firm in my insistence, citing her short time getting out of the hospital.

Mom capitulated, but she was near tears. Therefore, I offered to and did drive her to the beauty shop on the condition that she would call me when she was done. Mom failed to keep her word. The doorbell rang while I waited for her call. It was Mom. She had walked, or taken the bus from the beauty parlor, against my strictest admonishment!

Mom's healthcare provider telephoned shortly after Mom broke her promise. According to Mom, the last thing I was to do was to prohibit her from going out or exercising. In truth, I thought that Mom should've exercised on Ted's exercise bicycle for at least a month before venturing out in any manner. Otherwise, I would NOT have had an objection to her going out in the community. I still hold that Mom cared more about her hair and appearance than her recovery.

Mom was like both mayors Daley in Chicago. Whatever she wanted, she got. And she was the boss! During her hospital stay for her first stroke, she explicitly stated: "I am the boss!"

Paradoxically, Mom had to be "the boss." She got minimal, if any, support from either of her two spouses. Dad didn't buy my developmental problems one iota, and let Mom know it.

Mom did, however, scrutinize and nitpick me to death-from my mode of dress to the way I ate my food, and yes, she also complained about the strength of my voice-even when I had no intention of getting loud at all.

With Ted, I already mentioned his Dr. Jekyll and Mr. T type of personality. That's what I term as being tough but fair.

Ted's greatest attribute was that he taught by example. It was because of Ted that I ever even heard of automotive magazines! His was a diverse array. Hot Rod Magazine and Motor Trend were the bulk of what he read. However, he got Car and Driver, and rarely, Road and Track!

Ted liked the big-inch musclecars of the 1960s. Don't even talk to him about anything else. In fact, I have reason to believe that he owned one of Chevrolet's famous COPO cars! COPO stands for Corporate Office Production Order.

The COPO car that Ted owned was a plain 1965 Chevrolet. Impala Sport Coupe-no SS badging or Super Sport Option. However, under the hood lurked a 396 Cubic Inch (6.6 Liter) V8. The thing was rated at 450 SAE Gross Horsepower. However, the manufacturers sometimes liked to lowball their horsepower ratings to keep from unnerving the insurance companies! It also had a steering wheel tachometer and 4 on the floor standard! Please note that very few American cars put out anything close to one horsepower per cubic inch at that time!

I can personally attest to his making short work of a Plymouth Sport Fury on South Halsted Street between 93rd and 87th Streets, yuk-yuk!

Ted had a host of friends and co-workers as an optician. His coworkers came from all types of backgrounds, which is how he came to learn the game of Chess and pass the game on to all the other siblings, including me.

You can also blame Ted for fostering other interests in me, such as Stereo equipment and Photography. He set up a darkroom in his attic apartment, and when he learned that I was building rockets, he was so delighted that he subsidized Mike and me for a kit! You see, he became familiar with rocketry when he served in the military.

As similar as Ted and I were, we were just as different.

For instance, Ted liked Drag Racing, NASCAR, USAC Open Wheel, and Indy Racing. As for this Author, I liked Sports Car Racing, such as IMSA, Trans-Am, Formula 1, LeMans, and some Rally Racing. Ted liked his cars big. I liked subcompact sports coupes only-no sedans! I wasn't too happy when the automakers would put bigger engines in some of their pony cars.

Norm was far more conservative. He had a lead foot but was more into luxury cars. He was also into basketball, football, and baseball. He was a Structural Draftsman and was highly skilled in mathematics. Norm was quite delighted with me when he learned of my ill-fated attempt at Track and Field, back in high school. In turn, I provided him and his sons with some tales of my ill-fated attempt that had them rolling.

Norm wasn't too happy with Dad's tirades against me when I wasn't talking by the age of four and a half. However, he tried to persuade Mom to stop Dad from bothering me, rather than to confront him directly.

Raymond, my third-oldest brother, didn't last beyond the opening timeline of this book. He had, by this time, relocated to Toledo and gotten into a wad of trouble due to alcoholism. He was heinously murdered in 1983. The circumstances read like the Kennedy Assassination!

Milt Two went the furthest in terms of education. During the timeline of this book, Milton would go from downright bourgeois to conciliatory. We both liked Jazz. However, Milton liked what I called "Coffeehouse Style Jazz." I'd find out later that the more correct description would've been Free-Form Traditional Style Jazz, that included blokes such as Art Blakey, The Manhattan Transfer, Gene (Brother Jug) Ammons, Eddie Fisher, Julian (Cannonball) Adderley, Arthur Prysock, and William (Count) Basie, whom he saw thanks to Mom!

I, on the other hand, liked Jazz Fusion and Smooth/Light Jazz. Examples of which include Ramsey Lewis, Jeff Kashiwa, Spyro Gyra, Steve Oliver, Dave Koz, and Dave Grusin.

There was some crossover. We both liked The Crusaders, The Rippingtons, David Benoit, and Earl Klugh.

Milt Two, like Ted, also liked hot cars. He was like me insofar as he liked the Z-Car, Camaros, and had himself an Austin America.

Like Ted, Milton also liked Stereo equipment. However, when I took the plunge, Milton thought I was going way too far in terms of the equipment I was getting and why.

Mom relayed a message to me when I told her about my Asperger's Autism. He responded that they were only recently discovering these types of problems. Since I was diagnosed in 2001, he was probably right.

Marciea was the only girl in the family. She had a sweet side, and she had a domineering side! It was she who introduced me to books such as Thor Heyerdahl's Aku-Aku, as well as some fictional works such as

The Pit and The Pendulum, and the Most Dangerous Game. It was Marce who introduced me to the music of Leandro "Gato" Barbieri. I thought that it would be a change of pace before his Caliente album. Once I heard Caliente, I was hooked on Gato for life!

Marce and I initially feuded in a jealous relationship. She initially thought that I was self-indulgent, childish, and cheap. She also felt that I spent my days reading.

When Mom was sick with her first stroke, Marciea, out of nowhere, and for no reason at all, turned her attention towards me and told me: "I'm sick of you and Ted, in your own world!"

However, once Marciea had Olivia, she began to see that there was more to me than what met the eye.

Most importantly, Marciea would insist that I continue to have myself evaluated for autism, and that was long before my bug was ultimately discovered in 2001. Tragically, she would NOT live to see how right she was.

Dwight was the one I had the most issues with. There was no longer the scrapping and fighting as we did as children. However, in terms of philosophies, we were still like the Hatfields and McCoys, pre-2000! He, too, believed it or not, was very domineering, or tried to be. We both liked hot cars. Like Ted, Dwight was strictly a big-inch engine guy, as opposed to my small car philosophy. Dwight liked the idea of putting Chevrolet engines in Ford cars. I detested that idea. In my mind, Chevys should be put in Chevys; Fords should be placed in Fords, and Chryslers should be put in Chryslers. Dwight even proposed putting a Chevrolet 454 into a VW Beetle!

Dwight and Raymond were Rat Rodders, long before the phrase became an accepted part of the motorsports culture. Raymond had a

1948 Ford. It had a classic Flathead engine and a cinderblock for the driver's seat! Dwight, on the other hand, had a 1963 Chevrolet Impala that was sold to him for a bargain basement price of $100! The car ran authoritatively but was severely chewed by rust and/or dents!

Dwight also liked big motorcycles too. I liked my small bikes.

Dwight also liked big motorcycles too. I liked my bikes small. Mikey was the youngest one -and the most supportive of me. That's NOT to say that we didn't have our issues. However, it was Mikey who joined me in my efforts to build rockets and birdhouses. Mikey also liked smaller sportscars. Together, we dreamed up what a punked out Austin America 2-door sedan would've been like-and even drew it up too!

Yes, together, we worked on his mini bike too. Mikey thought that I was too bookish and played too much by the rules. I thought that Mikey was a bit stubborn at times. Then again, he thought the same thing about me. He also thought that I played by the rules too much. For instance: I finally was in the process of forming a song that Mikey might Honey have been able to use. I had listened to Patti Austin's From The Bee , then permutated a few of its notes around while retaining the same key. Patti's song used what sounded like the Common Time Signature, and that was good enough for me as well.

Mikey's Korg synthesizer had four slots for putting voices in. Although I could not put a whole phrase in one of the slots, I used one slot for one word, one slot for my second word; one slot for my third word; and the last slot for the last word. Thus, Honey From the resBee became Fish or Cut Bait! Weeks earlier, there was an annual bill-fishing tournament on the Kona side of the Big Island. During this tournament, it is NOT uncommon to catch large fish such as sailfish, Ahi Tuna, and in this particular case, a 1,069-pound (about 475 kilograms in SI units) Marlin! It took a forklift to hoist the catch and haul it around!

Although the annual bill-fishing tournament was in the back of my mind, there was also a popular expression that people use to refer to those who promise without delivering results. Such people are oftentimes told to "Fish or Cut Bait!"

I had to battle the Korg to finally get a song out of it. Sometimes, the song would linger on a note, then drone on and on. However, I ironed that problem out too. I then decided to record my results on a cassette before the system changed its mind. Thankfully, it didn't.

I proudly played my results before Mikey, who, in turn, liked it, but cautioned: "That's great. But now you need to get out of that one-dimensional thinking."

By that, Mikey wanted to hear other voices added to what I had. Then an argument ensued. I told Mikey: "How the (H) am I going to be able to put in a bass line when I don't even know the Bass Clef?"

Mikey, in a seemingly simplistic manner, responded: "Man, you

shouldn't worry about the Bass Clef. It's all C. It's not like you're go into a whole different dimension or something." The next morning, I was once again back at work trying to program in a bass line for Fish Or Cut Bait. Once again, I had to deal with the synthesizer sticking on a note. However, I wrestled with it, and was able to give Mikey a finished product a couple of nights later. Mikey liked it, but now, I was tearing my hair out trying to convert the synthesized trumpet waveform I used to a waveform sounding close enough to the Alto Saxophone that Mikey used. I felt I needed to do that to give Mikey a model for what Fish or Cut Bait would sound like.

At that point, I would be projected into a whole new and unexpected world.

I told Mikey: "Now if I can just get the waveform to sound like a sax."

Mikey gruffly retorted: "Now there you go again, always following the rules!"

At that precise moment, Mikey stormed over to a sax stand containing his Alto Sax and picked it up. He then had me turn on the synthesizer and had me play Fish or Cut Bait. He would accompany the part that the trumpet synthesizer was covering.

I got Mikey to go to Middle C and above staff, rather than lower to Middle C, and the results sounded very good. Then, something delightfully strange happened. I had the lead instrument "lay-out" or pause during a bridging section I had programmed in. However, Mikey played through that bridge, using improvisational riffs so slick that I had no idea he could do it, and no idea even how to step-write in!

Then it was back to the melody line!

Even back at the melody line, Mikey was finding ways to stick improvisational riffs into the body of the song. Delightfully, these riffs followed the form of the song in ways I could NOT have conceived.

There was a part I added, towards the end of the song, that contained nothing but percussion. Remember! I had NO idea that Mikey could perform the type of improvisational grooves that he was doing; yet the grooves fit seamlessly into this section! Fish or Cut Bait had taken on a life of its own-a life I never could've dreamed about in my wildest dreams!

Mikey and I were both getting off on Fish or Cut Bait. But the next step was to print it. In a twinkling, Mikey turned on the tape recorder, and we were at it again!

This time, the synthesizer didn't stick, and I yelled: "That's it!"

I did it. It took me nearly four months to learn how to put a piece together, and about a week or so to complete it. But now my attention was on Mikey and those amazing improvisational riffs.

I asked Mikey: "How were you able to do that? I wouldn't have even been able to think of programming the stuff you were able to do in!"

Mikey said: "It's all about feeling. There's this Japanese dude down at CJ's, I work with sometimes. Believe me! He knows everything there is to know about music-all that technical stuff! He can do it. He can play it, write it, score it, mix it, produce it-all kinds of (Sugar-Tea)! You name it! He's a whiz at all that technical (Sugar-Tea)! But he doesn't deliver that feeling, and that's what music is about-feeling!"

Meanwhile, I was so awestruck by what I finally accomplished that I couldn't see, for obvious reasons, the Glass Monolith that lay ahead of me.

Mikey then said, "That piece is good, but it's more of a Jazz-oriented piece. What I was looking for was something along the lines of Dance Music."

I surely thought Mikey and I would follow in the footsteps of Moon and Jerry in the studio for a final cut. However, it was not to be. Although I intended to have a vocoder in the bridge section, Mikey was not convinced that he could sell the piece as a Dance song. I must take some culpability here, too. I had toned down the hand claps sound to prevent listener fatigue. In the final piece, I should've added extra hand claps to convey that the piece was meant to be danced to think about it. Seven strong-willed siblings and two strong-willed parents. You have all the ingredients for overload.

My Health

Asperger's Syndrome is classified as a MAJOR medical problem. Therefore, you can imagine the fireworks being generated because of all the testing I had done on myself during my childhood. Some persons even suggested that I be carted off to the proverbial "booby-hatch!"

Oddly, I was experiencing chest pains during training as an Operator in 1987. I felt sore in the chest above the heart. I would rub the sore area. Princess was concerned. I assumed that if there were any real problems, I would not have passed the medical examination I was given days before.

I had a variety of medical tests in 1992. Those tests included a complete psychological evaluation at the University of Chicago. There were all types of tests: cognitive, memory, and storytelling. As for the inkblot, there was always a blot that looked like a Surinam Toad! I had them before, but never this exhaustive. Since the psychological evaluation was also recommended by Professor Chung's friends at the University of Chicago, it fit right in!

It took about a month or two to get the results of that evaluation. However, when I did get the results, I went in and got a considerable shock.

The resident psychologist felt that I should be taking psychoactive medications. Even more insidiously, the resident psychologist recommended anti-psychotic drugs or mood stabilizing drugs!

At that point, I pointed out that when I was a child, I was already on psychoactive medications. I recall an orange-brown medicine I took. The most insidious side effect I noticed was that I was experiencing SKY-HIGH fevers, and prolonged sleeping! Of course, what else could I do when I had the sky-high fevers?

I told the resident psychologist that I regard psychoactive medications as highly dangerous. Not only was that based on my experience, but also my observation. I saw and heard about too many people who engaged in behaviors more bizarre than the original illness. Those behaviors could include histrionics, boomerang effects, or even, in some cases, death! Certainly, there were times when I was on that stuff, when I thought I was dead! I was completely in black for several hours!

Neither the resident psychologist nor his assistant was buying. They shook their heads and told me to at least try these drugs in the short term.

Part of the resident's reasoning lay in the answers on a test I took, as part of the evaluation. That test was the Minnesota Mental, and I forget the rest of it. Anyhow, this test had a series of thoughts or statements. If you agreed with them, you answered yes. If you don't, you answered no. There was NO varying degree of agreement or disagreement.

I was bothered by two things during this review. First off, I was effectively told that I was one step from the "puzzle-factory"! Second, who do these psychoactive medications really benefit? I know of no pharmaceutical manufacturer who is strapped for money! That includes those who manufacture psychoactive drugs. The resident psychologist cautioned me against my using the term "drugs" because these medications might be confused with street drugs! The resident psychologist made another point for me.

Does it really make any difference if it is sold on 119th Street or sold to a pharmacy? If it is a psychoactive drug, it will be harmful in some way.

My mind harkens to the American Broadcasting Company's failed attempt to compete with Saturday Night Live. ABC's effort was called Fridays! What attracted me to the show was that the cast could do almost exact impersonations of many popular figures of the day, such as Senator Edward Kennedy of Massachusetts!

What I also found noteworthy, as well as funny, about Fridays was a cast member named Mark Blankfield. He did a skit that underscores another problem with psychoactive drugs.

For instance, Blankfield would play a pharmacist who was "using up the profit!" Also, his most noteworthy line was: "Take a pill! Take a pill!"

This Author holds that the drug addicted pharmacist, in the short-lived and defunct comedy series Fridays, underscores what is wrong with society today, particularly American society! Every time someone has a problem, the prevailing answer seems to be "Take a pill-Take a pill!" As for any issues that may cause the mental illness, those issues are merely masked over or ignored!

Ironically, we Americans drop our jaws when school-age children and teenagers become addicted to alcohol and other mood-altering substances!

Another concern that This Author has always had with psychoactive drugs is that bizarre, unusual, and barbarian means have been historically implemented in the treatment of mental illness. Those means included various racks and machines, Electro-Convulsive Therapy, and drugs! I must ask: Just who do these psychoactive drugs serve? Is it the patient, or is it a society or decision-maker that doesn't want some person who doesn't fit in around?

I hold that it is the latter!

It is essential that anyone reading this chapter watch the movie, The Fifth Floor! For the uninitiated, an innocent victim had a Mickey slipped into her drink after she had her heart broken. She was then mistaken for someone who was suicidal and committed to a mental institution! I found that movie so frightening because I came perilously close to being that victim.

Sometimes, you can have thoughts such as these, without consciously realizing that you have thoughts such as these. However, with these thoughts, I politely told the resident psychologist where to go and what to do with psychoactive medications!

The Operator's Lounge, at that time, was so clogged with cigarette smoke that my sensitive lungs could NO longer handle it. I was still coughing with very little provocation. Even more insidiously, anything from perfume to the smell of Lady Ditka's coffee in the Training Room was sufficient to send me into a coughing frenzy. Fortunately, there was a lounge to the north of the Operator's Lounge that was quieter and relatively smoke-free. I took my breaks in there.

Unfortunately, one morning, there was a mixed group of Black and White people that had gathered at one of the tables in the lounge. They all had a large pizza and were digging in. I simply kept on with my magazine. About two to five minutes into my break, a very big, burly, bearded White man yelled: "We're having a meeting of the Just Imagine Committee!"

I must reiterate how much of a coward I was because I did NOT respond to them directly in any way. I simply left that lounge. I did, however, report the incident to Pat Schwartz. She was of little help. Instead, she said: "Direct Marketing doesn't like Operators using their lounge. They think Operators are on the low end of the totem pole.

While my situation at work was stabilizing, my state of health was, in Lady Ditka's words, "giving me the flux"! Lady Ditka already knew of my coughing episodes. They were so bad that anything from Lady Ditka's perfume to the smell of Lady Ditka's coffee was sufficient to send me into a coughing frenzy!

One episode was severe enough to send me to the Emergency Room! However, when a lady ER physician asked me whether I was using Prednisone, my response was that I wanted to avoid using that evil drug at all costs. She then chided me for not committing to improving my health. Her attitude towards me was that I had no business being in the Emergency Room.

The following night was even more insidious. Mom had fried a delicious meal of catfish with a side of spaghetti. The catfish was fresh because I was with Mom when the butcher at the fish market beheaded the things. Therefore, the fish was not old at all.

Nevertheless, I broke out in an intense itch on my arms. That itch soon turned into an all-out rash. Then, my forearms swelled. The worst was yet to come.

Soon, I noticed a lump on my right cheek that itched. Mom, however, insisted that I merely try to relax.

A few minutes later, I returned to my basement den. When I looked in the bathroom mirror, I noticed that my entire head and face had ballooned to the size of a large softball or basketball, nearly doubling in size!

Like an idiot, however, I failed to go back to the Emergency Room that night. I needed to. I didn't want to have to put up with that snippy ER physician. Therefore, I just suffered.

Meanwhile, back at work, the chronic coughing spells would also plague me. Joyce Brewster, one of the Service Assistants, was friendly enough to show me how I could prevent coughing in the customer's ear by hitting a certain button. The problem was that the same button that prevented offending the customer also prevented me from hearing the customer whenever he/she had necessary details. Therefore, I used that key with the greatest of reluctance.

Stac, being an old-school type of conservative, believed that most cases of Asthma were strictly psychological in nature. She cited the example to a friend on how a granddaughter of her's tried to get her way by threatening an Asthma attack. Stac said she promptly spanked the girl and dared her to carry out her threat!

What was most insidious about me were the chronic, hacking, coughing spells I was now having. The coughing spells were so bad that Ms. Cole gave me a box of cough drops for posting an error-free observation!

Dr. Herzon did a CT scan of my sinuses. His diagnosis was that I needed surgery. But before I was to have surgery, I was to have a Mandatory Second Opinion for health insurance reasons. That second opinion said "No". While all of that was going on, the stress of the impending surgery was setting off chest pains. So, Dr. Herzon chose to put the surgery off for a while.

Insomnia

What was NOT so comical was a series of sleep disorders I was experiencing. In fact, I was so concerned about the problem that I consulted NU Medical's Sleep Disorders Center in the Fall of 1990.

Once there, I met with Dr. Phyllis Cheung. She was an expert on the subject. After an initial interview, she conducted a complete upper body exam and a complete neurological exam on me. Almost immediately, Dr. Cheung suspected that I may have been experiencing depression. She scheduled a sleep study on me. In the interim, she put me on a very effective medication. However, it would take me 30-35 minutes to open my eyes the following morning. I also felt like lead going down to the washroom to wash up in the morning. The medication solved my failure to get to sleep, but did nothing for my daytime drowsiness problem.

I was afraid of my sleep problems because I was on a job where I thought daytime drowsiness would be fatal to my job! Dr. Cheung, at one point, even thought I was obsessive, and gave me some medication for it. However, I was leery of psychoactive medications because of what I call a boomerang effect. Some psychoactive medications can also be very dangerous.

Dr. Cheung did, however, have some friends at the University of Chicago Sleep Disorders Center. I met with two of their staff physicians in late Fall 1990. The University of Chicago Sleep Disorders Center conducted a more comprehensive Sleep Study than even NU Medical did. That study would cover two nights and the following day!

There was already a strong bite in the air that late Fall evening in 1990. Fortunately, my car was up to the task. I was also a hop, skip, and a jump from work. Therefore, there was no problem getting to the University of California.

By this time, I knew the drill. I arrived early, showered, changed into my bedclothes, then was hooked up to an EKG and clothespin Oxygen sensor on my finger. This time, however, I would also be hooked up to a bar-like device that went across my chest. This would check my breathing and was called a Polysomnogram.

At that point, it was lights out, at least, until one of my electrodes fell off! That occurred frequently throughout the night.

The next day, I went home, then returned to U of C the following night. Although there would be no bar across my chest, the drill would be the same. I had virtually no episodes of electrodes falling off of me throughout the night.

The next morning, I had a different technician meet me. He was Black and male. However, he was not one of those types who was menacing to me in any way. He cautioned me not to go home yet. Come to find out, I was to take a series of monitored naps throughout the day. There were times when I slept very peacefully-until that blasted helicopter would take off and land! That interrupted my sleep. There were times when I would not go to sleep at all!

The technician knew it and could even record everything that went on with me.

Ultimately, the two sleep studies I took added to Dr. Cheung's suspicion that I may have been experiencing Clinical Depression, or as I called it, Clinical D!

Additional Medical Concerns March 1993 would bring additional medical concerns. For instance, Al Bennett was upset with me for my written ultimatum against Shellie. Paradoxically, Al Bennett was also concerned about my health. I had an episode where I experienced momentary faintness during my last break. She stopped my work to ask how I was doing the next day. She worried about the startling episodes that I was having. And she concurred with Ms. Williams over whether the job was getting to me. Therefore, Al conferred with me and asked me for permission to submit to a Medical evaluation.

At first, I thought that it was over the top. Then, I relented because at least I could explain to Medical about findings concerning my Functional Hypertensive Dysphonia. With those thoughts in mind, we set the date for the evaluation for late May 1993.

Now that I am back to work again, I was sent a letter from Medical. That letter gave details about my Medical Evaluation that I agreed to. It was now late May. I was too fast for a full 12 hours before arriving. I would not need to go to work. However, I would get a full day's pay if I kept my appointment.

A couple of weeks later, I got another reminder to go for an appointment. But it wasn't with the Doctor. It was with a company-appointed psychiatrist! She, too, was worried about the company's concern that I was becoming a time bomb! I had a hard sell to convince the Psychiatrist otherwise. However, she was satisfied that I was NOT the time bomb the company feared it had. I am sure that if I were such a time bomb, she I would've recommended that I not go back to work, or perhaps I would have petitioned for my termination!

Two more weeks later, I made another return to the company doctor. Although only basic vitals were taken, the doctor merely interviewed me to "determine my mood."

At first, I thought that it was over the top. Then, I relented because at least I could explain to Medical about findings concerning my Functional Hypertensive Dysphonia. With those thoughts in mind, we set the date for the evaluation for late May 1993.

Meanwhile, I was prompted to see an allergist for my allergies. Dr. Eugenia Grasser was NO longer in the Northwestern Medical system. Therefore, I needed a new allergist. Through my internist, I was referred to Leslie Grammer, M.D.

Dr. Grammer's student allergists conducted a fairly good evaluation on me. However, it was not as comprehensive as I expected. She knew of my Cough-Variant Asthma, as well as my Rhinitis. I was also having skin problems at that time. She prescribed Prednisone!

Prednisone, to me, was like a cross to Dracula! Recall that I had a book called The Pill Book. In the book, it described the wicked, serious, and sometimes even fatal side effects of Prednisone! I wanted to avoid that stuff at all costs.

However, Dr. Grammer's students scoffed at what I stated. The student who worked with me even noted that some people would die without Prednisone. With that, I was given a sheet that described the drug, how to take it, and when to take it.

In the meantime, I was scheduled for a second Sinusostomy in three years. My first Sinusostomy was concurrent with the extraction of four wisdom teeth! I wanted one knockout and one hurt to do for all!

During the week of May 10, 1993, I once again had Pre-Ops. I also had an appointment with my Urologist, and my allergy shots, along with pre-operative instructions from Herzon. I also told Herzon that I was on Prednisone. Herzon not only understood, but he also suggested a schedule for tapering off that wicked, vile medication without injury. When I called Dr. Grammer, she concurred with Herzon.

I would be fortunate enough to have all of these appointments scheduled on one single day!

First came my Pre-Ops. I was fortunate enough to have the same person take blood from me who took the blood during my pre-op for my first Sinusostomy. He knew me very well. Next came the Anesthesiologist. Then, I had my other Pre-Ops at Herzon's office, and I had my Urologist's appointment that afternoon.

Mom said that she couldn't deal with what she went through when she accompanied me to surgery the first time. Therefore, she had Milton take me to the surgery. He agreed to it. On a bright, sunny May 18th, Milton pulled up in his van. Meanwhile, Mom was fussing at me because I chose to wear Mexican-style Huaraches and bare feet, rather than heavier shoes and socks. However, the Pre-Operative Instructions specifically stated that I should dress in a manner that I could easily dress and undress. This, I did.

Milton got me down to NU Medical on time. In a twinkling, I was in surgical garb. Once again, I was on a gurney while a nurse attempted to insert a tube that would eventually be my IV. When I asked her if she got it, she became a little salty with me as if she disapproved of my asking. I didn't think to tell her that I had rolling veins-making it difficult to find and hit the vein for that purpose.

I also presented a letter from Herzon about the Prednisone I was tapering off from. I was to give this letter to the anesthesiologist One aspect of my Glass Monolith had always been that I would forget some things, to remember other things! In this case, I remembered to bring that letter. However, I completely forgot to bring the canister of the Albuterol that I was taking, like an idiot! Would the surgery be messed up because of it?

Fortunately, the answer was no. In a twinkling, a student anesthesiologist had a canister of Albuterol on hand. Before I took the hit of Albuterol, I was prompted to ask whether it would defeat the purpose of the anesthesia, since I knew that Albuterol can keep a person awake. The anesthesiologist allayed my concern and again prompted me to take the hit.

The IV medications were started. The anesthesiologist produced a syringe that he would add to my IV. He told me that Dr. Herzon was delayed, so he would add the medication while we were waiting for him to finish with another patient. According to him, I would start feeling sleepy.

I was fully conscious when they all started rolling me into the Operating Room. To my surprise, however, they didn't roll me into the Operating Room. Instead, they rolled me into my room! I was done already!

I experienced no fade or flash to white, unlike during my first surgery! I experienced absolutely NO feeling of drowsiness or sleepiness! I experienced NO fade to black. I experienced NO discontinuity in my consciousness whatsoever! For a surgery, that's fine! However, my concern is that some knucklehead might, someday, try to steal the powerful anesthetics used in my surgery for illicit purposes. I am thinking of such purposes as date, or acquaintance rape-hetero or homosexual, pedophilia, or robbery!

Milton was present when they rolled me into my room. Therefore, he would bear witness to a couple more things I'd experience. For starters, I experienced seeing two satellites flying around my head, the way two electrons may fly around a Helium nucleus! Milton would also bear witness to seeing me puke! Fortunately, I felt it coming on. I then motioned for Milton to get a nearby wastebasket. Once I got the wastebasket, I was then able to throw up without creating unnecessary work for NU Medical's Custodial Department!

After Milton telephoned Mom to let me know I was alright, he left me with one issue of Sports Illustrated and one issue of Road and Track, then left for home. Meanwhile, a svelte, statuesque figure walked into my room with red stiletto-heeled pumps. That figure turned out to be Dr. Grammer herself. I was in Post-Op, and although my transition wasn't particularly smooth, I was glad to have at least advanced to the Post-Operative phase. A couple of hours after Dr. Grammer left, Dr. Herzon came in. He, along with several students in tow, visited me. It was then that I would learn that I would once again need to stay at NU Medical overnight.

Just as before, I had packing inside my nose where the Sinusostomy took place. Unfortunately, the packing fell out over several hours.

Those several hours weren't the most comfortable hours of my life. For starters, I still wasn't very comfortable. Secondly, I felt my heels ache, apparently from lying on my back for so long. Most insidiously, I felt as if I had lost all feeling in my back. I thought something was terribly amiss. Fortunately, I had a very capable young, White, Male Nurse Practitioner who not only saw to the problem, but also kept my Mom apprised of my condition. Come to find out, I was so congested that I could NOT go home right away.

I got up to urinate and couldn't! Fortunately, I had strong pelvic muscles that were able to will my bladder to get it out! If I had it to do all over again, I would've summoned the Nurse's Station!

As the night wore on, my packing eventually fell out. I was also experiencing a mild fever, 101°F (about 34°C). Fortunately, I had a nurse of Filipino extraction, by the name of Pirie, who promptly took care of these issues. Since I had vital signs taken all night and an already established history of sleep disorders, it would be well into the morning before I could finally get any sleep at all. However, I eventually did get some.

At about 9 AM, a White, full-figured, tall nurse walked in and told me that I would be sprung before long. I still had to go for my Post-Op with Dr. Herzon across the street.

Once again, the nurse at Otolaryngology saw me and offered me pain medication. I declined pending the approval of Dr. Herzon.

I was lucky this time. There weren't as many rocks that Dr. Herzon had to pick out of my nose as last! It was almost worth the trouble to have the work done the second time around.

I had to go back to my room and floor after I concluded my post-op to sign the discharge papers. Once that was done, I shook hands with the nurse and went back to my pick-up point, where Ted awaited. Once again, I had to be driven home, where Mom hastened me to bed. Since I was on vacation this time, there was no immediate worry about time lost from work. However, any talk about seeing the New Orleans Grand Prix again, was just that-talk!

Now that I was back to work again, I was sent a letter from Medical. That letter gave details about my Medical Evaluation that I agreed to. It was now late May. I was to fast for a full 12 hours before arriving. I would not need to go to work. However, I would get a full day's pay if I kept my appointment.

A Nurse that took vitals, then had me wait in one of several examination rooms met me. That same nurse was quite impressed when I told her that I had a Sinusostomy a scant three weeks prior. When she took my blood pressure, she noted possible White-Coat Anxiety. Soon, I would meet the company physician, an upper middle aged lady of Polish-American extraction. It was then that I found out why I was referred to Medical in the first place. That reason was that the Middle Office was very worried about having a time-bomb in their midst-that time-bomb, being, me! The company doctor and I discussed these issues and why they were affecting me. Then, the examination began.

The doctor rechecked my blood pressure and found it to be within normal limits. The nurses were quite nice during this time. I had fasted, per the instructions of the letter. They really had fun taking blood from me. Remember! I still had rolling veins! Fortunately for them, they had a Vacu-tac device that sucked blood out. This consisted of a vacuum-sealed vial that was opened when I got the dart. As a result, blood rushed into the vial to fill the vacuum. Next came the all-important Urinalysis and Blood Screen, although they acknowledged my total abstinence. As for the EKG, they used clothespins and conductive tape for leads! After the Chest X-ray, I was done. I didn't even tell Mom about it.

A couple of weeks later, I got another reminder to go for an appointment. But it wasn't with the Doctor. It was with a company-appointed Psychiatrist! She, too, was worried about the company's concern that I was becoming a time bomb! I had a hard sell to convince the Psychiatrist otherwise. However, she was satisfied that I was NOT the time bomb the company feared it had. I am certain that if I were such a time bomb, she would've recommended that I NOT go back to work, or perhaps, would have petitioned for my termination!

Two more weeks later, I made another return to the company doctor. Although only basic vitals were taken, the doctor merely interviewed me to "determine my mood."

During my return visit to the company-appointed Psychiatrist, she and I both agreed that the best tack to take would be to see the very Psychiatrist that Dr. Cheung recommended earlier.

My coughing episodes returned in early 1996 with a vengeance.

It was at that time that I was getting harassed by management in such petty ways, such as my keystrokes, phraseology, or work time, that I was drawing suspensions.

I was also coughing more intensely as I asked how long my suspension would be. Come to find out, it would be a three-day suspension. I continued to cough when Ducky #2 said, "Go home."

Another health scare occurred just before I was to start at Underwriters Laboratories in 2000. Oddly, instead of a "Company Doctor," there would, instead, be an Industrial Nurse who would conduct my physical. At this juncture, it was important to make sure that all explicit directions were followed, since a drug screen had to be conducted. However, Sally, the lady I met at Oakton, explained all of that to me when she phoned me.

The Industrial Nurse was thorough and conscientious. That proved problematic. She turned up a problem that threatened to become, yet another Glass Monolith.

She asked: "Have you ever had an Electrocardiograph before?"

The Industrial Nurse turned up a blip that could've indicated Pericarditis! She stated that the danger in Pericarditis is that if it is left untreated, it could lead to Congestive Heart Failure! At first, I thought that my slight movement of my head forward might have disrupted the readings. However, the Industrial Nurse ruled that out.

I was concerned. Recall that I had some chest pains back in 1984 that felt as if one of my ribs had locked with another one. That was at Alpha Metals. When I was taken to the clinic, I was told that I might have had a heart abnormality that was common to Blacks. Even this doctor ruled out heart trouble, however.

Now, was it Déjà Vu-plus an unexpected Glass Monolith?

I was told that I would need a clearance from another doctor before I could be approved for starting work!

After my physical, I met with Sally and was formally offered the job. To which, I softly answered "I ACCEPT". I then blazed out of Underwriters Laboratories to see what I could do about that abnormal reading. Once I got past O'Hare Airport, getting from Underwriters to Christ Hospital's Vocational Services unit took me only a matter of minutes.

Shortly after I started out at Underwriters Laboratories, I was making a myriad number of operational errors, despite my best efforts at correcting them. I was even written up for the errors. However, I knew I was on medication, and wondered if the medication was contributing, in part, to the errors. I visited at least two websites about the side effects of Claritin. BOTH of those sites described MEMORY LOSS as a possible side effect. "Could this be the reason why I would have a problem with my work performance?" I thought.

I paid a visit to the Industrial Nurse to find out further.

According to the Industrial Nurse, it was not common for Claritin to cause the memory drop-offs that I was experiencing. However, it was more than possible for the drop-offs to occur.

After I conferred with the Industrial Nurse, I paid a visit to Rich's office, along with the necessary proof. Rich was skeptical at first; however, given the magnitude of the problem, he begrudgingly gave me the benefit of the doubt.

I stopped taking the Claritin in the following days after my conference with the Industrial Nurse. The operational errors, while not coming to a screeching halt, also diminished in number. In fact, I would be working on a couple more projects that Rich had in mind. Rich ultimately liked my work.

I also took Underwriters Laboratories up on its network of professionals that help employees deal with personal problems.

It was here that I discovered that there was a psychologist/counselor who had an office that was just a few blocks from NU Medical! I was sold on him for simplicity's sake.

It was here that I got an unexpected revelation.

According to him, the experiences and events I was experiencing at UL that caused Rich to write me up were actually the delayed effects of Norman's Death!

Sometimes, I Got It Right

Mom would occasionally beam when she thought of the time that I took her to a double bill with B.B. King and the Spinners back in 1974. This concert had something for both of us: B.B. King for Mom; the Spinners for me! The Ramsey Lewis -Sarah Vaughn concert of 1989 represented the potential for a delightful case of deja-vu!

But not so fast! Although Mom loved Sarah Vaughn, and until the seventies, liked Ramsey Lewis too, the stroke that sent Mom to the hospital in October 1987 was now causing her trepidations as to whether she could, or would be able to, attend another concert. What concerned Mom the most was the possibility of another incident that required immediate medical attention. Mom raised an excellent point.

Fortunately, the David Benoit-Lee Ritenour concert came about two weeks prior, giving me an opportunity to get the lay of the land.

More specifically, Ravinia had an infirmary on campus. The infirmary assured me that in a case like Mom's, that they were more than capable of handling a sudden medical emergency, such as a stroke, until help arrived. The nurse was quite nice about accommodating me when I inquired to boot.

I also tried to arrange with the nurses to have my allergy shot administered at Ravinia's infirmary. Dana thought that I was out of my tree until I explained a secondary motive. That motive was to have the nurses meet my mother. Then, Dana commended me for contemplating taking Mom to Ravinia to see the double bill in the first place

Now that Mom's potential Glass Monolith was broken, before it was even cast, I immediately purchased two tickets from a still open Ravinia Box Office for the Ramsey Lewis-Sarah Vaughn double bill.

Author's Side Note:

I will always remember Mom for the time she put one over on my butt-but good!

I was a fan of Ramsey Lewis, (whom I considered to be The New Chairman of The Board). Give me a pile of dirty dishes, or a dirty kitchen, and now I had the perfect excuse to listen to a Smooth/Light Jazz record, or two. I failed to realize that I liked Smooth or Light Jazz, more than I knew about Smooth or Light Jazz!

Ten years prior, I had just purchased Ramsey Lewis's More Sounds of Christmas and put the 33 1/3 LP on the turntable. Then, I started cleaning the kitchen. In an instant, I heard a very heavy voice singing words to what I thought was a strictly instrumental piece by Ramsey Lewis.

I craned my head towards Mom, and interrogatively shrieked: "You know the words?"

Mom replied: "Why of course!" "That's Snowbound!" "You should hear Sarah Vaughn sing it!"

Ten years after Mom fixed my clock, it appeared that I would get a chance to see and hear what Mom was talking about!

There was also an interesting series of events at Midway Drive. For starters, the Queen Bee noticed that I lived closer to the South Suburban Remote #2 office than I did to even Chicago Southwest #1, or even Midway Drive. With those thoughts in mind, she asked me if I would go on loan to South Suburban Remote #2. I accepted. After all, I still had a civil rapport with the Queen Bee.

It just so happened that the very first day that I started at South Suburban Remote #2 was the very evening of the Ramsey Lewis-Sarah Vaughn double bill! I wouldn't have a Glass Monolith to run into. However, I would have one long, challenging day!

My week with South Suburban Remote #2 would send me into a whole new world that I would not have expected from an Operator's office. There were cubicles. However, each of the cubicles was very neat, very decorated, and very personalized. It was very common to have family pictures decorate each of the cubicles. Not surprisingly, eating and drinking at the positions, one of my pet peeves with Operators, was NOT going to happen here.

What would happen at South Suburban Remote #2 would be that I would see some of my old pals from South Suburban Remote #1. Then, there was a Bible-slinging kook there. Although there was a Bible-slinging Operator at Midway Drive, this one was a little more fanatical.

It wasn't until between my first break and lunch that I met my Group Chief Operator for South Suburban Remote #2. She was White, with blonde hair. She was slightly taller than me. She wore a white shift with red candy stripes. She wasn't bad looking as Group Chief Operators went.

I only had one caution about the strength of my voice, then never again throughout my entire week at South Suburban Remote #2. The rest of my first day there would be uneventful. That was more than I could say for when I got off work that first day! I made a mad dash to my car, then rushed home and jumped into the basement shower.

Although the concert would be at an outdoor venue, Ravinia's Pavilion was, nonetheless, a classy place, as was the rest of the campus. In fact, even picnickers choosing to hear the concert, rather than to see the concert, would light candelabras and dress to the nines. I couldn't bear the thought of going without showering for this extra special event.

Meanwhile, Mom was already dressed and ready to go. As soon as I jumped out of the shower and into a change of clothes, I jumped on the Tri-State Tollway at 127th Street and Cicero Avenue. Forty-five minutes later, we would be involved in the bumper-to-bumper traffic that comprised Ravinia's attendees that evening. My car almost stalled while we waited in that bumper-to-bumper traffic. Fortunately, I was able to relight the engine before things got any worse.

Now that Mom was safely inside Ravinia's Pavilion, I took time out and ate at one of Ravinia's several outdoor cafes. This was a cash-and-carry café with picnic tables. My hoagy and cheesecake would be all the dinner I would need for this night.

It was shortly after I rejoined Mom in the Pavilion that the concert started. First up was Ramsey Lewis. I had seen him so many times that his show was now standard fare, old hat, so to speak. He did do something different for his finale. At that time, he had an all-new album out called Classic Encounters. Lewis did a track from that album called

290

With a Gentle Touch. What I liked about his choice of track was that Ramsey Lewis used a very convincing string ensemble synthesizer! Mom found the synthesizer very pleasant.

I took another short break at intermission, then rejoined Mom. I turned towards her and told her, "Now comes your half of the show!"

Judging by the predominance of old-timers at the Pavilion that night, I would say that most of those in attendance were waiting to see and hear "The Divine Miss Sarah!" They'd get their wish.

Mom, however, would be left justifiably dumbfounded! Sarah Vaughn would walk out to a very high barstool with a back on it. There, she would sit and sing throughout her portion of the show. Meanwhile, a rhythm guitarist, a drummer, keyboards, and a bassist would accompany Sarah Vaughn. That bassist had the oddest Bass Viol that I would ever see!

When you think Bass Viol, you'd think of a monstrous instrument that has a large, bulbous chamber at the bottom of it. However, this Bass Viol had the bulbous chamber missing. It was an electronic Bass Viol! It was still tall; it still had the long spike at the bottom of it; and it still had those fat strings that characterized Bass Viols. Fortunately, Sarah Vaughn's band also had someone that could play that Bass Viol-magnificently!

I would hit one Glass Monolith -even at Ravinia! When I ordered my tickets for the Ramsey Lewis -Sarah Vaughn show, I inquired about getting them both to perform Snowbound Ramsey Lewis on keyboards; Sarah Vaughn on the vocals. I offered to pay extra for having them do the piece together. Alas, this epic performance was not to be.

The Ramsey Lewis/Sarah Vaughn double bill at Ravinia ended delightfully. Although Mom still liked the B.B. King -Spinners double bill better, this one was not short-stopping either. Our trip home was rather interesting-even though I missed a turn of that I needed to get me back to the Tri-State. I decided to continue down Green Bay and, eventually, Sheridan Roads, for the ride back home.

Sheridan Road, from Wilmette north to Lake-Cook Road, was very poorly lit. Therefore, Sheridan Road was a downright spooky-high beam or not! Combine a very dark, single lane per direction Sheridan Road, with numerous twists and turns, and you've got one problematic route in which to drive. Fortunately, once we reached Wilmette, Sheridan Road would prove more beautiful than problematic.

Mom would wind up receiving a bonus. Mom always wanted to see the Bahai Temple. She got her wish, albeit only through a drive-by. We also passed by Northwestern University in Evanston. There, I attempted to take a three-course battery of Physics in a matter of just eight weeks! Mom reiterated that what I did was not only crazy, but unnecessary!

Finally, Sheridan Road would lead to North Lake Shore Drive. Although we would not get back home as quickly as we arrived at Ravinia, it would no longer be long. In a twinkling, we got it done. After work the following day, Mom still made it a point to thank me for, in her terms, "a very lovely evening" as I sat down to a plate of her spaghetti.

The Ramsey Lewis-Sarah Vaughn double bill had a special significance. Sarah Vaughn was supposed to have returned to a nightclub called George's in the back of the Merchandise Mart a few months later. She had to cancel out to treat some malignancies that formed on her hands. A few months later, Sarah Vaughn would die of Lung Cancer! Therefore, the Ramsey Lewis-Sarah Vaughn double bill at Ravinia was positively the last concert that Sarah Vaughn would perform in the Chicago area!

I Broke One of Mom's Glass Monoliths

Raymond, my third oldest brother, loved photography and would take pictures of the family's record collection. Mom was looking for a replacement for an album that left the house called "Hymns of all Faiths"

One of the pictures that Raymond took was that Johnny Mathis album! Once I took the magnifying glass to the album, I found out that the title was NOT "Hymns of All Faiths" as Mom originally thought, but instead, was titled Dear Lord.

Mom jumped for joy, saying: "That's it! Dear Lord!"

It was about that time that I learned that the Skokie Public Library would be a source of information on celebrities, such as Johnny Mathis.

Now all I had to do was get the telephone number to the Skokie Public Library.

Lo and behold, I was able to get a mailing address for the Johnny Mathis Fan Club!

Once I got the information I needed, I wrote a letter to him stating that Mom was looking for Dear Lord for years. I figured that the album would be out of print. However, I also figured that Johnny Mathis would have a master copy.

So my plan was relatively simple. I would ask Johnny Mathis to provide me with a copy of his master copy, and I would give it to Mom. I also sent $25.00 to him and a blank VHS-Hi-Fi tape so that he can make a copy of the album.

Author's Side Note:

Before the advent of the Recordable Compact Disc and Digital Audio, any VHS Hi-Fi Stereo tape recorder could double as a high-quality audio tape recorder, provided you could vary the recording level! Remember! Since the rapidly spinning recording heads of a VHS Hi-Fi Stereo tape recorder spun in the same direction as the direction of the tape's movement, the effective recording speed of a VHS Hi-Fi FAR ECLIPSED THE RECORDING SPEEDS OF EVEN THE BEST OF ORDINARY REEL TO REEL TAPE RECORDERS! Since high recording speed is an ABSOLUTE MUST for high fidelity stereo sound, your ordinary VHS Hi-Fi Stereo tape recorder was an Audiophile's dream at that time! This trick also worked for Beta Hi-Fi, as well as Super VHS, or even Super Beta Extended Definition, since they were Hi-Fi recorders, as part of their standards!

As a result, I would now have a copy that would be useless to any thief-unless he had a VHS Hi-Fi Stereo Recorder, and most people "in the hood, still did NOT have such a recorder!"

Johnny Mathis International Fan Club

P. 0 Box 2066 • Burbank, California 91507-2066

April 6, 1993

Jon K. Evans

xxxxdxxxxxxxxxxxxxxxxxx Chicago, IL 60628—6014

Dear Jon Evans:

Thank you for your letter. I'm glad that your mother enjoyed

"Goodnight, Dear Lord".

I'm sorry that I can't be of assistance with the money order. We're not set up in our office to deal with money in any form. Therefore, I'm returning it to you. The best that I can do is to pass it along to Johnny's business office as a donation to one of Johnny's favorite charities. They can use it in this capacity, but can't accept it in any other form, even to deposit or send you a check. If you're interested in this, please let me know. The money would go to one of the following organizations: Childhelp USA, AIDS Project-Los Angeles, American Red Cross, and Union Rescue Mission.

Thank you again for your interest. I'm sorry that I couldn't be of further assistance to you.

Cordially,

Dianna Poling

Correspondence Secretary

Although my plan backfired, Mom still got what turned out to be Goodnight- Dear Lord! Come to find out, Johnny Mathis just happened to have just a handful of his remaining stock of the album on a Metal particle cassette! As for the $25.00 check I sent him for his trouble, he turned it down!

Once I got the cassette from Johnny Mathis, I immediately dubbed a plain-bias copy of it from the Metal Particle tape that Johnny Mathis sent. That way, Mom would always have a copy of it that would be compatible with ANY tape machine she chose to play it on. Mom and I both agreed to keep the Metal Particle copy from Johnny Mathis as a Master copy, and promptly put that copy under Lock and key!

The bottom line was that Mom was so pleased as punch that she promptly excused me from having to worry about having to give her anything for her upcoming birthday, Mother's Day, or even Christmas, that year! But wouldn't it be ironic that I could break Mom's Glass Monolith-but NOT my own!

I must credit Smooth/Light Jazz as a catalyst for bringing Mom and me closer together than we otherwise would have been.

Recall that when Ms. Cole admonished me to give Ducky #2 a chance, she also told me that I would always be a part of her team. That was very evident when I returned to Midway Drive from South Suburban Remote #2. I was off that Sunday, a Sunday that was between pay periods. I got a call that Sunday afternoon. Ms. Cole asked me if I could come in and work from 6 PM to Midnight, a six-hour tour that credited the person working it for eight hours! Duty called. I jumped into my car and arrived at 5:30 PM. Then, I declared it available. I started 1`/2 hour early.

When I arrived, it didn't seem busy at all. In fact, it seemed manageable. What I also found odd was that Ms. Cole admonished me about referring so many calls the minute after I started work.

Still, I had one of the smoothest nights since I returned to the telephone company, and the most profitable! Whenever an Operator was "hauled in" the way I was, that Operator got paid double time. Even if I weren't "hauled in", I still was eligible for time and a half! Then comes the matter of the initial thirty minutes I spent when I arrived. My six hours would ultimately pay me the equivalent of thirteen in straight time! It was just an easy day, or evening, down at the office!

The next day put me in a dilemma. I had to work the next day from 9 AM to 5 PM. Since I did not get off until midnight the night prior, I had to ask, Would I be eligible for a differential, due to a ten-hour span violation? Come to find out, no. Once I accepted the "haul-in," I was told that I effectively waived the span violation.

For good money, getting "hauled in "on my day off was still worth it.

But now I had another dilemma. Sunday always started the work week. I was scheduled from the day after my haul-in until Friday. If I completed the work week as scheduled, I would have earned time and a half for that sixth day! Would I get it?

You can have quite an adventure, without even leaving home!

There was also a series of seminars that were sponsored by Northwestern Memorial Hospital's Health Education Series in the Spring of 1993. These seminars ranged from simple lectures to whole screening examinations, and all points in between! The cost of these seminars ranged from free to $75 US Dollars! The latter case came only if there were complex medical procedures that came along with it.

I would attend Northwestern Medical's seminar on Strokes. I considered Stroke to be a Glass Monolith for Black Americans. Naturally, I would be interested in prevention and treatment options. This seminar also included a screening examination called auscultation. This seminar was free! However, advance registration was required.

I came prepared for the seminar. I drew up a family tree. However, this family tree included everyone in my family who suffered a stroke at some point or another in their lives. That included my grandmother, aunt, cousin, and mother. I included both sides of the family in that family tree. That family tree also discussed the outcome of the incidents they had.

There were two lecturers at the seminar. The first person was a nurse BSN/RN by the name of Kathryn Wirtz. She worked in Neurology. The other one was named Vicki Fahey. She, too, was a BSN/RN. She worked in Vascular. After the lecture, there would be a doctor present to conduct the auscultation.

Ms. Wirtz went first. Briefly, she discussed the window-shade effect common to some strokes and introduced the concept of Transient-Ischemic Attacks (TIAs) or Mini-Strokes. Her contention was that a Transient Ischemic Attack was to be interpreted as a signal to get to an Emergency Room immediately, lest a more serious incident ensue further down the line. Ms. Wirtz also touched on how debilitating Strokes could be in the long-term.

Ms. Wirtz touched on a point I had never heard of prior to the seminar. That point was the "Drawn Window Shade Effect." In a Stroke, or even a Transient Ischemic Attack, vision would sometimes fade out like a drawn window shade. This effect would NOT be the result of opening or closing one's eyelids. Instead, the actual internal eye would momentarily wipe or fade the way some scenes would wipe themselves on movie shows. This effect would be like a drawn window shade!

I could concur with Ms. Wirtz on how debilitating a stroke could be. For instance, my Grandmother, on my father's side, Olivia Coleman Evans, suffered the worst stroke I saw of anyone that suffered a stroke! Her face was distorted-her body, twisted-her speech, ruined. She felt self-conscious about what happened to her, and how I reacted to her when I first saw her after the stroke. I nauseated!

So when Ms. Wirtz lectured, I hung on every word Kathryn Wirtz had to say, so much so that when she concluded and turned the lectern over to Vicki Fahey, I handed Ms. Wirtz my family tree. Ms. Wirtz took a keen interest and told me that she would want to speak to me about it. Meanwhile, Ms. Fahey took over and discussed the role of plaques and Cholesterol in the cause of Strokes. She also clarified that a Stroke need NOT necessarily involve the brain. Instead, it could include blood vessels leading to the brain!

Ms. Fahey, like Ms. Wirtz, touched on groups of people and behaviors most likely to lead to a stroke. Those factors included lack of exercise, diet, cholesterol levels, alcohol consumption, drug use, age, Diabetes (Classical, as opposed to Insipidus), and heredity. Both lecturers noted that Blacks were at a higher risk of contracting a Stroke!

A scant few minutes later, Ms. Wirtz called me out into the hall, and we conferred. She then told me, "You have a hereditary predisposition towards Strokes."

That statement alone was enlightening!

Ms. Wirtz and I engaged in other small talk relevant to the problem of Strokes. Then, we both returned to the lecture hall. At that point, Part

300

Three of the seminar on Strokes was to begin. That was the Auscultation by the doctor who was present.

In an Auscultation, the doctor places a stethoscope up to the neck of the patient. That way, he/she could listen for what are called "bruits" (pronounced "brew-E"). That's French for a racket or a noise. As Ms. Fahey stated, the absence of a bruit does not necessarily rule out the possibility of a stroke because if there is a clot deep within a brain, no auscultation can detect it. Conversely, if a doctor can detect a bruit at ANY TIME, that patient is urged to seek medical attention IMMEDIATELY!

My turn came up. I removed my tie and unbuttoned my top button. Per the doctor's instructions, I held my breath while he listened for a bruit. He could detect no bruit.

All those in attendance got scads of literature on Strokes and the dangers of stroke, so much so that we were all given small bags to put it all in. That included me.

What was most surprising about the Stroke Awareness and The Screening Seminar revealed the demographics of those in attendance. I was the youngest person (age 39 at the time) in attendance. I was also the only Black person in attendance at that seminar!

That thought didn't go wasted just on myself. As the Seminar concluded, an upper-middle-aged to elderly White man commented to me: "Gee! You people are at the greatest risk, and yet, you're the only Black person here this afternoon."

My reason for mentioning the Stroke Awareness Seminar and Screening was that Cerebro-Vascular Disease is one of several Glass Monoliths of Black Americans. When I discovered that this Glass Monolith was present, I effectively could work towards breaking it.

It was late afternoon that day-just shortly after dinner hour. Still, there was light out, and the weather was picture-perfect. Therefore, when I gave Ted my car for the day, he had no problem picking me up from Northwestern Memorial Hospital, or as I called it, NU Medical. Once we got home, both Ted and Mom were more than a little interested in the brochures and literature I obtained from the seminar and screening.

My Pre-Ops ended with the conclusion of that Stroke Screening Seminar. Had I tested positive for a bruit, I would've reported it to Dr. Herzon, and consulted him relative to adjusting the schedule for the Sinusostomy he planned. I was fine. Now, the problem turned towards getting me to and from surgery the next week.

I loved fine cuisine. That led me to take in The Taste of Chicago. Speaking of fine cuisine, I would stir up some controversy in a most humorous way. For instance, Justin Wilson, the famous Cajun Chef, would appear at the Taste of Chicago, or as disk jockey Richard Pegue would call it, Ratfest!

Author's Side Note:

Pegue referred to the Taste of Chicago as "Ratfest" due to the hundreds of tons of garbage that would be produced during the event. Pegue surmised that the rats would have themselves a feast!

Justin Wilson would appear at a special tent at the Taste. WKQX, Chicago's Country Music station, sponsored this exhibition.

I made it a special point to see Justin Wilson. He appeared on Public Television, and he made many of his Cajun dishes for demonstration purposes. I would even tape many of Justin's recipes as he worked. I wanted to be able to make the food if I were to do his type of cooking.

Justin Wilson also taught me some food preparation habits that I consider quite good. For instance, when he fried foods, he used nothing but Olive Oil. Come to find out, Olive Oil is a monounsaturated, or so-called "good fat." I decided that I, too, would use Olive Oil in my cooking. I did cook occasionally. The Super Bowl was one such time of the year that I would give Mom a rest and do the cooking that day, for instance. Justin Wilson also believed in using Onion and Garlic in all of his seasonings.

Justin Wilson would talk about some of his experiences and then pose some questions to the audience. It was at that point that I asked Justin: "What is the difference between Cajun cuisine and Creole Cuisine?"

Justin Wilson responded: "The only difference between Cajun cuisine and Creole cuisine was that the Cajuns had to go out and get all the stuff they needed. The Creoles already had theirs. I'll tell you this! Both kinds of cooking are pretty damn good, I guarantee!"

Mom and Ted were delighted to learn that I met Justin Wilson that afternoon. However, when I told Mom about the difference between Cajun and Creole cooking, Mom took issue with him.

Mom said, "I don't know where he got his information from. The Creoles were just as poor as the Cajuns!"

I still snicker when I think about how Mom reacted when I told her what Justin Wilson told me. In the meantime, Justin Wilson's shows would be a favorite with Ted. However, it wasn't the cuisine Ted liked; it was those TALL TALES he told that exceeded anything that other comedians could tell.

Not All of My Lessons Were Losing Lessons!

Even Midway Drive's Ducky #2 told me that I was a good researcher. If that were indeed true, not only did I save my own life, but I was made aware of a life-threatening, limb-threatening condition that I did well to learn about.

Since I regularly visited NU Medical for my allergy shots, I would stop off and pick up NU Medical's Lifetime of Health newsletter. It was now the Fall of 1993. I just happened to notice that NU Medical was holding a Seminar on circulation in the feet and legs. This seminar included not only a lecture but also a screening examination. That screening examination was similar to the Stroke screening I attended during Pre-Ops for my second Sinusostomy.

What piqued my interest was that when I went to a podiatrist one time, she noticed abnormally weak pulses in my feet. That indicated a potential problem. As a result, I was more than a little interested in this seminar.

Vicki Fahey BSN/RN, the same Nurse Practitioner who co-moderated the Stroke Screening Seminar, moderated the Foot and Leg Circulation Seminar!

This time, Ms. Fahey had a slide show. That slide show introduced the term Peripheral Artery Disease (PAD). Her slide show also very graphically showed the long-term results of untreated PAD. Those results ranged from pain to wholesale gangrene! The ultimate result would, therefore, be the loss of that limb!

Ms. Fahey covered the various types of PAD. Those types ranged from intermittent claudication, characterized by pain on walking, to aortic aneurysms, which cause the main blood vessel leading to the legs and feet to rupture. Once that occurs, bleeding is so quick that death can and does occur within minutes.

What caught my attention was the part of the lecture where Ms. Fahey discussed the risk factors for Peripheral Artery Disease. They were smoking, had a lack of exercise, had high blood pressure, had high cholesterol, had diabetes, had heredity, and used alcohol and/or recreational drugs. Ms. Fahey also mentioned that Blacks and Hispanics were at high risk for Peripheral Artery Disease. I THOUGHT TO MYSELF: "THEY'RE THE SAME AS FOR STROKES"!

I ALSO DISCOVERED THAT THE ETHNIC GROUPS CONSIDERED TO BE AT HIGH RISK FOR PERIPHERAL ARTERY DISEASE AND THE ETHNIC GROUPS CONSIDERED TO BE AT HIGH RISK FOR STROKES, WERE ALSO ONE AND THE SAME!

Nurse Fahey had several assistants on hand to conduct the screening. That screening consisted of the screener placing his/her hand on the veins of the patient's foot. What the screener would look for is the strength of the pulses in the foot. If they were strong or adequate, the result of the screen was considered normal. If the pulses were weak, that was an indicator of trouble.

I had already changed into a pair of shorts and my huaraches for this screening. When the assistant placed her hand on my foot, it was positively dead! She could feel nothing! She said, "I need a consultation here!" In a twinkling, Nurse Fahey came over to me, tested me, and she could also feel nothing.

I let Nurse Fahey know that I had attended the Stroke Screening Seminar back in May 1993, and that I noticed that the risk factors for Strokes and Peripheral Artery Disease appeared to be the same. Nurse Fahey agreed. She also liked the idea of my attending both seminars the way I did.

Obviously, Nurse Fahey and her assistant recommended that I see a doctor about what they found as soon as possible. Given the severity of their findings, I took their advice. My internist, however, thought that the acid test consisted of the Doppler that I learned about during the Seminar. With those thoughts in mind, he set the Doppler up.

It was now mid-November 1993. I went back to NU Medical for the Doppler. There was no preparation necessary for the test, although I did take my shorts and huaraches for ease of disrobing. I soon would lie on a bed while a technician wrapped an oversized blood pressure cuff around my left thigh. When it was pumped up, it felt as if I had a Boa Constrictor wrapped around my thigh! It wasn't particularly uncomfortable, just weird! At that point, a probe was touched to various points along my groin first, and then parts of my leg.

As the test went on, cuffs would be wrapped around my calf and even my big toe. Again, the probe would be touched to several points along the way. Then, the test would be repeated for my right leg.

After my feet and legs were tested, a cuff was then wrapped around both of my arms for a standard blood pressure reading. The only difference was that this time, I would have a sensitive probe, rather than a stethoscope, to take my blood pressure in both arms.

I ultimately tested negative for abnormalities. The test was quick and painless, although having a Boa Constrictor wrapped around one's thigh was an experience I thought to be unusual.

There were two reasons why I was looking forward to 1994. The first reason was that Chicago would, for the first time, be one of several sub-venues for the World Cup Soccer Tournament! Remember! I was a two-time Olympic visitor. Secondly, I saw Olympic Soccer at the Los Angeles Olympic Games of 1984. Thirdly, I was not too long coming off seeing the Chicago Power Indoor Soccer team defend its home carpet, then go on to sweep the Dayton Dynamo out of the Major Indoor Soccer League Finals in Dayton!

Another reason why I looked forward to 1994 was that the late R&B Soul singer, Edwin Starr, mistakenly said: "war has only has one friend; that's the undertaker!" What the late soul singer failed to realize was that an alternative venue to a sporting event would also be a friend of war!

For instance, the World Cup Basketball Tournament was originally scheduled to be held in Belgrade, Yugoslavia. However, Yugoslavia had a despot by the name of Slob Milosevic, who was conducting some "ethnic cleansing." As a result, war ensued. Consequently, FIBA, the sanctioning body for the World Cup Basketball, decided to move the venue for the tournament from Belgrade, Yugoslavia, to Toronto, Ontario!

Toronto, Ontario, was only 513 miles (825 kilometers) east-northeast of Chicago. I was just a ten-hour drive from yet another world-class sporting event. I even had the option of taking Amtrak or Canadian National Railways!

The Summer of 94.

I had so much planned for the Summer of 94 that I had to cut some of it loose. I had the World Cups of Basketball and Soccer. Therefore, when Quinetta, my niece, was about to graduate from high school, I had to let that go due to cost. I didn't have enough money to go around.

By this time, Marciea had left Keith for Hawaii. She grew tired of his pettiness and psychological abuse. For instance, Keith would park the Z-Car he had at a remote location and have Marciea walk a long distance, even though she was in high heels. Speaking of the Z-Car of his, she would pay to have it repaired, yet would not lift a finger to repair her Volkswagen! In Marciea's mind, Keith was a Peter Pan!

Although Marciea was in Hawaii, Quinetta was not happy. She wanted someone from the mainland at her graduation, and as it stood, no one would represent the family. That's where I stepped in.

My idea was to send Mom. I was so quick about sending Mom at the time until I learned that everything on Quinetta's end wasn't finalized. However, when I told Mom that she was to leave for Hawaii two days after I made the reservations, she balked. I had to call Marciea and cancel the whole thing.

Marciea wasn't going to give up that easily. About another two days later, we were able to reschedule Mom's trip to Hawaii in time for Quinetta's graduation. I wired a whopping $600 to Hawaii to pay for Mom's round-trip airfare.

Ted and I hustled Mom off to Continental Airlines and had her on a DC-10 early that morning. However, Ted told me that Mom wasn't ready for such heavy-duty travel. She started shaking, and tremors would set in. Once we got Mom to the terminal, I took the Blue Line back downtown for work. Nevertheless, it was Mission Accomplished, for now!

Once Quinetta completed her graduation, Mom would subsequently make a host of friends at a luau provided by the local hotel where she stayed. Quinetta also stayed by her side. Quinetta was the right person to be with Mom at the right time.

Meanwhile, back at home, I prepared a welcome home meal when Mom flew back in. As luck would have it, my days off coincided with Mom's flight back. I chose to marinate and barbecue a set of boneless, skinless chicken breasts on our grill. Once completed, I then popped the breasts into the refrigerator and waited for Mom to return.

However, Mom had a wrinkle for all of us. She wanted to show us how dreadful airline food was. In this case, she showed us a hoagie and a salad she kept with her. The salad, at least, had croutons.

Mom wasn't enamored of the chicken breasts I barbecued. She complained about the dryness and immediately demanded the ribs she had barbecued and had kept in the freezer during the Memorial Day holiday. She usually liked chicken, and I always cooked boneless, skinless, wasteless, fatless meats, poultry, or seafood. I guessed wrong. However, that was usually par for my course.

But at least I got one issue out of the way, and got Mikey's thanks for getting Mom to Hawaii.

The next issue of the summer was the World Cup. First off, there was the FIFA World Cup of Soccer; that is, if I could get tickets to the FIFA World Cup of Soccer! Believe it or not, the Glass Monolith here was politics!

At the outset, I had to telephone somewhere in Los Angeles to get any information at all, even for the events in Chicago that I was interested in. Then, come to find out, there were published reports that tickets were only being sold in lots of four. Then, I found out that the ticket brokers had the World Cup all sewn up, and they were making a killing on it!

Now that I had a line on tickets to the World Cup, I asked Norman if he would've been interested in going to a World Cup event. Ted was with us at the time. Norman looked at me and said: "Shoo! Not me!"

Norman then turned to Ted and said, "Soccer people are crazy! You should see them, man! They go getting into fights and starting riots-all that kind of stuff. People get killed at those things, man!"

Meanwhile, I cracked up at an unexpected reaction by Norm. I could understand it if I were teasing him. However, I did not expect the type of reaction that Norm exhibited.

Little did Norman know that Chicago was the perfect venue for a soccer event. For one thing, no one was going to show up in Chicago. Let us not forget. Chicago was the venue for the 1968 Democratic National Convention, where the police went on at the Yippies' expense. I also doubt if Mayor Daley (Jr.) would allow any form of disorder or let the city fall victim to embarrassment the way that his father would allow it.

Now that I had settled the issue of getting a ticket, I had to do something about my camera equipment. I had bought a Mamiya 500 DTL Single Lens Reflex camera from Ted; I needed some serious telephoto lenses, not just the 135-millimeter telephoto lens and the 2x teleconverter, which effectively doubled its focal length to 270 millimeters.

Unfortunately, I had to search for lenses for the Mamiya. Since the 500 was manufactured, Mamiya decided to exit the consumer camera market. That meant that I had to chase to the Near West Suburban Oak Park, Illinois, to find some telephoto lenses that would fit my camera. I could see them. However, the camera consultant cautioned that too much tele power was as bad as not having enough. For instance, I would've had to anticipate my shot if I chose the 1,000-millimeter lens I had my eye on. Instead, I decided on a 270 millimeter zoom lens. With my 2x teleconverter, I would still ultimately get 540 millimeters of total focal length when I needed it!

Steve Winkler, one of my co-workers, told me about the lots of fours. I made a bet with him. I bet him that if they indeed came in lots of four, he would get one of the tickets. Although Steve held me to my promise, it didn't turn out that way. Meanwhile, I had to get an early dismissal from work to go to an outfit called 94 Sports Marketing. Once I paid my money, I had to go to the U.S. Soccer Federation in the old 18th Street Historical District to pick up my ticket!

Now, check this letter from 94 Sports Marketing, the outfit that sold me my World Cup Soccer ticket!

May, 1994

Jon Evans   ORDER NUMBER 1165

xxxxxxxxxxxxxxxxxxxxxxxxxxxx

Chicago, IL 60628

Dear Jon Evans

Soon, you and your guests will be joining an exclusive group of people who will witness "Sports History in the Making." For the first time, the World Cup will be played on United States soil, and you will be there live. '94 Sports Marketing has gone to great lengths to ensure that this is a most memorable event for you.

With just a few weeks remaining before the 1994 World Cup begins, you will need to consider your options for obtaining your World Cup USA '94 tickets and package contents. Enclosed is all of the information detailing your options. Please read and follow the instructions carefully.

ADDITIONAL WORLD CUP USA '94 EVENTS

If you have not already reserved your place at the following World Cup events, don't put it off any longer. Tickets are limited, for more information about these events call 1-800-455-KICK.

• The Chairman's Opening Night Gala on Friday, June 17, 1994 at Navy Pier's Grand Ballroom featuring Liza Minnelli, hosted by Alan I. Rothenberg, chairman, president & CEO of World Cup USA 1994, Inc.

•World Cup USA '94 Golf Event on Monday, June 20, 1994 at Medinah Country Club,

Championship Course No. 3.

• Chicago '94 Soccer Cruise Series on the Odyssey II Cruise Ship, June 17, 18, 25 (Venetian Night) and July 2 & 3 (City of Chicago Fireworks), 1994.

If you have any questions or need to schedule an appointment, please call (708) 559-9737 extension 530.

Sincerely,

'94 Sports Marketing

60 Revere Drive   Suite 550   Northbrook,   Illinois

60062 708/559-9737 Fax 708/559-9744

WORLD CUP USA '94

—

PACKAGE VOUCHER

Jon Evans

ORDER NUMBER: 1165

(PRESENT THIS TO REDEEM ALL PACKAGE CONTENTS OTHER THAN THE WORLD CUP USA '94 GAME

TICKETS)

60 Revere Drive   Suite 550   Northbrook,   Illinois

60062 708/559-9737 Fax 708/559-9744

Did I ever have to pay, too? Although the face value was just $100, the actual cost of my ticket was more like $300! Even more insidiously, tickets to the Opening Ceremonies of the World Cup Soccer Tournament were available-but only as a package deal that included a boat cruise on the lake, and a Liza Minelli concert. That package costs $1,000!

Please! If it were someone like Roberta Flack, Basia, Angela

Bofill, the Spinners, Lani Hall, Alpert, or even an acoustic guitarist, Steve Oliver, I could see myself paying $1K for a soccer game-cruise-concert package.

If it were someone like Yanni, Sadao Watanabe (if he brought the same orchestra he had from his How's Everything album), or the then-alive Barry White and the Love Unlimited Orchestra, I may have killed to see them, regardless of price!

313

Even Doc Severinsen or John Tesh with their orchestras could've also made me want to drop a G-Note on a combined soccer game-cruise-concert package!

However, Liza Minelli, to me, did not rate spending that type of money to see her!

I almost messed up when I got my ticket. I specified the Greece versus Bulgaria match on Sunday, June 26, 1994, on my order form. Ted saved my butt! He saw that my ticket was for the next day, June 27, 1994, and the Spain versus Bolivia match. He then told me about it. The next day, I was able to exchange my days off so that I could see Spain versus Bolivia, rather than Greece versus Bulgaria, as I intended!

The weather was wonderful, albeit stinking hot! However, it was perfect for seeing a soccer game! When I saw my seat, I jumped for joy, and even a couple of White dudes sitting above me knew it! I was a scant eight rows from the front. I was also equidistant between midfield and the goal to the south end of Soldier Field!

Never had I such a prime seat, for ANY sporting event, in my life! However, I would hit a Glass Monolith! Come to find out, the same seat that made me jump for joy also made me too close to use my telephoto lens-teleconverter combination! Although I could get the focus correct, the light meter would tell me that if I attempted the shot, I would burn (overexpose) the picture!

I had to experiment. I was restricted to two choices. I either had to use the original 135-millimeter lens with the 2x teleconverter or use the zoom lens alone, without the teleconverter! Since I elected to put my shots on slides, anything less than perfect was unacceptable.

Turnout was lighter than the media hype made it out to be. There was a host of no-shows. The match did NOT sell out! I had a shot at being able to see the Second Round of the World Cup Soccer Tournament, on July 2, 1994, provided that the United States did not advance to the Second Round. Had that occurred, I would NOT have been able to get a ticket!

Fortunately, I was able to pull it off. It only cost me another $300! I was also able to trade into a late afternoon shift with Malaika, a Generation X-er who always begged me to trade with her on Saturdays so she could go out and do the do! However, when Malaika discovered that I traded with her to make it possible for me to see the Second Round of the World Cup Soccer Tournament, she was provoked!

This time, it was Germany versus Belgium. Once again, I had my camera equipment ready. Since I was much higher up in my seating, I could get better shots with my zoom lens teleconverter combination. Unlike Spain versus Bolivia, this day would be comparatively dank, almost soupy. Still, I felt as if I had attended a third Olympic Games! To sweeten the deal, I'd also stop off at Ratfest (The Taste of Chicago) on the way to work, and it was just across Lake Shore Drive!

The FIBA World Cup Basketball Tournament was next. Once again, I had to ask the Tournament officials about policies and particulars. Come to find out, NO cameras were allowed! Since Canada was nice but highly strict, I was unable to take any camera equipment of any kind to the World Cup Basketball Tournament.

I telephoned Dad and let him know that I would stop off at James' house on the way to Toronto. I didn't mind seeing Dad at any neutral site. However, I would NOT stop to see him at his house, on account of that messy divorce of 1986. Dad didn't show up, and I had to move on. I was on a schedule.

As I drove along the MacDonald-Cartier Freeway, I noticed that every driver had their headlights on, even though it was bright and sunny.

Come to find out, that was the law in Ontario. I already knew that Canada converted to the SI system. However, I knew that if I kept my speed at 65 SAE miles per hour, I would be within legal speed limits.

Once I hit Metro Toronto, and my Choice Hotels International affiliate, I was already a touch late for my first game. However, I made it. I saw a great game too.

Toronto had an old but still capable subway system. However, what caught my eye was that Toronto still had trolley-based, fixed-rail streetcars, unlike Chicago, which had dispensed with electric trolley buses.

As I returned from my game, I decided that I was just a scant four blocks from my hotel. Therefore, I could walk from the Yonge Street Subway. Boy! Did I get an eyeful as I walked? For one thing, there was a White woman in a flesh-toned bikini thong combination who danced on the street in front of a bar along my way! This drew such a crowd that I momentarily had to walk out into the street to continue my walk! Once I finally got to within around the corner of my hotel, I saw another unusual sight-prostitutes! There was one White one that was in sky-high, spike-heeled pumps. Her pimp was boldly sitting nearby. I knew not to look too hard, lest I get caught up in something I couldn't handle. Instead, I bedded down for the night.

The next day, I had one wild game-Croatia versus Russia. The atmosphere was downright jingoistic! Remember! The Balkan States and Russia had some bad blood stemming back to the old days when the Balkan States were Satellite states of the former Soviet Union! There was even one Croatian fan who carried a bass drum into the Sky-Dome, where the tournament was being held. That made me wonder how officials at the Sky Dome would allow someone with a big bass drum into the stadium in the first place!

This game featured Toni Kukoc, who at that time was playing for the Chicago Bulls! Just as the burden of bringing a fourth championship to Chicago would fall on Toni Kukoc's shoulders, the burden of beating Russia would fall on Kukoc as well. However, Kukoc could not carry the whole team, much to the chagrin of a Croatian who was keeping me company. Before the game would end, he would swear, grimace, and groan, but he would NOT go home happy! I felt his pain. I pulled for Croatia as well.

I don't remember the other semifinal game. However, I would remember the Final. That final involved the United States and Russia. Although Larry "Grandmama" Johnson appeared heavy and slow, the rest of the team more than compensated for him. The United States showed excellent defense, courtesy of Shaquille O'Neal, while Reggie Miller provided a long-distance shooting presence.

When a basketball team can shoot 2/3 from the field alone, the odds favor that team winning; and the United States was no exception! I am not sure whether it was Puerto Rico or Croatia that came in third that year. However, this type of basketball beat the kind I was more familiar with, hands down!

Now that I concluded the World Cup of Basketball Tournament, I ate, exercised, and then swam for an hour. It was then that I discovered the joy of a hot tub. Its warmth nearly had a sedating effect. I retired to a movie that night, then retired for the night.

The next morning, I said goodbye to Toronto and headed for Detroit. It was here that I committed a tactical error. I tried to get rid of all my Canadian money. However, I only had mixed money with me when I hit the Ambassador Bridge. I therefore had to back up without presenting a hazard, park my car, and raid an ATM to pay my toll!

Once I was safely on the American side, the rest of my trip was anticlimactic. That was more than I could say for when I got home. Dad telephoned me from Detroit, and he was not happy with me. I vowed that I would NOT set foot in his house or apartment on account of the divorce. I did, however, tell him that I would be at James' house, that didn't satisfy Dad one iota. He wanted me to stop in at his house on the way back. Come to find out, Dad had the gout, making him unable to meet me. Had Dad told me about his illness, I would've made other arrangements.

There was also a Glass Monolith between me and Sadao Watanabe, who was coming to Chicago during the early month of September 1994!

For the uninitiated, Sadao Watanabe was Japan's Number One musician. He played the Alto, Soprano, and Sopranino Saxophones, plus the flute! Once I heard his How's Everything album, an album that featured at least a forty-piece symphony orchestra, I was so wiped out that I became a Sadao Watanabe fan from then on!

I had already missed Sadao once, due to protracted unemployment and NO income! I was NOT going to miss him again!

The initial report from WNUA, Chicago's former Jazz Station, had Sadao Watanabe appearing at the Pick-Steiger arena of Evanston, Illinois, Northwestern University. However, when I telephoned their box office, they had NO knowledge of Sadao Watanabe's even being booked! I telephoned WNUA itself and told them of my difficulty getting information on the concert.

WNUA's Rick O'Dell came to my rescue. According to O'Dell, the concert was to be held at Chicago's Park West, a theater club located on Armitage Avenue, and Lincoln Park West, hence its name! O'Dell also apologized for the runaround I was getting. Here was one Glass Monolith that I would break.

The Sadao Watanabe concert was positively one of the most unusual concerts I ever attended. For starters, 90% of the audience at the concert was Japanese! For another, children were allowed inside the Park West along with their parents! For another, those children were very well behaved! Try that with some Black families, and I could assure you, some form of stuff was going to hit the fan!

If I am not mistaken, even the two-drink minimum was waived!

What Sadao didn't waive, however, was the quality of his performance. Although the Park West was too small to carry any semblance of a symphony orchestra, I still noted a marked difference between a piece of his that I had on CD and that same piece performed live. The piece was called Pastral, a piece he recorded without the use of a symphony orchestra. The notes were the same as on the CD, as were the arrangements. And yet, when Sadao Watanabe performed Pastral live, and on stage, there was a sharpness and clarity that my CD could do no justice to, whatsoever!

Ultimately, I would rate this concert as at least equaling that of the B.B. King/Spinners concert that wiped both Mom and me out! Considering that this concert was staged 20 years beforehand, the Sadao Watanabe concert was an improvement, to say the least.

As I was working on my Post-Baccalaureate in 1995, I was experiencing a challenging period. Dad would succumb to Metastatic Lung Cancer just ten months after I came back from the FIBA World Cup Basketball Tournament! I had to force myself to stay focused on my post-baccalaureate studies and a course I was taking in the weeks following Dad's death.

Professor De Forrest offered optional presentations for students. It was up to the students to choose whether they wanted to do a presentation. It was our responsibility to come up with a topic related to Regulatory Policy and Politics, his course.

That was where I stepped in. I felt I could use the grade and even felt energized at the opportunity to make good. I met with Professor De Forrest during the break and told him that I had thought about the Betamax Case. This was a case in which Sony was being sued for the development of its VCR, the Betamax!

Professor DeForrest liked the idea but felt that I could've even expanded on that theme, rather than just sticking to the Betamax Case. It was with those thoughts in mind that I decided to do a presentation on how the consumer, himself, is a regulator! It was up to me to sell the idea.

I started off at IIT/Kent College's Law Library. There, I met a very friendly librarian named Gretchen Van Dam. She looked like your classic German fraulein! However, she was more than capable and helpful. First, she directed me to the area where I could find references to the case. Next, she saw me in the back and brought me some more books related to the case.

I was also surprised to learn that it wasn't Sony versus Walt Disney Productions, as I thought, but it turned out to be Sony versus Universal Pictures!

Since I had a ton of buff books from the consumer electronics industry, I was now able to combine the notes I took from the Law Library with the notes I took from the buff books to come up with my topic: Consumer Electronics and Regulatory Policy!

Professor De Forrest wanted to see the drafts of our papers first. I met him at his home to review my draft. That way, if changes needed to be made, I could make those changes by the deadline.

The long and the short of it was that I pulled it off. Not only did I complete the paper, but I also gave my presentation on the role of the consumer in regulatory policy. I also had my camcorder on. However, like an idiot, I did not have anyone behind the camcorder as I gave my presentation. The result was that I was more off-camera as I talked than on-camera!

Nevertheless, the class bought it.

I only gave the SECOND-best presentation in the class. The

The best presentation went to a classmate who was also a Chicago Police Officer! His name was Police officer Deo! Officer Deo discussed the role of the V-Chip as part of upcoming standards in television viewing. The overall theme of Officer Deo's presentation was that the V-Chip was being used as a substitute for responsible parental supervision!

When the smoke cleared, and finals were given, I would wind up with a B for this course. Were it not for the opportunity to give that presentation I gave, I would not have made it. Now, however, a bigger challenge lay ahead of me.

Ascension Thursday or: V-IIT Day or: Daggerboard Found!

In the Roman Catholic Church, the Feast of the Ascension was marked forty days after the Resurrection of Jesus Christ. This ceremony was always celebrated on a Thursday. Ascension Thursday is usually celebrated in the middle to late Spring.

The only difference between Ascension Thursday in the Roman Catholic Church and my feast of the Ascension was that my version of it was a touch belated. It was, however, just as sweet.

Also consider that when the Allies won World War II, they referred to the surrender of Japan as VJ Day, while they referred to the surrender of the European Axis nations as VE Day. Since I was in an absolute war, why not refer to my version as V-IIT Day?

Author's Side Note:

The VJ stands for Victory in Japan. The VE stands for Victory in Europe. My version stands for Victory at the Illinois Institute of Technology Day!

My version of Ascension Thursday started with the bright and sunny morning of August 28, 1996. I turned in my materials for the last time and met with Dr. Feinberg that afternoon. Feinberg already introduced me to a Black lady who would ultimately replace me. The program would continue well into the Fall.

As I met with Feinberg, she confirmed the credit hours I completed and that I was, indeed, eligible to receive the Certificate in Technical Communications. Feinberg then told me that she would petition the Dean of the Graduate College to award me my Certificate. I did it!

There would be no formal commencement exercise or formal ceremony. No matter! I didn't need it. I celebrated this blessed day by jumping into my car and driving from Chicago's Illinois Institute of Technology to the Dominick's Food Store in Merrionette Park, Illinois. There, I purchased a raspberry flavored coffeecake and shared it with Mom and Ted.

I especially didn't need the music of "Pomp and Circumstance." I had a better song that I would choose as my graduation theme song. I chose Bob James/Fourplay's track Dream Come True! This was much smoother.

Unlike my graduations from Grade School and High School, this graduation was under the most delightful weather possible. That paralleled the most delightful circumstances possible, leading up to my graduation.

There were times, however, when graduation, even from college, would prove problematic. For instance, I had to decide what kind of apparel to get from the IIT bookstore. There were class rings. However, since I rarely wore any jewelry other than a watch, I passed on that. I also passed on an IIT Alumni sweatshirt, figuring that I might have wanted to return to school someday. I did, however, decide to get an Illinois Institute of Technology jacket. This one had a cushioned liner for use in moderately cool weather. I chose that jacket instead.

Another problem occurred in mid-September 1996, and here it was!

Graduate College

 Illinois Institute of Technology

Graduate College

3300 South Federal

Chicago, Illinois 60616-3793

Illinois Institute of Technology

Telephone: 312-567-3024

Fax 312-567-7517

18 September 1996

Jon Evans

Chicago IL.

Congratulations! The Graduate College and the Department of Humanities hereby present to you the Certificate in Technical & Professional Communications.

The enclosed certificate was awarded upon the completion of the requirements and the recommendation of your advisor

Sincerely

S. H. Shadidepour

Dean

A couple of days after I wore that jacket for the first time, a Black Male saw me on the Dan Ryan, or Red Line southbound, and saw that I was from IIT. He then told me, "I tried it, man, but the math was too much."

I responded to him: "Don't let that stop you, because if you have any kind of work ethic, you will be found out."

I had already applied for and paid my membership dues for joining the Society for Technical Communication. When I got my membership kit, it included a certificate that certified me as a member. Now I had to buy myself not one, but two picture frames!

I had temporarily put my Certificate from IIT into a picture frame, but found it too large, so I had to fold it on the corners. This time, I decided to get myself two large black picture frames and put my letter of notice of intent to award in the smaller one. I wanted nothing left out of this experience.

1996 would roll into 1997 with the same results. It was also at that time that I had attended my first Society for Technical Communication meeting. This one was an Independent Consultant's meeting. Unfortunately, I didn't know that these were Independent Consultants and not sources of employment.

In the Pre-Spring of 1997, there was a General Membership meeting of the Society for Technical Communication at the William Tell Inn in a suburb called Countryside. I arrived early and met a young graduate of the University of Illinois at Chicago (formerly Circle Campus). He was white, and thin.

As we chatted, I mentioned buzzwords such as the types of software that I lacked knowledge about. After this graduate stepped away to the cash bar, a relatively tall White woman slipped up behind me, and spoke, in a low voice: "It's best that you try to pick up the Microsoft Word. I think that's the most important."

I began to think about what she said as I sat with several other women at my table and had dinner with them. They seemed happy to take my resume. The dinner wasn't bad either.

As dinner concluded and the announcements were made, I found out a little more about that mystery woman. Her name was Anna. She was on the Education Committee of the Chicago Chapter of the Society for Technical Communication.

All of the Committee Chairmen/Chairwomen sat at a long table at the entrance to the dining room. As I concluded the meeting, I stopped at that table and presented Anna with my resume. She began to be more than a little interested. She insisted that I exchange contact information with her.

That weekend, Anna telephoned me. When she told me that she thought that I had excellent credentials, I promptly told her, "Ha!" She then faxed some changes that she felt I should make to my resume. It took two tries. Come to find out, I had to set up my computer not only to receive the faxes, but also to print them out! There were some Glass Monoliths that I could break, just not enough.

My training for what Anna suggested would come most oddly. For instance, as I visited my email, I hit some spam! However, that spam would deliver some important, timely, and relevant information. The spam was from the Illinois Education and Training Center at the campus of the old Wilbur Wright College on the Northwest Side of Chicago.

This training center was funded by the State and dealt with those who were involuntarily displaced from their jobs. That, of course, would include me! Therefore, I made further inquiry.

My first step in the process was to take the L-Subway and bus out to Wright College and the IETC. Come to find out, I had to take a qualifying test first. Even college graduates had to take this test. Formerly, they were granted an automatic exemption.

Since my track record on qualifying tests was very poor, I cringed. Fortunately, the test consisted of basic skills such as reading, math, comprehension, etc. Unlike my performances on pre-employment screening tests, I did very well, according to the test interpreter.

Mom and I regularly visited Ted at Veterans Westside Hospital when he sustained a stroke.

During one of our visits, however, I was faced with an incident that was downright bizarre. Ted had a Hot Rod Magazine. When I got up to use the washroom in his room, I inadvertently knocked the magazine onto the floor. When I picked up the magazine, it was soaking wet! I saw a stream of water that ran from where I dropped the magazine to Ted's bed. It wasn't water that ran from Ted's bed. It was Urine! The source of the urine was his urine bottle, which had leaked.

What was most insidious was that this urine bottle was made out of CARDBOARD!

I was angry. I slammed what would've been a perfectly good car magazine into a nearby garbage can and yelled: "Ain't this a bunch of (Sugar Honey Iced Tea) a cardboard urine bottle!" I thought to myself that it was bad enough touching my own pee, but somebody else's?

I was highly grossed out, and it took a lot to gross me out! I was also offended. Who was the knucklehead who came up with the idea of using cardboard to hold urine?

I used those exact words, or similar ones, when I got home from VA Westside that night. I got on America Online and really gave it to one of the officials there. Although my email didn't reach the right official, he was just as shocked and as offended as I was at my experience. As a result, I got the following letter from the Veterans Administration:

DEPARTMENT OF VETERANS AFFAIRS

VA Chicago Health Care System

West Side Division

PO Box 8195

Chicago IL 60680—8195

April 10, 1997

Mr. Jon K.

Dear Mr. Evans:

We received a copy of your letter to Dr. Hoffman regarding the incident that you experienced at our medical center. To ensure we provide you with the correct information, we contacted the supplier of these products (biohazard control) and conducted an investigation of nursing use of this product.

After investigating the incident, we concluded that the urinal leaked because it had not been emptied as often as recommended by the company. We have reinforced to staff to follow the company's recommendation for product use.

Enclosed, for your information, is a copy of the company's response regarding their product. (biohazard control) System was chosen because of its infection control capability (no aerosol spray of urine during emptying) and quality control.

Thank you for bringing your concerns to us and for giving us the opportunity to respond. (biohazard control)

Dear Sir:

We are both disturbed to learn of your experience with our product at the Veterans Medical Center — Westside Chicago — and appreciate that you have brought this situation to our attention.

Firstly, let me assure you that (biohazard control) products are manufactured under strict quality control standards to ensure they will not leak if used properly. We draw on our firm's 35 years of experience producing leak-proof utensils for the collection and disposal of human waste. Products undergo a 12-hour water retention test to ensure they are resistant to leaking, and we are confident medical practitioners utilizing the (biohazard control) System will receive several hours of leak-proof performance on all our products.

Unfortunately, something failed in the case of the urinal used by a member of your family, and I offer my sincere apology for the distress this may have caused. Please be assured that if this urinal leaked under proper use, this is not in any way acceptable to (biohazard control), and we will do all we can to investigate the incident and take corrective action. Our system has been used for decades throughout the United Kingdom. It has been adopted in hundreds of hospitals across North America for our ability to provide a safer and more hygienic means of collection and disposal of human waste. Leaking products are totally unacceptable, and our review of incidents is quite diligent.

Your initial reaction to a paper product used for human waste collection is understandable. Still, unfortunately, you were only able to view a small portion of the overall system. Naturally, you were unable to witness the full benefits we can provide hospitals like VA Westside. Allow me to explain our system in its complete form.

The (biohazard control) System is made up of a series of pulp-molded collection vessels (bedpans, urinals, emesis basins, etc.) made from recycled newsprint. A natural wax is added to render the vessels leak-proof. This represents only one part of the system. The part you were not able to see involves a disposal unit located in a soiled utility room, which is designed to macerate the urinals and their contents into a biodegradable pulp in a closed disposal unit. This process is done quickly and conveniently, and greatly reduces the chance of splashing and spraying and the accompanying contamination of the environment around the soiled utility room that may occur during older cleaning methods. It also eliminates the use of ineffective bedpan washers and the myriad problems their use can involve.

Printed on recycled paper The biohazard control System is successfully used around the world because of its ability to potentially reduce nosocomial infection in hospitals and provide a closed, safe, and effective method of human waste disposal. Leaking product would eliminate any of the infection control benefits our system can offer. We diligently investigate any complaints, and I wanted to respond to your letter personally.

I certainly do not expect you to be pleased with any response I can return after your experience. Still, I felt it was important you understood fully the (biohazard control) System and the benefits we do provide. The decision to implement the (biohazard control) System by VA Westside was made for the reason of improving infection control, certainly not to in any way compromise the high standards implemented by the VA Westside for the prevention of nosocomial infection.

Truly,

General Manager

In atypical Jon Evans fashion, I would NOT hit a Glass Monolith this time. In a twinkling, I got a letter of apology from the manufacturer of the cardboard urine bottles. Come to find out, the engineering was sound. According to the manufacturer, however, the nursing staff was asleep at the switch! There were practices and procedures in the use, care, and maintenance of cardboard urine bottles that were not followed. The manufacturer acknowledged that I was unlikely to agree with its position.

Ted informed me that the VA Westside Medical Center would almost immediately stop using Cardboard Urine Bottles after I complained to the Hospital and the manufacturer!

In late October of 1997, I was fortunate enough to secure a temporary job with the Resurrection Healthcare network through the auspices of Advanced Personnel, where I trained for my MS Office and typing.

One of the Information Technology workers at Resurrection Healthcare was a beautiful, statuesque, and, understandably, married woman. I didn't know whether she was from India or Pakistan! Her name was Shashi Ohri. As I sat at my receptionist's console, on the telephone, I suddenly found a gold-colored box placed on my desk, addressed to me. It was from Shashi. It was a Christmas present!

Shashi only knew me for a scant two months; yet, she thought so highly of me to want to include me on her Christmas list. I hardly think that Shashi was merely trying to be civil. In fact, it was downright poignant.

I didn't have the heart to tell Shashi that I was allergic to the chocolates that were inside. They were Frango Mints, a premium, prized, set of chocolate to boot. So my plan was to give the box of chocolates to Marce and the girls.

However, the best-laid plans, aren't. Once Mom found out about the Frango Mints, she sent me downstairs to get the mints, confiscated them, and devoured them post haste-without Marce even knowing about them-until I told her!

As I told Marce that night after she got off work: "I've only been there for two months, and for someone to think highly enough of me to want to give me a Christmas present, made me think to myself: "Look! You dope! Some people care about you!"

Marciea enthusiastically agreed.

1997 would roll into 1998 and give me a few new presents as well.

Chicago's winters are known the world over for their harshness, brutality, and severity. It would not be uncommon for heating bills to exceed $1 $1 $1K per season from October through April, inclusive.

So you can imagine how delighted I was to have a Saturday, January 3, 1998, that saw temperatures reach 58 degrees Fahrenheit (14 degrees ABOVE zero, Centigrade)! January 3 was This Author's 44th birthday! Rarely did I celebrate birthdays that weren't cold and/or nasty, and/or snowy, and/or blustery. I thought that the only way for me to celebrate a warm-weather birthday would be to fly to a tropical island. Yet, the temperature in Chicago on this day was as warm as a night on the resort island of Bermuda!

I was also heartened that Mom wanted to take me out on my birthday. She chose the Red Lobster. She would spring for the meal! Mom thought that there was a Red Lobster in Lansing. There was not. However, Mom insisted that there was. When we failed to find it, we wound up substituting an Old Country Buffet instead.

There was drizzle that afternoon. It was, however, a warm, misty drizzle. As a result, I felt warm in my blue and yellow jacket. Once inside, I found the food inviting, but disconcerting. I liked the variety of food. However, there were no labels on the food telling me what it was. I saw what looked like seafood cakes. I had that, then returned for what looked like a seafood salad. Of course, on the side, I had garden salad. I more commonly referred to it as G-Salad!

Mom had a simpler choice. Give her some chicken, some mashed potatoes, and/or a G-Salad, and she was fine. She also had string beans.

I also had a dessert salad.

What I also found disconcerting about the Old Country Buffet was that it was crowded, and mostly with my soul brothers to boot! They seemed to be under control for the moment. However, I was hoping for a quieter, more intimate surrounding. I'd not get that today. However, since Mom was springing for it, I thought not to make too big an issue of it.

The heartening experience of January 3, 1998, would continue that evening. Marciea had to work that afternoon. As I picked her up from the Stewart Ridge Metra Electric Station, she asked me to take her to Dominick's in Merrionette Park. There, not only did she get some food, but she also allowed me to pick out my choice of cake for my birthday. I chose a yogurt-iced carrot cake. Marciea enthusiastically approved of my choice.

Those devious daughters of Marciea's hastened me into the basement den, and admonished me not to come upstairs to the kitchen just yet, as if I didn't know that they were planning to surprise me with a birthday party. I played along. I was right. They sang "Happy Birthday" to me and had a spread at the kitchen table already laid out. I did not, however, produce another episode of the Livie and Nicki Show, for the occasion, like an idiot!

I spent so much time running around with Marciea and the girls that Mom had grown to value whatever little time we had together. Consequently, I would be rewarded for not making too big an issue of my displeasure with the Old Country Buffet. On January 10, 1998, another warm Saturday, Mom would spring for yet another meal at the Red Lobster in Oak Lawn.

My co-workers were also quite gracious. They were also quite appreciative of my efforts at work. For instance, there was a high-level meeting at the job one afternoon. Wherever there were high-level meetings, there were also lots of hungry bodies and lots of coffee to be served. As a result, I employed the large, industrial pot and all the smaller ones to boot.

I had a stroke of luck. I figured that the two secretaries present couldn't lug around all of that coffee or food. However, they could easily roll around a cart I found in one of the classrooms. I handed it over to the secretaries and let them have at it. As a result, I was commended by not only the secretaries, but also Ms. Hammerton, and most importantly, Ron Yoder!

To underscore how easy it was to get along with a very conservative Ron Yoder, the Information Systems Manager at Resurrection Healthcare, there was another incident that left the office without a working fax machine. There were procedures that I had to follow for working with the fax. However, the lack of a working fax machine in the office was downright intolerable. Therefore, when I told Ron that I wished that I had the authority to call the repairman for the fax, Ron interceded: "I authorize you! If anybody has any questions, they can talk to me!"

During this period, I decided to finally get off my BRQPW and find an exercise regimen that I could do every day. To that end, I decided that I would try swimming every morning before breakfast.

One of the advantages about living in Chicago is that Chicago has a fairly good park system. Chicago's Park system included a network of indoor swimming pools! Since I was finding my weight machine less than satisfactory, I thought that swimming would be a viable alternative.

There was an indoor swimming pool that was a scant four blocks south of my home. However, Los Negros (pronounced "Lows Negg-Rose"), that's my term for Blacks that were rowdy or otherwise undesirable, overran West Pullman Park! Fortunately, the Beverly Historical District also had an indoor pool and a diverse, but comparatively civil, clientele. Beverly Historical was also a short fifteen-minute drive from my home.

On the first day that I decided to get off my donkey, I packed my swim trunks, a towel, and some shower shoes that I just happened to have with me. I took the girls to school, and then I went to Beverly Historical after dropping them off.

I could only swim a few lengths of the pool at the time. Otherwise, I spent time at the shallow end of the pool kicking my legs while sitting. I used up a lot of air very quickly, since I had Cough-Induced Asthma. When I got home, I left Mom very surprised that I would take a side trip to Beverly Historical to go swimming.

In subsequent days, I decided to use the same snorkel I had from my trip to Hawaii. I didn't need my fins, but I did pack a set of swim goggles. The plan worked. Now I could swim without worrying about gasping for breath.

The one bright spot in 1998 was Nicki. She was having a rookie season that would've been the envy of any athlete, even though she was only in Kindergarten! Nicki didn't play any football, basketball, or baseball; however, she was becoming one of the premier students in her class. If Nicki wasn't the "Student of the Month," her grades were making a case for it! Consequently, Nicki would soon be graduating from Kindergarten with honors!

Best of all, while Marce, the girls, and I were shopping at Safeway/Dominicks, we passed by the floral section in the store.

Lo and behold, there was a rose called, ironically, The Nicole Rose!

The Nicole Rose was a beautiful pearlescent white. However, it also had a coral red color around the edges of its blossom. Those blossoms, in turn, were fairly large. The result was a rose so beautiful that I had to tell Marciea about it. Nicki and Livie found it hilarious that there would be a rose that literally had Nicki's name on it. Meanwhile, I was hitting a Glass Monolith in all areas -except one-Health maintenance!

I had been dutifully doing my morning swims after I dropped the girls off at school. However, the pool at Beverly Historical had closed so that annual maintenance and cleaning could be performed during the month of May. That left me with a whole month that I was not exercising.

Nevertheless, I appeared to be getting a payoff. For one thing, Mom swore that the reason why I could snap up the end of a large dining room table was because of the morning swims. I declared that I hadn't been doing it long enough to make that significant an impact.

However, I discovered a clever health awareness screening program that I wish would be duplicated throughout communities throughout the United States! I found out about the program while reading the Chicago Sun-Times.

Loyola University Medical Center had sponsored a program called "Let's Stroke out Stroke!" This one-day program was held at the Westchester Country Club. This program consisted of a health assessment questionnaire, a blood pressure screening, and an electrocardiogram-all at absolutely NO charge to its participants!

There was a White, delightful, refined, and attractive Nurse Receptionist in civilian clothes who called me. She had a refined, but not snobbish, look about her. In a twinkling, she conducted the questionnaire. She was amazed when I told her that I swam every day. After she interviewed me, she took my blood pressure. It was 110/74. Afterward, she added up the score. This score included the results of my blood pressure measurement, plus the medical history.

Despite my telling her that I did get chest pains under stress, and/or rare, nondescript incidents, I only scored a "one" in risk factors for a stroke. Had my blood pressure read 105 or less, according to their charts, I would've registered a "zero!" Anything between five and ten was considered a "moderate risk." "Eleven or more" was considered a significant risk. I was classified as having a "low" risk.

After my questionnaire, I sat in the Shaggon Wagon for forty-five minutes, then had my electrocardiogram. I lay quietly on the table as conductive tape and alligator probes were placed on my chest and ankles. At that point, the attending cardiologist looked at my strip, then declared that I was a poster child for cardiovascular health!

I thought that it would be highly implausible that a scant onemonth of exercise would result in such apparently dramatic benefits to my cardiovascular health-especially when you factor in not being able to swim because my pool was closed for maintenance. However, the "black and white" said otherwise!

Tragically, Loyola Medical never again staged its Let's Stroke out Stroke health awareness and screening program. I speculated that the cost of such a program, plus manpower and logistics concerns, doomed the program. Ironically, such health awareness programs are necessary in ALL communities, and POSITIVELY ESSENTIAL in minority communities.

I was fortunate enough to get a job at Espo Engineering. Their client had been Montgomery Ward, which had moved out of its main building and was doing all of its operations in a big, tall building across the street. That was in March of 1999. My supervisors were a dream. But the job was short.

It had been 7 ½ months since Espo Engineering sent me out to Montgomery Ward for that Data Entry assignment. I had no assignments from either this agency or any of the other temporary agencies that I had been working with. That would change on October 19, 1999.

This time, I got a call for a Data Entry job out at a place called Miller Fluid Power. This was a Hydraulics Engineering firm in Bensenville, Illinois. That was just in back of O'Hare International Airport.

I pulled up and announced myself as one of the temps. In a twinkling, I was escorted to my workstation. For once, I would meet a very delightful Black Male by the name of Leroy Bryant III. He had a slightly husky build and was slightly taller than I was.

Leroy showed me the ropes of the job, which turned out to be a simple data transfer and nomenclature assignment. Miller Fluid Power was about to scrap its DOS/486-based record-keeping system and replace it with a Windows/Pentium-based system. That required someone to transfer the records from one computer to the other. That project also required someone to standardize the nomenclature. Later that day, Leroy phoned the supervisor of the department to say that I had indeed shown up.

The next day, I'd meet that supervisor. He was White, short, svelte, and very knowledgeable about the system. His name was Rick Sarver. Rick designed the system that Miller Fluid Power had been keeping. Rick was also responsible for heading up the changeover.

I enjoyed every aspect of working at Miller Fluid Power for the time I worked there; that is, except for having to navigate through a minefield of goose poop on the parking lots! However, once I was inside the building, I could see myself working full-time if the opportunity presented itself.

Each of the co-workers was clean-cut, well-dressed, and pleasant. Even Leroy spoke the King's English, and NOT Polluted English. He knew well about the crazies from the hood. Come to find out, Leroy was from one of those areas where crazies abounded.

Not only was Leroy very easy to get along with, but we also shared a common interest: sports compact cars. In Leroy's case, he had a snowy white Eagle Talon Turbo Coupe that would've caused me to envy him, had he not sustained a slightly buckled hood.

The data transfer project at Miller Fluid Power was nearing completion. On Thursday, November 4, 1999, Mr. Sarver had me sit down at his desk as I was walking by. The next day would be my last day, and he was notifying me so that I could inform Espo Engineering in hopes that I could latch on to another assignment. Nevertheless, the assignment was considered successful, and Rick appeared to have no problems whatsoever rehiring me if he were so inclined. The next day, I parted company with Leroy, then worried about my car's radiator.

It was late in 2000 when I landed a job at Underwriters Laboratories. I had to go through an adjustment period. However, some good things were finally occurring in series after the hiccup that nearly cost me my job at Underwriters Laboratories in Late 2000.

Rich, the Engineering Group Leader, asked me to take an early lunch, as opposed to the usual late lunches I took each day. Although I enjoyed this early lunch and a better selection of food from the cafeteria, in the back of my mind, I had to wonder if the reason for my early lunch would be to fatten me up for a disciplinary or exit interview. I couldn't be complacent. There were too many times that I thought things were easing on a job, when in truth, I was about to be terminated.

Author's Side Note:

For instance, everything seemed so smooth at Pheoll Manufacturing Company, where I worked in the spring of 1979. I had NO idea that I would be charged with slowness and subsequently dismissed!

When I reported back from my early lunch, Rich walked me down to a section of the building where another supervisor awaited. He was White to Hispanic, a touch husky, and had long hair. He was generally friendly. His name was Marty Magiera.

Marty, Rich, and I walked to a nearby workstation where there was a screensaver with a vintage Rover sedan on it. There was a short, pudgy, but again, very friendly, White gentleman by the name of Aaron Walker. I asked Aaron if that was a Rover 3500. However, Aaron corrected me and told me that it was a Rover 2000 TC. However, that screensaver broke the ice between Aaron and me.

Aaron was fascinated that I would have an interest in classic sports compact cars such as Rovers, Triumphs, MGs, Mercury Capris, etc., especially the British sporting coupes and some sedans, mostly the former.

Aaron would move on to greener pastures. In so doing, that created a need for someone to clear up a massive backlog of Data Entries. Aaron would be spending his final days at Underwriters, training me on making the entries. To make matters sweeter, Marty and Aaron gave me the option of using Microsoft Excel, which I was somewhat familiar with, for making the entries.

After a few minutes of working the system, Rich decided that he was no longer needed, and he returned to his office. Meanwhile, I made entries and otherwise chewed the fat with Aaron. As I said before, he and I hit it off immediately.

For that matter, Marty and I also hit it off immediately. The next day, there would be a few instances where I would have to interview some of the people that made these entries. However, Marty gave me his fullest backing. That alone was comforting enough.

I didn't forget about Rich, though. I decided to spend the mornings at my new assignment, while I spent the afternoons completing Rich's work. However, I failed to communicate that to Rich. I left him with the impression that if I didn't get Magiera's work done, I would be fired! Although that thought crossed my mind, I assured him that I would be splitting my time between Rich and Marty. That would leave me busy. However, indications were now tending towards my keeping my job for, at least, the duration of this backlog.

I kept Ms. Bazan at Christ Hospital Vocational apprised of my situation at work, mostly by email. Ms. Bazan was delighted. She also agreed that perhaps I was turning the corner on the job.

Although I was feeling a sharp bite in the late autumnal air, I felt a sense of relief that I had, for the moment, escaped getting fired. Now, I could look towards Thanksgiving 2000 without having to PRETEND to be thankful for any of my blessings. I decided to rent a subcompact car that weekend. It was a Geo Metro Sedan. It wasn't half-bad either.

Once I got that car, I was able to beat the Thanksgiving 500, a series of mad holiday rushes that included early store closures and heavy traffic. The next day, I helped Mom do the cooking. It was at that point that I lamented not being able to roast the turkey on the kettle. Mom was, however, amenable to roasting the turkey on the kettle for the last half-hour. She, however, detested barbecuing the turkey from the very beginning as she had a problem with the redness of the meat. As a result, I built a charcoal fire on a biting Thanksgiving 2000, and the end result was a downright yummy turkey!

There was a realty company in the Mount Greenwood East district of Chicago that needed someone to replace their regular Group Secretary on 13 March 2002. As luck would have it, it was not too far from the Southfork at all! That's why I got the note. All I had to do was to telephone the managing owner of the company, then show up!

And show up I did! Once the lady with the health problem explained what I had to do, I was in business! Now all I had to do was call Mom and explain that I would be delayed in getting home because this sudden shift in fortune would have me working, albeit temporarily.

This would be absolutely the first day I had worked since I was cut on August 7, 2001. Therefore, it was my first day of work in 6 ½ months. That was important because my Unemployment had run out, with NO possibility of an extension. After all, the current administration did NOT want to declare an unemployment crisis. Before that afternoon was done, I would meet "Brains", the managing owner of the company.

I would work two full days, then would need to attend an appointment. However, I notified "Brains", and he assured me that he would have a replacement for that day.

On that first full morning, I came in early and was prepared. As I manned the receptionist's chair, a tough, burly-looking White gentleman walked in and promptly picked up mail from a mail slot in the office. He spoke to me, and I was prompted to say: "Let me guess. You went up to Sturgis."

I was right on that account.

"What else do you know about me?" asked the mysterious realtor.

I asked: "And let me guess. You own a Harley."

This burly chap replied: "Is there any other bike?"

I told him: "That's open for debate."

It was clear that one of the realtors was a chauvinistic Harley-Davidson man, the way Dwight was chauvinistic about Chevrolets! This man recognized NO other motorcycle.

However, since he was the first of the realtors that I would get to know, I would refer to him as "That Biker Dude"!

Once I came back to pick up my check, the word had gotten out about my chance encounter with the mysterious realtor-the person whom I called "That Biker Dude". Even Brains would have himself a considerable roll when he learned about that encounter.

There were many things I liked to do, in terms of my hobbies, my travels, and my interests. There was also an irony in these hobbies, travels and interests. If I said that I were a people person, I would've been telling a boldface lie-even if I didn't have Asperger's Syndrome!

And yet, my hobbies, interests, and travels sometimes brought many people together!

For instance, when I worked on going to the 1984 Summer Olympics in Los Angeles, many of Mom's co-workers would stop by to see Mom and ask: "How's Jon?" The same held true with some members of the family. I also wound up networking with Milton's girlfriend at that time, plus Rod (The Dude), my cousin.

Then, there was the New Orleans (IMSA) Grand Prix. This event served as a catalyst to bring together many relatives of the family who were on Mom's side.

Finally, these events revealed one of my strong suits-my ability to research. I did a lot of reading to find the correct lodging and/or hotel arrangements for my particular adventures. Of course, I also had the good sense to choose that Volkswagen Rabbit Hatchback Coupe car that lasted almost five years after I bought it, a ten-year-old model.

Then again, whenever you are talking about Asperger's Syndrome, you can study any topic whatsoever.

Final Justice Final Vindication

I made three attempts at applying for Disability. The first attempt was sometime around March, 1998. This first time, I was called before a physician that gave me a Psychological and a medical examination. The result of that was that I was deemed not disabled enough to warrant Disability.

I didn't even consider myself so medically impaired that I couldn't work. Yes, I thought that protracted unemployment was causing me emotional problems. However, protracted unemployment was NOT preventing me from working, unless some employer decided that he did NOT want to hire someone experiencing a protracted period of unemployment. As for the Asthma, I made it clear, and up front, that I had Cough Variant Asthma, and NOT what I called Classical Asthma. As for the Functional Hypertensive Dysphonia, what I was experiencing was an image problem, rather than a medical problem, although there was some of that, too.

Given these guidelines, of course, I was going to fail. However, Mom wouldn't hear of me quitting. It was under duress that I would appeal this initial decision. As you can see by the document above, I would once again fail.

That was it. I had enough. However, I would be deemed NOT ready for placement after an evaluation by The Center for Personal Development. Once again, I submitted an appeal in 1999. Once again, I was rejected as the document above stated.

When I met Jeremy Sadlier at Christ Hospital Vocational Services Unit, he urged me to continue to apply for Disability, despite the failures I had at securing it. That was BEFORE I underwent the Job Readiness Workshop and Training. When the Job Readiness Workshop and Training ended for me, Jeremy expressed concerns about my fitness for placement.

I underwent a third appeal. This one did NOT include a medical examination, but DID include yet another psychiatric evaluation in July 2000. The psychiatrist correctly asserted that I was disgusted with my life, which I was. Two months prior, I washed out at Xerox.. Once again, I was rejected.

It was at this time, however, that I connected with a law firm that I was referred to by Christ. Hospital's Vocational Services Unit. It was expanding. That law firm thought I should continue appealing.

All of these events occurred before my diagnosis of Autism Spectrum Disorder in 2001. In February of 2002, I received a court summons! It was an administrative hearing that was like a court of law. It even featured a judge! For brevity's sake, I will simply refer to the hearing as "court".

The first thing I did was to mark my calendar. My court date was April 4, 2002.

I had my work cut out for me. I had to round up all of the people who were involved in my case. I had the power of subpoena, and I used it. I decided to ask if some of the people at Christ could help me in court. It was here that I would hit a Glass Monolith.

Lisa and Melissa could not attend the session. They were busy in one way or another, running the day-to-day operations of the Christ Hospital Vocational Services Unit. Also, Jeremy was running a personnel unit elsewhere in the network. Jeremy did, however, keep in touch with his former colleagues at Christ.

I asked Dr. Harrison, Dr. Darren, and/or Dr. Folisade about appearing as an expert witness in court. It would be here, too, that I would hit another Glass Monolith. Dr. Folisade had already gone on to another assignment. Dr. Darren was unable to get away.

As for Dr. Harrison, she also phoned me to tell me that she could not appear in court as an expert witness either. She added that she didn't think that it was necessary to have an expert witness from NU Medical present in court.

I wasn't so sure. I had three rejections already. After each rejection, I had even stronger insistence that I apply for Disability benefits. One such clamoring was from Mom. However, Mom was not an objective professional. Therefore, I doubted whether she would've been effective as a witness even if I wanted to have her present, which I didn't. She was too old, too frail, and too vulnerable to the stress of a court hearing.

It was clear that if I were to have any possibility of success at all, I had to have more than good looks, charm, or even the documentation I had.

I had to have some of the principals document the issues that I was facing, and I was having tons of trouble in getting a witness in court.

At this point, I decided to make a compromise. I decided to use my subpoena power to get written depositions from the principals. I would NOT try to haul any of the principals into court. I also considered having one or more of the principals participate in a teleconference during the court session.

So I gave options to the principals. For some, I subpoenaed them for written depositions or teleconferencing at the option of the principal. For others, I decided to have them submit a written deposition ONLY.

While all of that was going on, I would get a stroke of luck that would break my Glass Monolith as far as getting an expert witness to testify in court for me. Ms. Bazan expressed willingness to testify in court, even though she had retired from the Christ Hospital Vocational Services Unit. It just so happened that she had some business to conduct downtown anyway, so it would be NO problem for her to testify.

In the meantime, the law firm that I was working with contacted me very frequently, and I made it a point to do whatever they asked me to do, to the letter. The associate attorney informed me that my appearance in court was mandatory and that she would represent me.

April 4, 2002, was a sunny morning, albeit, with a bit of a bite to it. The associate attorney I was working with asked me to come in for a pre-court briefing. I agreed to that, and the attorney explained what would go on. After that briefing, I would meet her in court. I still had considerable time left. I didn't know if the court would allow me to sit for upwards of two hours waiting for my case to come up on the docket.

So at first, I stopped by Roosevelt University's Placement Center to get some job leads. Next, I went to Union Station's Great Hall. There, I sat

348

out and waited. I was making myself careful not to nod off in the Great Hall. If I did, I ran the risk of being late and causing problems.

My court date was at 2 PM, and it was 1:15 PM that afternoon. At that point, I decided to start towards the court and my session. I arrived at about 1:30. Shortly after I arrived, Ms. Bazan, true to her word, arrived at court. All I needed was the final piece of the puzzle, the associate attorney that I was working with. About fifteen minutes before the start of my court date, that final piece of the puzzle fell into place. I made one final pit stop before the court was to begin.

A courtroom was already set up for my hearing. Come to find out, my worries about having expert witnesses in court would prove to be unfounded, according to Dr. Harrison. The court had its witnesses.

In keeping with the confidentiality of court testimony, I will ONLY describe my reactions to the events during court, and NOT the backgrounds of the witnesses. However, I will state that the judge gave me instructions on how to respond and conduct myself. My lawyer was also with me. Ms. Bazan was also instructed as to when her testimony would be required. She would wait until she was called in.

Court testimony corroborated everything that Dr. Harrison asserted concerning the Autism Spectrum Disorder she diagnosed. That same testimony also corroborated the occupational evaluation done on me by Dr. Julius March. Court testimony also documented evidence of my having Clinical-D!

Court testimony also revealed that it would be difficult for me to obtain a job because I would want more than just being an Operator, or any other lower-level job. That testimony contradicted statements made in one of my rejections. That statement was NOT true anyway because I was also rejected outright for other Operator's jobs, even though I had previous experience as a Telephone Operator.

Once the court proceedings were done, my lawyer, Ms. Bazan, and I all met at sidebar. She stated that in her expert opinion, I won. It was with that that my lawyer gave me some final instructions before we all parted company.

Delighted, Ms. Bazan needed instructions on how to get a commuter train back to her home. I walked with her towards Union Station and directed her to the commuter train she needed. I stayed with her until it was time for that train to pull out. It was the least I could do after she took the time out that she did. That time out, ultimately, put me over the top.

As Ms. Bazan and I walked towards Union Station that chilly, cloudy afternoon, she admonished me NOT to worry about looking for such jobs as Technical Writer or Lab Technician. She was worried that I could mess up my newly found Disability benefits. Instead, she thought that I should get a light-duty job.

About one month later, I got the official word from the Social Security Administration. I was approved for Disability. It was at that point that I felt a sense of final justice, and even more importantly, a sense of final vindication.

But if I felt vindicated at receiving the letter of acceptance and approval, imagine how Mom felt. It was she who had to put up with myriad criticisms for the time she spent with me at various specialists to try to find out what my Glass Monolith was.

Remember! Asperger's Syndrome wasn't even discovered until 1943 by Hans Asperger. I wasn't even aware that I might have a major problem until ABC/WLS-TV aired a piece about Hyperlexia. That piece was broadcast in 1990. Prior to that, I thought that I was merely bombarded with stress to the point that my ability to function was threatened.

Marciea also proved to be ultimately correct. She didn't live to know how accurate she was.

A few weeks later, Ms. Bazan cringed when I was getting information about alternatives and rules on earnings for persons on Disability. She thought that I should keep it simple, and that would be that.

But the fact of the matter is that rents were four figures, car prices were five figures, and houses and/or condominiums were six figures. That was at the time of this writing. Inflation and diminishing employment would be very pervasive in America. Given the political climate of the day, I would NOT be optimistic. What made matters even worse was that I would later discover that the unemployment rate for persons with disabilities was seventy percent!

It would be with these thoughts in mind that I would continue looking for work as long as I had a lead to work with, and as long as the job prerequisites of that lead do not eliminate me.

Despite repeated rejection of me by my so-called Black Brethren, what I was grateful for was that I found out what my Glass Monolith was, and that court testimony corroborated evidence of my having a medical problem. That, to me, was Final Justice and Final Vindication.

Epilogue

The best way to end this book is to describe a couple of hopeful events I experienced. For instance, in August 2002, I started receiving benefits and found myself a used Pontiac Fiero SE with a 5-speed manual transmission. I spent the first few weeks of ownership debugging the car.

I dreamed of what a restored version of my car would've been like as Milton took Mom, Ted, and me to our niece's wedding in Cheyenne, Wyoming. Milton had a large GMC custom conversion van with "the works." Mom found the ride very comfortable. Once at Cheyenne, we would meet Mikey, Quinetta's new baby, and Shonta's new baby, and generally have ourselves a good time.

After the wedding, I immediately renewed my suspended membership in the Society for Technical Communication.

As I renewed my membership in the Society for Technical Communication, I inquired about forming a Specialty Interest Group, or SIG, among the many Specialty Interest Groups within the organization.

The SIGs covered such activities as Independent Contractor, Scientific, Usability, Science, International, for covering translations, and on and on. Each of the SIGs costs an extra $5.00 to join.

I joined the Science SIG, and then I inquired about forming a SIG.

I surmised that I was probably NOT the only disabled Technical Writer in the Chicago Chapter, let alone the entire Society for Technical Communication's system. I didn't know how right I was!

Come to find out, there was already a SIG for the very purpose of advocating for disabled Technical Writers. That SIG was called "Special Needs." As the representative explained it to me, the Special Needs SIG was designed to do the very thing that I had thought about in forming a SIG nationwide.

It was with those thoughts that I signed up for the Special Needs SIG. The question was whether to form a Special Needs SIG at the Chicago Chapter level. For that, I needed to present my proposal at the next meeting in September 2002.

That meeting was held at a very quaint microbrewery/restaurant in far west suburban Downers Grove, Illinois. I forgot the name. However, the place had a delightful charm of an Old English pub motif. The food was NOT half bad either.

While I was there, I reintroduced myself, and well, I should have. There was a whole new cast of characters. For instance, the The Employment Committee was now chaired by a fairly young White gent who favored jazz guitarist Steve Oliver. Actually, his name was Steve Madison.

When I bandied my idea about forming a Chapter-level Special Needs SIG to Steve Madison, his interest piqued so much that he was introducing me to people, over and above those I had already known from my previous association with the STC! It was during the "announcements" phase of the meeting that Steve suggested that I go before the meeting and present my proposal. I took Steve up. Come to find out, I would not be alone that evening in learning that some members could've benefited from a Special Needs SIG.

My ride from Downers Grove back to the Southfork was like a road rally. For instance, I had finally debugged the Fiero enough for it to be expressway worthy, without any appreciable calamity. Speaking of the Fiero, Mom was ecstatic about the car, as she felt the joy at my finally finding myself a car that was a semblance of what I wanted. She laughed as she tried to get her increasingly frail body inside of it. However, she confessed that once inside the Fiero, she found it not only roomy enough for her, but fairly comfortable as well! She and Mrs. Marsh, Mom's longtime friend, had a good laugh when I showed Mrs. Marsh the car.

Ted liked the Fiero too. What he wanted was the apparent power that the little four-cylinder engine had. What he didn't like was the lowness, or riding in it. He also had reservations about having Mom ride in it.

Once I got back from the September 2002 meeting of the Society for Technical Communication, I began drafting a preliminary charter and mission statement for the Chicago Special Needs SIG. I chewed the fat with the Chapter brass, then presented my proposal to the next meeting, one month later. However, I teleconferenced with the meeting rather than going to it this time, as it was in a different location. Once I presented my proposal at that meeting, I seemed set. All I needed to do was to provide a meeting place and get myself a quorum.

My idea was to form the Special Needs SIG, have members caucus, then recuse myself from any leadership role in the SIG. Instead, I would continue as a rank-and-file member of the Chicago Chapter Special Needs SIG of the Chicago Chapter of the Society for Technical Communication.

I had a devil of a time finding a meeting place for my SIG. Initially, I chose the same Beverly Historical area where I swam every morning. However, the Park Commissioner told me to consider that an upstairs meeting room may not be appropriate for people with disabilities, and there were no elevators. That sent me to some nearby parks. At one, I got the meeting room without the stairs, but was warned to act fast because this park's winter activities were about to be staged. That would leave the park's fieldhouses or meeting rooms unavailable until the following March.

Shortly before that September 2002 meeting, Melissa Bos found a brand new job, on top of the brand new husband that she would also acquire. Rawda, on the other hand, graduated with a Master's in social work.

That left Ms. Leander to run the day-to-day operations of Christ Hospital's Vocational Services Unit-but not for long! In about the middle of September 2002, Christ Hospital decided to close its Vocational Services Unit permanently. Fortunately, Ms. Leander sensed that her job would be eliminated, and she had already landed another job serving people with disabilities. Although Ms. Leander had to leave right away, Christ Hospital had Ms. Bazan run the Unit for the last two weeks of operation. Meanwhile, I felt it imperative to say goodbye to Ms. Leander one last time.

In fact, Ms. Leander worked on transitioning each Job Club member into other programs, rather than simply leaving them hanging. She made no bones about being particularly concerned about my case.

Meanwhile, back at the Southfork, Mom was fairly skeptical about my forming the Special Needs SIG. She complained that I might incur some costs. I took great pains to ensure that any meeting of the Chicago Special Needs SIG would be sanctioned by the Chapter at large, so that I could get the money. However, that would be moot if I didn't have a quorum. I had to work on that.

I also received an invitation from the Northeast Ohio Chapter of the Society for Technical Communication. That chapter was to stage a seminar and meeting called a "Life Planning Workshop." This meeting would be staged at a Hilton affiliate hotel in Twinsburg, Ohio, a suburb of Cleveland.

If anyone needed to attend a "Life Planning Workshop", I thought I would. However, there were a few catches. First off, there was a $90.00 charge for registration at the workshop. That would cover the cost of materials for the workshop. Secondly, there was the matter of getting there.

Mom had reservations about my driving to Cleveland/Twinsburg. In her mind, the Fiero was NOT suited for highway, let alone cross-country driving. Therefore, she thought that I should either fly or take Amtrak. I had reservations about driving because I had yet to debug the windshield washer. I did NOT want to be on the highway with caked salt spray on my windshield. Remember. The meeting was around March 13, 2003. Also, remember that Cleveland had a reputation for being very snowy at that time of the year.

Fortunately, I just happened to be in Amtrak's Guest Rewards program. By that, I could accumulate points by NOT only riding Amtrak trains, but also using vendors that were affiliated with the Guest Rewards program. As luck would have it, the hotel where the workshop was to be held was also affiliated with Amtrak's Guest Rewards program.

It was with those thoughts in mind that NOT only would I heed Mom's admonishment, but I would also even use the affiliated rent-a-car and accumulate more points for using that vendor as well.

Mom gave me her blessing for the one-day trip, despite my concerns about her health. She was confident that Ted could handle her needs if any were to arise.

So it was on.

I didn't bother ordering a sleeper. After all, I would be in Cleveland in a scant few hours anyway. It was, however, around 8 PM in the evening when my train left Chicago Amtrak. It was late. However, dinner was provided. I spent the rest of the evening pondering my move from Downtown Cleveland to suburban Twinsburg, and well, I should have given it some thought, too.

Although Amtrak's right of way passed right by Cleveland's Hopkins Airport, there was positively NO station there. I had to go to Downtown Cleveland, then order up a cab to take me all the way back out to Cleveland Hopkins Airport, at a cost of $26.00! Cleveland had a stellar public transit system that ran towards Hopkins. However, Cleveland's entire public transit system shut down after 11 PM, unlike Chicago's at the time of this writing. Keep in mind that Amtrak's trains NEVER arrive in Cleveland before the wee hours of the morning! Fortunately, the cabbie was White, and far from the type of person predisposed to ripping off an out-of-towner, so I tipped him $5. I also had the fortune of having the rent-a-car agency reimburse me all but about six dollars of my ride out to Cleveland Hopkins.

Now that I had arrived at my rental car, I had to start the car, then spend about half an hour scraping ice off my windshield. Cleveland sat on the shore of Lake Erie. As a result, any winter winds would make their presence felt in the form of snow, ice, or both.

By the time I was able to remove the ice from my windshield, my rent-a-car was now warm, and the defrosters were at full operation. Now I'd have no further problems with caked-on ice. What I did have a problem with, however, was finding my hotel, where the meeting would take place. I had to make several stops along the way, then backtrack. Come to find out, my hotel was at a slightly out-of-the-way place where a sign was barely visible.

It was sunrise before I finally got myself squared away. Fortunately, I had a very loud electronic alarm watch. I placed that alarm watch by my head as I bed myself down in order to get a scant few hours of sleep. It wouldn't be that long before the meeting and workshop would begin.

Once my alarm watch went off, I dressed in my brown business suit and proceeded downstairs. Once there, I registered, was given my pass, and scanned the meeting area to familiarize myself with the layout.

It wouldn't be long before I would meet someone. It was a short, full-figured, White woman. She just happened to be a Technical Writer from Indianapolis. It wouldn't be long before word got out among attendees that they had someone from Chicago from their midst. I was one of only two Black people in attendance at Technicom 2003. The other Black person was a Black woman from the Cleveland Chapter. Nevertheless, I was very warmly received by my fellow attendees, and would soon be the topic of hot conversation. I felt that I fit in in this setting.

That thought didn't go unnoticed by Beth Williams, the Regional President of the Northeast Ohio Chapter of the Society of Technical Communication. She smiled as she said, "I'm happy that so many people came from such places as Indianapolis, Columbus, Dayton, and Chicago!"

I knew she was referring to me.

Ms. Williams would introduce the keynote speaker of the day. She would introduce the entire day's proceedings, as well as moderate the Life Planning Workshop that would bring me to Technicom 2003 in the first place. Her name was Judy GlickSmith.

Judy Glick Smith was a short, svelte White woman from Dallas, Texas. Understandably, she had the stereotypical Southern twang to her speech and wore cowboy boots. Her hair was also short, and she wore a midi-length skirt. She was an active member of the Dallas Chapter of the

Society for Technical Communication. She also had her own Independent Consulting firm.

Ms. Glick-Smith's svelteness belied the fact that she had, and beat, a severe weight problem. Ms. Glick-Smith's energy belied the fact that she was a breast cancer victim and survivor! Her successful raising of her family belied the fact that she underwent a divorce, which may or may not be as stressful as an illness itself.

Ms. Glick-Smith outlined the principles that made up the quality of how life decisions were to be made. She categorized some decisions that were made on factors such as love, fear, duress, and possibly finances.

Meanwhile, I was hanging on to much of what Ms. Glick-Smith said. Therefore, I stuck my neck out and proposed a hypothetical question on how these principles could be applied towards a real-world problem I would face one year later. That problem was my 50th Year Medical Exam. For that, I had planned to go to a top-flight national medical clinic where I would get the full monty, not just a checkup or a regular medical examination. My problem was that the "full-monty," as I called it, could cost me hundreds, if not thousands, of dollars!

Ms. Glick-Smith noted that the class would offer me some solutions to this daunting but straightforward problem, as well.

I remembered Blanche from Ameritech's River West Directory Assistance Office. Blanche chided me for "trying to get the big picture." I noted that you had to do that to make credible and viable decisions in Life Planning. Ms. Glick-Smith agreed with me and became very leery of people who would treat getting the big picture as the wrong thing to do.

The workshop would go on until approximately noon, or shortly afterward, Eastern Time. At that point, lunch would be served. It was

Lent at that time. Therefore, there was a separate spread to accommodate us Romans, as well as others. I was under the impression that poultry was also permissible on Fridays during Lent. However, the caterers impressed upon me that only dairy, vegetarian, or seafood-based foods were permitted during this period. According to them, Romans were referred to as "fish-eaters" for that reason.

There was also plenty of sodas and Tea. As for the fire-water, you had to pay for that, and that was fine by me. I didn't touch the (smack).

There was a second session. Here, we had the option of attending a session on Single-Sourcing or a panel discussion on the Technical Writing community's activities. I opted for the second session.

That second session was anticlimactic after the conference in the morning. Nevertheless, I attended it to see what was going on. The results of that panel discussion were that there was a recession in the Cleveland area for Technical Writers, as there was in the Dallas area.

However, travel lag was starting to set in on me. I was fading in and out. Still, I was gaining valuable insights into what the Technical Writing industry was doing nationwide.

After the session ended, there was an informal Cash Bar/Reception period. It was during that period that I met Judy Glick-Smith, again, who was sitting outside the meeting rooms. She and I chatted at length and traded secrets about each other. It was at that point that I told her about my case of Autism Spectrum Disorder. In turn, Ms. Glick shared a secret with me.

We exchanged telephone numbers and emails. Shortly after Technicom 2003 ended, I met with the lady I had met initially and her husband from Indianapolis. The husband and I then chatted outside of the gym and pool room about Technicom 2003.

I went upstairs and looked forward to a swim. However, I had a problem. Since my arrival time was so early, and my checkout time was also early, my electronic key card would be rendered useless. Fortunately, I settled the problem with the front desk and got myself a new key card.

Once I had a new key card in hand, I was able to get back to my room, where I changed out of my suit and into my sportswear. Under that, sportswear was my swim trunks. I was now able to swim some laps at the hotel pool, as I resumed doing at Beverly Historical every morning since I debugged my Fiero.

Just as I did every morning, I figured that all I needed was forty-five minutes worth of swimming laps and I would get in a round of exercise.

After my swim, I didn't immediately go upstairs. Instead, I soaked in a hot tub right next to the pool. There, I was met by a curious pre-teen to lower teen-aged White girl. Although I was apprehensive about telling her my name when she asked me, she was friendly and even kind enough to turn up the bubbles. In time, I felt very warm and very comforted by the hot tub.

After I soaked for forty-five minutes, I went upstairs, showered, and went to bed until approximately 7:30 PM Eastern Time. Then, I checked out. With all the food I ate during Technicaom 2003, I didn't bother with dinner. Instead, I drove from suburban Twinsburg to Cleveland Hopkins Airport, then was able to catch the shuttle to Cleveland's counterpart to Chicago's "L"-Subway train for the ride downtown. Otherwise, I would've had to drop another $26.00 to get from Cleveland Hopkins to Downtown Cleveland.

There was a station downtown that was the equivalent to Chicago's Washington Street Station. By that, I meant that you could transfer to ALL trains from that station. In Cleveland's case, I needed to transfer

361

to a Light Rail Vehicle to complete my ride to Cleveland/Amtrak. What I found odd, but delightful, was that Cleveland/Amtrak was near the new Cleveland Browns Stadium!

I arrived so early at the Cleveland Amtrak that no one was present in the station yet. Although this was an all-new station, it was very sparse.

In time, agents from Amtrak would eventually arrive at Cleveland/Amtrak. Now, all I had to do was wait for the east coast train to pull into Cleveland/Amtrak to take me home. Just as was the case when I arrived in Cleveland, I would have to wait until the wee hours of the morning for my train to arrive.

Like an idiot, I neglected to telephone Mom to let her know that I made it from my hotel in Twinsburg to Cleveland/Amtrak. I had thought about doing that when my train arrived. I wasted positively NO time about getting on my train. Once I did, I could truly say that I was on my way home.

It would've been better for me to have ordered the sleeper for my return trip from Cleveland to Chicago. I would've slept better, and my ride would've been more comfortable. Not only that, breakfast would've also been included the next morning with my sleeper at NO additional charge. However, a sleeper would've bumped my one-way train fare up to about four times above the fare for ordinary coach. Still, I'd return from Cleveland hopeful and enlightened.

A couple of weeks later, Ms. Glick-Smith emailed me from her Texas office. She wanted to know how I was doing. She also found it remarkable that I would take Amtrak from Chicago to Cleveland/Twinsburg and back and make it safely on top of that. Ms. Glick-Smith also gave me the names of a couple of black oriented family books that I might have found useful.

When I presented my model about Achievement versus Marriage, to Ms. Glick-Smith, she, like Lisa Leander of Christ Hospital and Bess Robertson of the Center for the Training of the Disabled, thought that I lacked self-confidence. It was as if I was a race on to myself, with my own brand of stereotypes that I had to face. I must reiterate that self-confidence was RARELY a problem; EFFECTIVENESS was!

The beauty of people like Judy Glick-Smith and Lisa Leander was that they could, at least, agree to disagree with me, and still be civil about it. They were still quite warm and supportive of my causes as a whole.

I was also getting regular newsletters from the Alumni Phoenix. That was Chicago-Cathedral High School's News Publication, which was dedicated to the now-defunct Cathedral High School's Alumni and former faculty. There was a section called "Birds of a Feather." In that section, alumni members were invited to submit articles about what they had been doing over the past year.

Some of the characteristics that comprised Autistics were evident when I was attending Cathedral High. I just didn't put two and two together. Nobody else did, for that matter. For instance, my Biology and Junior Year Math teachers noted peculiarities in me that set me apart from the rest of my classmates. Also, remember that the majority of information about Autism and ESPECIALLY Hyperlexia was uncovered in the years after I graduated from Cathedral in 1973.

Fortunately, the editor of the "Birds of a Feather" section understood what I was driving at. She correctly stated that I wanted to convey the message that Asperger's/Autism, my Glass Monolith, was a condition that was a serious medical problem. However, Asperger's/Autism was also manageable.

Final Thoughts

Remember! All the units and chapters of this book overlapped. Simultaneously, there was a crossover. For instance, issues about my speaking voice affected people's perception of me. People's perception of me affected whether I would get a job, irrespective of my voice. My health was a subset of any one of these factors at any given time. Still, people knew I sometimes got things right, which got me consideration for the interviews in the first place!

It is imperative that I alert my readers to the Autistic Conundrum. Yes, there was a problem with This Author.

However, it would've been a GROSS EXAGGERATION to refer to my Asperger's/Autism as an illness. That would be embellishing. Even the STC's Judy Glick-Smith and I agreed that the danger in referring to my Autism Spectrum Disorder as an illness would be tantamount to using it as a high-tech form of the "I Am Black" excuse! Conversely, Asperger's/Autism is classified as a severe neurological disorder that can affect social functioning. That's the conundrum.

It took me from the time I was awkwardly plodding through grade school until I became a middle-aged man before I learned that I had Autism Spectrum Disorder! Even then, I would NOT have discovered that I had the problem until I almost messed up a delightful job working for and with a quality company in Underwriters Laboratories.

There were many clues that led me to believe that I might have had some form of disabling condition. However, I couldn't put those clues together in a cohesive description. Keep in mind that Asperger's/Autism is a HIDDEN disorder.

I learned that there are more services for Autistic children than there are services for Autistic adults. I also learned that the majority of the American Hyperlexia Association's activities are geared towards children who are Hyperlexic.

This Author previously used the term "Autism Spectrum Disorder" to describe my problem. There was more to it than that. For instance, I was also found to have been Hyperlexic by two doctors who made separate diagnoses, and even Pervasive Developmental Disorder. Try telling a layman about any one of those conditions or problems. On the other hand, the typical layman has at least some grasp of what Autism is. Now, I call it Asperger's Autism for brevity to describe my Glass Monolith. Asperger's/Autism is a hindrance or a disabling condition.

Back in the 1970s, the television series Different Strokes aired. During one such episode, there was a disabled child actress who insisted that the character "Arnold", played by actor Gary Coleman, refer to her as "Handi-Capable"! Since then, that term has given way to the term "Special Needs." However, some old terms, cars, appliances, procedures, and systems are better than what is used presently. In my case, the term "Handi-Capable" hits the nail on the head when describing such persons as This Author. For instance, I wasn't handicapped enough to complete my primary and secondary education. I even completed a little postsecondary education on top of that.

The paradox to my perceived need to complete some form of postsecondary education was that I felt that a Black American needed to complete some form of education beyond high school. Whites, on the other hand, could probably get away with high school and on-the-job training.

I must temper my criticism of Black Americans who were born and reached adolescence between the periods of Reconstruction and

Emmitt Till's murder. This group didn't just experience overt racism. This group experienced what This Author will call IN-YOUR-FACE-ISM! That In-Your-Face-ism was capped off by Emmitt Till's murder in the Southern part of the United States.

Conversely, Black Americans born after 1950, including This Author's age group has had numerous advantages bestowed on this group. We were permitted to read, without facing any form of legal sanction. We were given access to information on Sex Education. Our schools are better. We weren't given shacks that leaned onto the neighbor's property, nor out towards the street. Yet, for all that Blacks in the Post 1950 upsets were given, we have thrown that groundwork we have been given out the window!

There was a host of educators, inventors, industrialists, engineers, and pioneering doctors in Reconstruction-1950 Black America. However, This Author can find very few corresponding samples in Post 1950 Black America. That is why I hit hard on my fellow Black Brethren throughout this book.

This Author's relationship with my fellow Black Americans served to hide my disabling condition over and above the difficulty inherent in uncovering Autism Spectrum Disorder. For instance, when I was ribbed about my voice, I thought it was because I didn't use Polluted English. It wasn't until 1988, and a three-year-old White girl who thought that I "talked funny," that I had any inkling of a voice disorder. Further readings on the Internet indicated that odd speaking mannerisms weren't out of the norm for people who had Autism Spectrum Disorder.

Black people, not just Black Americans, are like a breed of tropical fish called "Black Mollies"! Although Black Mollies are a wonderful breed of tropical fish, they are a home aquarist's nightmare! They are so delicate that any change in the pH (acidity to alkalinity) ratio from what the fish might be used to can and will easily kill Black Mollies! Mikey and I lost many Black Mollies in just a matter of days after we got the fish!

That parallel described above holds true for Black Americans as well. We have the highest incidences of Vascular disease, including Heart Disease, Cerebro-Vascular Disease, and Peripheral Artery Disease, compared to other ethnic groups! I see too many Black Americans who are half my age with most, if not all, of their teeth missing! I see more with whole limbs missing! This Author is probably NOT the only one with Autism Spectrum Disorder, including Asperger's Syndrome. So, the onus is on Black America to educate ourselves about wellness and practice it.

Most importantly, we Blacks need to learn more about ecology. Ecology isn't just cleaning up a garbage-strewn riverbank or planting more trees in vacant lots. Instead, the ecology is that and our relationship with people, other ethnic groups, social infrastructures, and on and on. I learned the most about ecology from a Zero Economic Growth advocate! Although I disagreed with some of his principles, his message was clear. There are checks and balances caused by social factors. For instance, my argument with Judy Glick-Smith and Bess Robertson was, and still is, that it is morally wrong for poor persons to have a family because poor persons are at a higher risk of having children who would come up short in some way. It is the poor person who often does not receive the educational care for their children. That same poor family is likely to wind up coming up short in getting the proper medical care for the family. That also holds true for dental care. The poor family is MOST likely to be a dysfunctional family.

Forget about social programs and community organizations! My experience with many of them is that they were and probably still are a sham at best!

This Author felt a need to write this book to defend my position on various points of view, and answer multiple charges that groups of people, as well as individuals, have placed against me over the years. There will be people who have their minds made up anyway. For those, I can accept the fact that hearts and minds cannot be changed. For those who are not prejudiced in such a manner, I can at least present an argument to keep an open mind about people who may not fit what is perceived as the norm. Remember. Although the Glass Monolith kept me from proper social functioning, it also kept others from understanding what I was about, even when my intentions were honorable. Sometimes, it is not what you say, do, or are, but how other people perceive you to be.

Throughout this book, I believed that I was always scoffed at whenever I presented a particular point of view, even if it were based on fact or evidence that was documented in some way. For instance, There was Dad with his contention that I could cure my Asthma with a daily regimen of Honey and Mineral Oil, Blanche with her contention that I could make Memphis in 5-6 hours driving from Chicago; Dad again, with his contention that my health problems were nothing but "nerves" or that interviewer at Taussig Manufacturing Company that told me that everyone that experiences protracted unemployment felt the need to take a job beneath them-even if it weren't suitable for them. Then there was Bess Robertson, who scoffed at my flowchart model when I attempted to show why people of poor or underachieving backgrounds should refrain from relationships, even sex.

Most troubling of all was that I frequently ran into situations where people in authority or power would try to choose my career! As a child, I constantly ran into a chorus of: "What Jon needs…" as if I had no say in how I lived my life. As a young adult, many officials would deliberately try to discourage me from choosing a career in science, whether from academia to industry.

Dedications

What Justine Mosely-Stevens, a former neighbor of the family and community activist, said about Mom was that, according to Ms. Stevens, Mom did not believe in just throwing people away. Considering what she put up with before finding out about This Author's Asperger's/Autism, I could concur with her.

I had next to NO problems making friends at Underwriters Laboratories, where I worked between August 28, 2000, and August 7, 2001.

Through one such acquaintance, Carol Pittl of Underwriters Laboratories, I met her daughter, Catherine. Catherine was, and at the time of this writing, still is, a victim of Cerebral Palsy! Catherine did tell me, however, that she had adjusted to her disability. Therefore, the things that usually affect her as a disabled person are less and less evident.

In truth, Catherine Pittl was, or is, very fortunate. At least, you can see what type of disability she was facing, or is facing. However, there are many people with disabilities who are not as readily evident. The only times when such disabilities may or may not turn up are when such persons hit what I call a Glass Monolith.

Part of this book is dedicated to Catherine Pittl!

Secondary Dedications

Noemi (pronounced Naomi) was an Emergency Room nurse who attended to my mother.

On January 9, 2004, Ms. Lillian Evans, my mother, went to her doctor. Her doctor told her that because of her illness, she thought it better that she enter the hospital for treatment. My mother balked at the doctor, went to the hospital, then balked again. On Saturday, January 10, 2004, her doctor sent hospice care workers to our home.

On January 30, 2004, while This Author was working on this book, Mrs. Lillian Evans died at 8:16 PM. This book is dedicated, in part, to the following hospice care workers:

Susie Austin RN

Marie, an Asian extracted hospice care nurse

Loretta Brown, LPN, who was in attendance at the time of Mrs. Evans' death

Luz, a Spanish-speaking hospice care nurse who always gave straight answers

Rev. Ed Stivers, a chaplain affiliated with Vitas Hospice Care

Reverend Father Thomas Kaminski of St. Helena of the Cross Parish

Justine Mosely-Stevens, a close friend of the family, who spoke at our mother's funeral

Family:

Quinetta Evans-She also spoke eloquently at our mother's funeral.

Dwight Evans, too, spoke eloquently at Mom's funeral.

Michael Evans-He came in from Hawaii to be at Mom's bedside during Mom's final days.

Milton Evans Jr. provided the leadership that the family needed at the time of Mom's death.

This book is also dedicated to:

Judy Glick-Smith of Dallas, Texas, and Atlanta, Georgia

The staff of Christ Hospital Vocational Services Unit, including:

Valerie Moreno-Tucker

Jeremy Sadlier-He was effectively on the right track as far as my having a problem that needed to be addressed.

Diane Bazan

Lisa Marie Leander

Melissa Bos-Hammer

Rawda Muhammad

Some Staff and Co-workers at Underwriters Laboratories, including:

Richard C. Winton-Were it not for Rich Winton, I would NOT have been forced to address the issues that were leading to loss of jobs, and what had threatened my job at Underwriters Labs.

Richard O'Sullivan, Chief Personnel Administrator, He supported and encouraged my efforts to identify my problem and to get help.

Mary Snyder BSN/RN-The Industrial Nurse at Underwriters Laboratories

John Hawley, Section Manager for the Waterlab and Engineering Groups

Thomas (The Singing Boss) Grant Jr, Engineering Group Leader.

Debbie Oates-She was my answer lady whenever John Hawley was unavailable

Conrad (C.L. or Connie) Parker-Whoever heard of a "Den Father?"

Dana Rivers, formerly of Project Strive

Bennett Leventhal, MD/Ph.D., formerly of the University of Chicago, Dr. Leventhal put me on the right track to solving my problem.

Deloris Marie Washington.

Albert G. Taylor of I AM CARES, now CARES CHICAGO-I appreciated his non-judgmental, can-do, let's get it done spirit.

Anthony & Michelle S. Pittman, MSW, who have sought to increase their understanding of, and about Asperger's Syndrome.

Finally, to my sister, Marciea Evans (3/22/1951-11/25/2000), it was that poignant afternoon in Oakland that prompted her to suspect that I might be Autistic. She ultimately proved correct, but NEVER lived to know how accurate she was!

A Short Synopsis:

There is a saying that goes: "If one man calls you a (donkey) Ignore him; but when another man calls you a (donkey), get a saddle!"

The Author's version of being called a (donkey) was having to run a gauntlet of charges against everything from his character to his sexuality.

Once those charges started to affect his career, The Author embarked on a long, exhaustive search for the reasons for the problems he was having, only to find out that he went from his childhood to middle age before learning that he had Asperger's Syndrome, an autism related disorder.

Today, there are a number of programs, treatments, and educational tools for young persons who are affected by Asperger's Syndrome. It is with early treatment that these persons can function almost as well as the Neurotypical community, or the mainstream.

The Glass Monolith is the story of one such person. It is clear that even if the Author were White, he would've experienced the problems described in this book. The fact that he was black cast a further cloud over his problem.

About The Author

Jon K. Evans
at a wedding Banquet
November 4, 2006

Jon Keith Evans

Jon Keith Evans aggnuy started his college education in his Senior Year at Cathedral High School in Chicago, Illinois. He picked up 18 credit hours through the College Acceleration and CLEP programs before graduating+ 3 more the following summer-starting him with a grand total of 21 Credit -Hours when college started. He then PROMPTLY STRUGGLED at severals Roosevelt institutions before graduating from Chicago ' University. Several years later, he earned a Post - Baccalaureate Certificate in Technical and Professional Communications from the Illinois Institute of Technology.